ROUSSEAU'S *SOCIAL CONTRACT*

Rousseau's *Social Contract*
A Conceptual Analysis

JOHN B. NOONE, JR.

The University of Georgia Press
Athens

Copyright © 1980 by the University of Georgia Press
Athens, Georgia 30602

All rights reserved

Set in 10 on 12 pt. Mergenthaler Janson

Library of Congress Cataloging in Publication Data

Noone, John B
  Rousseau's Social contract.

  Bibliography.
  Includes index.
    1. Rousseau, Jean Jacques, 1712–1778. Contrat so-
cial.   I. Title.
JC179.R9N66   320.1′1   79-28560
                  ISBN 0-8203-0511-1

IN MEMORY OF MY MOTHER AND FATHER

Contents

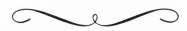

Acknowledgments

I am much indebted to two of my colleagues, John J. McDermott and Peter Manicas. Their constant encouragement has triumphed over my indolence. Peter Manicas has been especially generous with his time. He has read my manuscript several times and his many suggestions have proved most helpful. I must also thank two anonymous readers whose criticisms have saved me much embarrassment. Should they read this book they will know the full measure of my indebtedness. But my greatest debt is to my wife, Barbara, who has typed and retyped I know not how many thousands of pages. I offer my appreciation to Carol Sachs, who also assisted in the preparation of my manuscript. My readers should be especially grateful to Ellen Harris. As my copy-editor, she has spared them countless stylistic infelicities and has gently helped me resolve several ambiguities. I would also like to acknowledge the editors of the *Journal of Politics* and the *Journal of the History of Ideas*, who granted permission to reprint portions of my articles that first appeared in those publications.

Introduction

The resources of even the richest mine are finite, and beyond a certain point the law of diminishing returns makes further excavations unprofitable. Were the minds of esteemed philosophers like rich veins from which dutiful commentators extracted precious nuggets of wisdom, it might be assumed that there is a last explanatory work beyond which further exegesis becomes either trivial or redundant. It would be comforting to believe that the importance of a thinker is roughly measured by the number of his expositors. Were this the case, Jean-Jacques Rousseau would surely have to be ranked among the most important minds of history, because few thinkers have elicited such a host of interpreters.

Unfortunately this analogy, if indeed it ever holds, fails miserably when applied to Rousseau and his myriad judges. What is gold to one commentator is fool's gold or worse to another. The exegetical literature bulks so large that it is scarcely possible to imagine a position or attitude that has not been attributed to Rousseau. He has been located on all points of the political spectrum, from totalitarian to democrat, from reactionary to progressive.[1] He has been portrayed as an individualist, a collectivist, a conformist. He is an advocate of pure will; he champions natural moral law. His is a call to revolution; his is the voice of the powers that be. He is an optimist; he is a pessimist. Multiply these categories and combine them in every conceivable way. The chances are that somewhere in the vast literature that engulfs Rousseau each of these permutations will have its paladin. This no doubt is an exaggeration, but the point is that in an area so extensively and

minutely researched and explored, the probability of an over-
whelmingly original discovery is infinitesimal. One could almost
believe that whatever might possibly be said about Rousseau has
already been said. This is hardly a happy situation. Taking into account so many
discordant, contradictory, incompatible explications, it may be
wondered whether the excessive attention accorded Rousseau is
an index of his importance or, on the contrary, his importance becomes a function of the considerable and ever-growing corpus of
critical comment devoted to him. If Rousseau is, as by most re-
ports, such a momentous sage, why has the gospel he preached
and its professed importance continued in such dispute? It seems
evident that once a scholarly tradition is set in motion it can feed
upon its own contradictions and thus propagate itself indefinitely.
Like a ram jet, the faster it goes the faster it goes. The duration
and vigor of the tradition is no doubt unable to explain the original importance of its subject, but it goes a long way in accounting
for the perennial and ever-increasing importance of that subject.
Variety may be the spice of life, but it is something of a scandal
when it becomes the hallmark of a scholarly tradition.

Ask any commentator, "Why are there so many Rousseaus?"
The likely answer would be: "There are not many Rousseaus.
There is the authentic Rousseau as certified by my research and
the many counterfeits minted by the less astute." Nevertheless,
each would probably agree that his rivals were understandably
misled by Rousseau's penchant for rhetoric and his disdain for a
systematic, orderly presentation of his ideas. As far as my primary interest is concerned, it is difficult to overstate this criticism
of Rousseau.

The *Social Contract*, when read from the perspective of the
problem it purports to treat, is the most unsystematic, disar-
ranged, confusing classic of political philosophy with which I am
acquainted. Though initially it focuses on the question of legitimacy, it is interlaced with observations on good and bad governments. There is a liberal assortment of random remarks. Formal
considerations and substantive issues succeed one another with
no intelligible order that might give unity to the whole. Perhaps
Rousseau's greatest and certainly his most vexatious weakness is

his inability to adhere to a single temporal perspective. To the reader's dismay and confusion, frames of reference are constantly shifting, never with prior warning. It is not always clear whether Rousseau is referring to the past, the present, the possible future, or to some utopian "ought-to-be" that never was, will be, or can be.[2] The redemptive role he assigned to the legislator is but one worthy specimen of his failure to organize his reflections on a single temporal plane.

Lack of organization all too easily suggests a simple lack of system. And where no system is suspected the tendency is to treat each concept atomistically, as though it had an autonomous life of its own independent of other concepts. It is like attempting to determine the properties of a triangle without reference to the type of space in which it is conceived. The general will, for example, when detached from the correlative ideas of sovereignty and law, can become something of a mystical chameleon, changing its import according to the hope and fears of the beholders. When Rousseau's basic concepts are disjoined and quarantined they become free-floating fancies anchored neither in time nor space nor history. It is little wonder that they can become all things to all minds.

A lot of obvious misinterpretations of Rousseau can be explained by this process of fragmentation and isolation. This is especially true of expositions that are at several removes from the original source. However, I cannot think of an important Rousseauan scholar who isn't in one degree or another sensitive to the organic character of his thought (note the tautology!). Nevertheless, when attention is directed to the problem of legitimacy, I have been unable to find a single complete, systematic presentation of Rousseau's argument. Yet it is only in relation to this system that the thoroughly organic character of Rousseau's thought reveals itself. It is only in relation to this system, fully explicated, that it is possible to determine in a meaningful way whether his solution to the problem of legitimacy is valid.

There is only one way to convince doubters that there is such a system, and that is to lay it out in all its logical splendor. This I intend to do, and this I offer as a justification for yet one more book on Rousseau. I offer no explanation of how there came to be a system in a work whose central argument is so poorly organized and so unsystematically distributed among elements that are foreign to that argument. No Euclidean neatness will be found in the *Social Contract*. On the contrary, it is more like a jumble of jigsaw pieces, some of which—but not all—fit together to form an intelligible picture.

I personally doubt that Rousseau ever had this picture, whole and entire, before his conscious mind. Rousseau was quite capable of delicate subtlety in veiling an argument when there was an understandable reason for concealment. A good example, as I will try to show in chapter 3, is his devastating attack on monarchy in the *Social Contract*. It is not that he disguises his contempt for monarchy. But underlying all his obviously negative appraisals is an even more fatal assault: monarchy by its very nature is illegitimate, and, worse yet, its nature prevents it from being a good form of government.[3] It makes sense to speak of reconstructing this argument because one feels fairly certain that Rousseau was fully conscious of the argument as a whole.

Prudence might well have dictated some circumspection in his case against monarchy, but I can think of no motive that might have induced Rousseau to conceal the mediating links between an explicitly stated problem and the clear conviction that he had solved it. For this reason I am at a loss for a description of what I have attempted. Can one reconstruct the argument of an author when that argument in its logical fullness probably never existed in the author's mind? 'Retrieval' as a description is hardly better. Yet somewhere in the darkness of his intuitive genius Rousseau must have known what he was doing, because scattered throughout his writings there are to be found all the elements of a surprisingly tight, consistent, and persuasive argument on behalf of legitimacy. I hasten to add that, though sound, this argument has no literal application to the world we know.

The logical form of Rousseau's argument is dictated by the specialized meaning he assigns the term 'legitimacy'. Having established this meaning, the form of the argument is quite simple: There are x number of necessary conditions that collectively provide the sufficient condition for legitimacy. By the nature of the case each one of these conditions must be a separate clause of the social contract. The social contract, then, is Rousseau's unique solution to the problem of legitimacy. This being so, why is the contract generally disregarded or considered of minimal importance? The answer is plain: with or without reason, Rousseau took great care to conceal the fact that his was a contract of some complexity. As a matter of fact, the contract consists of eighteen or nineteen separate articles, not one of which is explicitly designated as such. Small wonder, then, that the contract's true significance has never been appreciated. Its terms are only inferentially present. They are scattered piecemeal and always unannounced over the whole range of the *Social Contract*. Finally, Rousseau's rhetorical simplification of the contract was not only premature but also thoroughly misleading.

The contract promises to reconcile freedom and obligation. The obligation in question is that decreed by law, and 'law' for Rousseau has a very definite but limited meaning; overlooking that meaning leads to some of the more lamentable extrapolations of his theories. The freedom in question is neither natural freedom nor moral freedom. It is political freedom, and this in turn is unintelligible save with reference to the social contract as a whole.

Government is established by the contract, and its authority is defined by the contract. Rousseau's treatment of government, however, must be approached with caution. Only a small part of his analysis relates to the theoretical exigencies of the contract. The rest is devoted to nontheoretical observations and especially to an analysis of monarchy as a form of despotism.

The general will, sovereignty, and law constitute an indivisible trinity. The general will is not a fixed, static entity. Substantively considered, the content of the general will can change, but I shall argue that some measure of this will must antecede society and form an explicit part of the social contract. Otherwise the contract would be incapable of instituting civil society.

The first four chapters of the present work contain all the elements, with one problematic exception, that collectively constitute Rousseau's rather ingenious argument as to how legitimacy may be secured. For the most part the analysis is formal. But once the several formal terms of the contract are made explicit, it becomes obvious that they are applicable only under extremely limiting circumstances. To understand why certain types of economies are incompatible with the social contract is to understand in large measure the root causes of Rousseau's war with society.

Once the contract is spelled out, it is evident why it is almost certainly unworkable. It may be defeated by any number of extraformal reasons, but in the last analysis it appears that the one constant and ever-present enemy is man himself. Others, notably Judith Shklar,[4] have sounded the depths of Rousseau's pessimism. To this tradition I would add a theoretical, nonpsychological source of his despair. There are any number of reasons that bear on Rousseau's pessimism, but there is one that has been completely overlooked. Though Rousseau was not a systematic thinker in any ordinary sense, he did have and make use of a method for determining the nature of things. It is a terrible method, but it is a method nevertheless. This method, which is explicitly employed by the vicar in *Emile*, predetermines his account of human nature in the *Second Discourse* and provides a theoretical justification for such other reasons as he had for his jaundiced view of mankind.

The account of human nature is not an integral part of Rousseau's theoretical argument, but it does help explain something that is a part of his argument—namely, the Civil Creed. This creed has long been a source of embarrassment for those who otherwise admire Rousseau. For his detractors it is further and decisive proof of his illiberality. Both parties share the common belief that the creed can be evaluated as some kind of independent entity. This is not quite accurate. In a formal sense the creed is not a necessary condition of legitimacy, but if there is to be a creed at all, it must be part of the social contract. I did not consider it with the other terms of the contract, because it is not, absolutely speaking, a necessary condition, and because its inclusion can only be explained by extraformal reasons and in particular in relation to Rousseau's account of human nature. I argue that there is nothing especially sinister about the creed, put in its proper context.

The social contract is designed to bear the whole weight of legitimacy; it contains not a word about some transcontractual source of moral obligations. This might seem to imply that there

is no other source. Were this the case, Rousseau's status as a moralist would have to be reduced to near zero, because the contract
is quite impractical. But it is not the case. Rousseau can be located in some stream that runs within the broad tradition of natural law. This, of course, is not a novel or an original conclusion.
But I have reargued the case in a different context, trying to show
how his theory of natural law relates to the contract and to the
theism that underlies the Civil Creed, and to show how a morality can, without contradiction, be at once conventional and
natural.

Just as the social contract, when fully elucidated, condemns
various economic organizations of society, so also it condemns
any number of attempts to put a label on Rousseau. But I must
append a caveat. My dominant concern has been with conceptual
analysis, an attempt to extract a system of ideas from what too
often seem to be random, casual and even purposeless particulars.
This I am presumptuous enough to hope is a significant contribution to the understanding of Rousseau. Yet at the same time I am
well aware of my many limitations. Even before Rousseau wrote
the *Social Contract*, history had ordained that his system was to be
stillborn. There is evidence that he recognized this, and so it is
not surprising to find that he had much more to say on matters
political and moral than could be comfortably accommodated
within his system. Though I think that the system can usefully
serve as connective tissue, giving unity to this "much more," neither my competence nor my interests have induced me to pursue
Rousseau into the realm of the second best, where ideas reluc-
tantly adapt themselves to the insistency of historical reality.
Even less have I been tempted to penetrate the shadowy recesses
of a psyche often at odds with itself, ever at war with an uncaring,
even hostile, society. That such a disordered soul could have unconsciously fathered a political theory *more geometrico* is existen-
tially perhaps Rousseau's ultimate paradox.

I do not know, nor do I pretend to know, who the quintessen-
tial Rousseau is. Why should we assume that the 'real' is some
consistent core of meaning from which all contradictions have
been exiled or explained away? How many lives in their fullness
attain the ideal harmony of axiomatic consistency? The career of

most lives consists of a conjunctive series of moments, not all of which can be made to coexist in perfect logical peace. For my part, I am perforce content to have reconciled some of the moments of Rousseau's intellectual odyssey. Whether all the moments of his journey unite *sub specie aeternitatis*, I gladly leave as grist for other more patient mills.

Chapter 1

The Unique Basis of Political Obligation

The *Second Discourse* was before the fact an elaborate gloss on that celebrated adage, "Man is born free, and everywhere he is in chains." [1] Man, it was argued there, not being by nature a social animal, was even less a political animal. The freedom man possessed in some far-distant state of nature was his natural liberty, and this was nothing more than the physical power nature granted him to satisfy his desires. In that state he had an unlimited right to everything he wanted and was capable of getting. [2] This right or liberty or freedom has absolutely no moral significance, because the related obligation is simply what is imposed by superior force. Rousseau's original man was for the most part solitary and independent, and thus subject to few if any obligations. By contrast, contemporary man is everywhere in chains forged by governments. Since a large-scale return to the state of nature is impossible, some form of governmental control is inescapable. The question Rousseau poses with this inevitability in mind is whether there is a legitimate way of circumscribing man's natural freedom. He thinks there is.

Rousseau takes for granted that all his readers have a common understanding of what it means to say that a given government is or is not legitimate. Having raised the question, he immediately, in chapter 2, proceeds to deny that there are any natural authorities such as fathers of families. In the following chapter, he dismisses might or superior force as a possible candidate for legitimate authority. This is an unfortunate sequence. Force is rejected, not because it does not meet the criteria of legitimacy as independently understood, but because in a negative way it defines what is meant by a legitimate authority. The crux of the matter is this: there is an essential distinction between a prudential obligation and a duty. A man who gives up his purse to an armed robber or the general who withdraws his troops in the face of a numerically superior enemy does what he is obliged to do, but this obligation is purely prudential, that is, a hedonistic determination that compliance is a lesser evil than noncompliance. Duty, by contrast, is a moral obligation. Moral obligations are seen as holding independently of personal desires or threats of retaliation. A person experiences a moral obligation in a situation where he wants something, believes he can take it without consequent risk, and yet feels strongly or knows that he ought not to take it.

The only chains that bind in a state of nature are prudential obligations. Here there is no question of legitimacy; here there is nothing but the wisdom of submitting to superior force. To speak of legitimacy, therefore, is to speak of an authority whose commands are moral obligations. This is a tricky point and deserves further elaboration. It is possible to accept this definition and nevertheless deny that a legitimate political authority is even theoretically possible. One could, for example, deny moral obligation and argue that any attempted distinction between de facto and de jure authority is indefensible. This is one way, though not an indisputable way, of interpreting Hobbes. Or one could accept moral obligation as objectively meaningful but argue that because morality transcends society, no human will, simply as will, can impose moral obligations. A government may happen to command what is morally obligatory, but it is not obligatory because the government commands it.[3] It is plain that Rousseau rejected the Hobbesean argument: otherwise the whole *Social Contract* would be unintelligible. He would also reject the second argument on the grounds that legitimate authority is at least a conceptual possibility. However, this second argument suggests questions concerning the relationship between the general will and a transcendent morality that must be passed over for the present.

Rousseau's original question can now be reformulated. Under

what conditions can a person's will be morally bound by political authority? When the problem is put this way, it becomes obvious that the question of legitimacy logically, though not necessarily temporally, presupposes the existence of a moral community. A moral community is a community of equals in that all members are subject to the same moral imperatives and in the same way. A moral community is a distinguishable part of society. It is distinguishable because it can coincide with all sorts of socioeconomic inequalities. In the Middle Ages, for example, a theory of natural law and moral equality coexisted quite comfortably with hierarchical conceptions of both church and state. No theory that fails to account for or defeats the meaning of a moral community suffices to legitimate.

Force being precluded by definition, Rousseau sees only four possible sources of legitimacy. An authority is legitimate (1) if it is perceived as such; (2) if it is ordained by God; (3) if it is certified by nature; (4) if it is based on a convention. I would hazard the guess that, outside of philosophy books, the perception of legitimacy is what legitimacy is invariably taken to be. Psychological acceptance of a regime—induced by habit, education, apathy, a sense of tradition, or whatever—is a sturdy bridge between de facto and de jure authority. Nevertheless, Rousseau rejects this possibility: "Nothing is more certain than that every man born in slavery is born for slavery. Slaves in their chains lose everything, even the desire to leave them; they love their servitude as the companions of Ulysses loved their brutishness" (*SC* 1. 2). This is perhaps an extreme case, but it points up the fact that people can come to accept anything. Were psychological contentment the sought-after criterion, the most diverse and incompatible polities would all be judged legitimate. The problem is not what people as a matter of fact do accept; it is what they ought to accept. The assumption underlying this rejection is most significant. Though Rousseau ultimately identifies legitimacy with a special convention, it is clear that he never takes the *meaning* of legitimacy to be conventional. Existing regimes and countertheories of legitimacy are all to be measured against an eternal standard of legitimacy. This Platonic ideal only slowly reveals itself; at first, little by little, as what it is not; then finally it manifests itself in all its splendor in the social contract. Stage one: it is not psychological satisfaction.

With regard to the second source of legitimacy, Rousseau is far more circumspect. Wishing to avoid theological thickets, he gets around such questions as God's existence and his authority in human affairs, and concentrates on the unknowability of a divine will. In the absence of a direct revelation, how are men to recognize which governors are divinely sanctioned? It is not possible (*SC* 1. 2). Stage two: legitimacy is a secular, not a theological, ideal.

Models of authority are not to be found in nature. The closest thing to a natural authority is the relation of fathers to children. But this is not a political relation, and the father's authority ceases when his children mature (*SC* 1. 2). Rousseau's examination of possible sources of natural authority is hardly complete. This, however, is not surprising. The *Second Discourse* is a protracted argument that no man has by nature authority over any other man. In simplest terms the reason is that even the idea of authority is alien to a state of nature. Authority takes on meaning only with the advent of civil society.

It is, I think, noteworthy that Rousseau did not consider a classical candidate for natural authority: the wise man or philosopher-king. If the end of political rule is to embody the truth, then those best equipped by nature and education to know the truth would appear to possess weighty credentials of authority. This would be so *if* political laws, like scientific laws, were simply a question of truth or falsity. But this is not, without many qualifications, the case. It will be seen later that the most fundamental ideals of a society are better evaluated as good or bad for that society rather than as true or false. Even when a legislator's services are employed, his 'truth' lacks authority independent of the people's consent. Stage three: legitimacy is not grounded in nature.

After the above process of elimination, conventions remain as the sole basis of legitimacy (*SC* 1.4). Historically there have been all kinds of conventions that determine legitimacy in a legal sense—for example, laws of dynastic succession. But this type of convention is not what Rousseau has in mind. These are not original conventions, since they presuppose the existence of a people as a moral community. And it is questionable whether any of them are ratified by the people as a whole; they are at most the determinations of the 'best part' of the people. Any convention that offers itself as a potential candidate for legitimacy must require the unanimous consent of the members-to-be of the nascent state. This is a necessary condition because once Rousseau has narrowed the alternatives to some form of convention, this convention has to effect a transformation of what is taken to be an amoral state of nature into what is at a minimum a moral community. If for some reason a person is reluctant to leave the state of nature, he cannot be morally obliged by the contractors. Consent as applied to the original contract means consent by each and every member.

Rousseau's rather summary dismissal of theories of natural authority is perhaps understandable: because he is firmly committed to his conception of a prepolitical state of nature, he must rely on convention. But his ultimate defense of a unique convention has credibility only to the extent that he succeeds in refuting all other possible conventions. And this in turn depends upon a classificatory schema that includes all possible conventions. Rousseau has such a schema, but it can be made explicit only by inference. Since the relevant conventions all seek to establish authority, some alienation of individual will is necessary. The individual will is transferred either to a part of society or to the group as a whole. To subdivide each alternative, the alienation is either total or partial. This leaves only four possibilities, and Rousseau examines each one.

Though he has one argument that suffices to refute both types of personal alienation (that is, total or partial alienation on behalf of an individual or a part of society), he employs two. What particularly draws his fire is any convention that demands total personal alienation. This is, in effect, a master-slave relation even if it is voluntary slavery. Total alienation of will is no more than an abdication of moral accountability for all actions done under the direction of one's master: "to deprive your will of all freedom is to deprive your actions of all morality" (*SC* 1.4). Without a concept of personal accountability the whole idea of morality, and therefore of legitimacy, is vacuous. It might be objected that a person cannot alienate moral responsibility, on the ground that one simply *is* responsible. One can no more cede one's responsibility than he can give up breathing. Rousseau would undoubtedly agree: man in a truly human sense is necessarily a moral being. But this otherwise-valid objection misses the point with respect to the case at hand. The objection presupposes an antecedent morality which is the very question at issue. Rousseau's point is that *if* a people were to alienate its will to some other individual, that alienation would preclude the possibility of a moral community, and all talk of legitimacy would be idle. Hobbes's convention fails because it does not succeed in bridging the gap between an amoral state of nature and a morally grounded civil state.

Slavery, whether voluntary or not, whether of an individual or of a people as a whole, far from terminating a state of nature, intensifies it. Moral discourse is impossible under this condition. A slave who disobeys his master may regret it, but there is no moral standard to condemn him. To say that he broke his promise presupposes moral standards prior to the convention, and this is contrary to the hypothesis. That aside, this particular promise is self-defeating, for it keeps the master in the state of nature, and where one party to a conflict is in the state of nature the conflict itself is one of a state of nature. The master is in a state of nature because there are no duties to which he is subject. "Is it not clear that you are under no obligations whatsoever to a person of whom you have the right to demand everything?" (*SC* 1. 4). Hobbes's contract may have terminated the war of all against all, but it has not terminated the state of nature, because it has failed to establish a moral community. A covenant that involves total alienation is only as valid as the sword that enforces it.

It seems intuitively evident that complete personal alienation is incompatible with even the most attenuated idea of a moral agent. An argument against partial personal alienation is not so intuitively evident. An indefinite number of arguments would seem to be required, because the class of personal partial alienation contains an indefinite number of cases forming a series that converges on total alienation at one end and no alienation at the other end. Nevertheless, partial alienation is also to be rejected on the general principle that the extent of alienation marks off exactly that area where one is not morally accountable. But this area similarly defines the scope of the state. The result is a contradiction: government's legitimate authority extends only to the area where subjects are not morally accountable.

Legitimacy can serve as a regulative idea only if it is a case of all or nothing. And this is Rousseau's strict interpretation: "the clauses of this contract are so completely determined by the nature of the act that the slightest modification would render them null and void."[4] If partial personal alienation were the convention in question, what could be the principle that selects one degree of alienation out of countless other possibilities? Can one conceive of a unanimous agreement among the people as to just how much will is to be alienated? This question suggests why partial personal alienation is not the convention sought. The transition from a state of nature where individuals are atomistically isolated to a condition where they are subject to government cannot be a one-stage process. No man can rationally consent to be governed before there are recognized social ideals and goals to guide a government.[5] In a word, before an aggregate can consent to be governed it must first become a people. Members of a mere aggregate, lacking common interests, have only particular wills, wills that look only to the isolated self. An association or a people, on the other hand, is a unity based on common goods, and it therefore has a collective will, a general will whose object is the common good. It is this community that gives itself a government, and this act is itself a civil act (*SC* 1. 5). Contract theories of government fail on two counts: they cannot account for the origin of a people as a moral community, and where they assume the existence of a people, they further assume that this moral community can be a party to a contract. According to Rousseau, the contract that creates a people is such that there can be no other public contract that would not violate the terms of the original contract (*SC* 3. 13). Why this is so will become evident when the terms of the contract are considered in more detail.

The social contract—that is, the original contract—cannot establish a government, and therefore a government cannot be a party to it. Thus, even aside from the moral dimensions of the problem, there can be no question of an original alienation of the will, whether total or partial, to an individual or a group less than the whole, that is, to a government. But alienation of some sort there must be, or else an aggregation would forever remain an aggregation, an unstructured plurality of individual wills. Since any degree of alienation to a person or persons is morally objectionable, there remains only individual alienation on behalf of the group as a whole.

Once again it may be asked whether this impersonal alienation is to be partial or total. If this alienation is only partial, what results is a situation where an individual is in part subject to the whole and in part the possessor of inalienable rights beyond social control. This might have eased the fears of those who look upon any kind of total alienation with unrelieved horror. The trouble, however, is that in Rousseau's state of nature an individual's natural rights are not moral rights; they simply describe an individual's natural power to effect his will. Consequently, in contracting in the manner to be described, an individual is not alienating a moral dimension of his being. Thus, for example, a man might have a natural right to the land he tills in a state of nature; that is, he has the power to resist encroachment. But this possession does not constitute property in a legal or a moral sense (*SC* I. 9).

The objection to partial impersonal alienation is the same as that to partial personal alienation. How could a multitude unanimously define and then agree upon a specific amount of natural freedom to be retained by all members? But there is no need for reserved rights, because the ideal contract is such that legitimate individual interests cannot be compromised. Moreover, reserved rights would lead to unmanageable conflicts and sooner or later would destroy the new but fragile union. "For if the individual retained certain rights, each, in the absence of any common superior capable of judging between him and the public, would be his own judge in certain matters, and would soon claim to be so in all; the state of nature would continue, and the association would necessarily become tyrannical or meaningless" (*SC* I. 6). Reserved rights contest authority and make it less than perfect.

At last the process of elimination is complete. Or so it seems. The convention that uniquely legitimates authority demands total alienation to the group. The clauses of this contract "can be reduced to the following only: the total alienation of each member, with all his rights to the community as a whole" (*SC* 1. 6). It may alternatively be summed up as follows: "Each of us puts in common his person and all his powers under the supreme direction of the general will; and in our corporate capacity we receive each member as an indivisible part of the whole" (*SC* 1. 6). These two formulas supposedly each provide a solution to the problem of legitimacy, which is "to find a form of association which defends and protects the person and property [*biens*] of each member with the whole force of the community, and where each, while joining with all the rest, still obeys no one but himself, and remains as free as before."[6]

Even granting that Rousseau's formulation of the problem is fully intelligible, it is plainly absurd to think that his condensed versions of the contract in any sense solve that problem. Rousseau generally had great difficulties correlating time and history with his conceptual framework. And this is surely the case here. At one moment we are presented with an aggregate of particular, self-regarding wills. A second later an unexplained general will comes into being, and everybody promises to obey it. Presto! we have a moral community and the problem of legitimacy is solved. The fact is that there is a lot more work to be done.

Rousseau's fundamental objection to Hobbes's version of the social contract was that it failed to institute a moral community. But how can a total alienation of individual rights to a group as a whole create a moral community? Indeed, given the state of nature as immediately antecedent, where is the community on whose behalf total alienation occurs? This is but another way of asking how the general will to which all agree to submit arises and how it is declared. To answer these questions one must first doubt whether Rousseau's capsulized summary of the contract does justice to that contract.

This must be doubted, because there appears to be no proportion between his formulas and the effects that supposedly derive from them. The contract confers sovereignty on the people. Now sovereignty is a right, the moral right to bind the wills of its subjects. Since, however, there is no moral community before the contract, the contract must somehow simultaneously generate both a moral community and sovereignty. This is at once a radical and a novel conception: a special type of convention not only justifies specific moral obligations as decreed by the sovereign, it establishes morality in general. This point cannot be stressed too strongly. Locke's contract is designed to justify new obligations, but this justification depends upon something that is not part of the contract, namely, an independent and transcendent moral code that includes among other rules one to the effect that promises ought to be kept. With some qualifications, consent once given is irrevocable. Locke's contractors are moral agents before they covenant. With Rousseau it is the covenant that makes them moral agents: "this passage from the natural to the civil state produces a very remarkable change in man, substituting justice for instinct as the guide to his conduct, and giving his actions the morality they previously lacked" (*SC* 1. 8). Duty becomes meaningful for the first time and, as a corollary, so also legitimacy.

But what can it mean to speak of the sovereignty of the people, beyond whose will there is no rightful appeal? Constant repetition in Fourth-of-July oratory may have given the phrase emotive impact, but its cognitive content is seldom clarified. Sovereignty as applied to a people is clearly not a distributive predicate, for it is the whole that is sovereign and not single individuals. Nor is each individual a part of the sovereign the way strangers are passive parts of an audience. Sovereignty pertains to that moral community which results from the transformation of what had hitherto been a mere aggregation. It is the sovereign's will that creates political obligations, and because the sovereign is legitimate these obligations are more than prudential; they are moral obligations.

Rousseau's explicit account of the contract is incapable of supporting these claims. A political community is not instituted by the mere affirmation of a desire to associate. It has no life prior to some collective decision that is realized in action. Before such a decision can be reached, however, men must at the very least agree on procedures for decision making and on some general definition of areas in which decisions may be made. Suppose, for example, a group declares itself an association. If no decisions are made, the declaration of association is pragmatically indistinguishable from the situation that preceded that declaration. If, on the other hand, a proposal is offered and voted upon, is it passed (that is, obligatory) when the vote is sixty yeas and forty nays? Without a prior definition of what constitutes passage, it obviously is not. Nor can the body vote to decide what the voting rule shall be until it resolves this definitional problem. In order to alleviate an infinite regress, the basic procedural rules must be part of the original contract. And there are many other clauses of the contract that Rousseau does not explicitly designate as such. As a methodological principle, it may be affirmed that the social contract includes all rules or commitments that require unanimous consent. This is completely defensible, because "there is only one law which, by its very nature, requires unanimous consent; this is the social contract."[7] This principle brings to light a surprisingly complex contract. A summary of the clauses, not all of which can be explicated in this chapter, follows.

1. All citizens are to have a voice and a vote in the general assembly (*SC* 1. 6; 2. 2; 4. 1). Or, to put it negatively, no citizen may be lawfully excluded from the assembly.[8]

2. Sovereignty is inalienable (*SC* 2. 1). Expressed as a rule, this means that the assembly cannot transfer legislative authority to any person or group. Even a unanimous vote to do so cannot effect such a transfer without abrogating the contract as a whole. This is a necessary condition for the moral authority of law. Total personal alienation had already been rejected by Rousseau as incompatible with the moral accountability of the individual. Should the sovereign alienate its will, it would cease to be sovereign, and its erstwhile members would no longer be morally obliged. The same is true when sovereignty is usurped, though here it is a case of involuntary slavery.

3. Sovereignty is indivisible (*SC* 2. 2). This is a specification of the preceding clause. It forbids dividing up legislative authority among various parts of the sovereign, as we, for example, do with our different executive agencies. All the citizens must have a legislative say in all areas of legislative concern. Divided sovereignty, with respect to any given individual, is the equivalent of partial personal alienation.

4. The assembly cannot bind itself, much less future genera-

tions. This precludes legislation in perpetuity. From the idea of sovereignty, "it follows that there is not, and cannot be, any sort of fundamental law binding on the body of the people, not even the social contract itself" (*SC* 1. 7). Rousseau well knew how prescription and the dead hand of the past have a way of legitimating inequality. Unlike Locke's contract, which exists independently and in its own right once an initial consent has been given, Rousseau's contract is not only created by consent, its continued existence depends upon continuous consent. Should this be withdrawn, the state of nature is reinstituted.

5. "Except for the original contract, the majority always binds the minority" (*SC* 4. 2). The size of the requisite majority is a variable depending on circumstances and issues. The precise percentages relating to various issues need not be spelled out in the contract; they can be formulated and even reformulated in subsequent legislation.

6. The assembly is a permanent constituent assembly (*SC* 3. 18). There can be no contract, as in Hobbes and perhaps Locke, between the people and its government, because the original contract does not even prescribe a form of government. The form of government is a product of a legislative and not of a contractual process. Since no law, according to the fourth clause, is in perpetuity, the assembly has the right to change the form whenever it so pleases.

7. Whatever the form of government, provisions must be made for periodic assemblies. With the exception of extraordinary circumstances, only those assemblies convened in accordance with law are lawful, "for the order to assemble should itself emanate from the law" (*SC* 3. 13). The contract does not specify any given timetable; this would needlessly limit the sovereign's response to changing conditions. The contract simply demands that there always be some law on the books requiring periodic assemblies.

8. Whatever the form of government, all magistrates are to be elected by the votes of all the citizens. The first act of each assembly is to approve or reject the existing form of government and/or the incumbents (*SC* 3. 18).

9. The criminal code may lawfully include penalties up to and including death (*SC* 2. 5). This may seem to be a gratuitous

clause, but it serves, I suspect, two purposes. Prospective members ought to be advised of the possible limits of jeopardy to which they expose themselves. More important, it denies that the right of self-preservation may, as with Hobbes, override the contract. This denial has significant consequences not only as regards criminals but also as regards blameless citizens. Once man enters the civil state, he ceases to be, as he was in the state of nature, the sole judge of what is best for his self-preservation (*SC* 2. 5). Self-preservation may have been a motive for contracting out of the state of nature, but the contract nevertheless limits this natural right.

10. Executive and judicial powers are the exclusive province of government.[9] Because sovereignty is inalienable, the government has no legislative authority whatsoever.

11. Legislation must be limited to areas of common concern, though it is the assembly that is the sole judge of what these concerns are (*SC* 2. 4). The first vote on any proposal determines whether it is an issue of common concern. If the answer is yes, a second vote determines whether the proposal is for the common good. These are distinguishable questions because one might agree, for example, that some set of traffic regulations is in the public interest but disagree that the proposed set is for the common good. Our Supreme Court embodies an analogous procedure: the justices first decide whether something is worthy of constitutional scrutiny and then, if it is worthy, whether it is constitutional.

12. Only those laws are binding that are universal and impersonal in form: that is, those that apply, either actually or potentially, to all. The sovereign may not single out a person or a group for special treatment, favorable or unfavorable (*SC* 2. 6).

13. Citizens are to vote, not according to personal desires, but on the basis of their estimation of what the common good requires (*SC* 4. 2).

14. When the very life of the state is threatened, the sovereignty of the laws may be suspended and a dictatorship set up. Survival is the ultimate common good and therefore the first and abiding dictate of the general will (*SC* 4. 6).

15. All claims to private possessions must be waived, and their

future distribution is to be determined by the sovereign (*SC* 1. 9). Property is not, as with Locke, an inalienable right.

16. All laws must be completely and fully enforced. Every would-be malefactor must "be forced to be free" (*SC* 1. 7). This is the very heart of the contract, because obligation depends upon mutuality and equality—qualities that are lacking where vice has an unfair advantage over virtue. So important does Rousseau consider this rule that he denies government the right of pardon, and "even its [the sovereign's] rights in this matter are not very clear" (*SC* 2. 5).

The above clauses are, as it were, the ground rules, determining what the sovereign may and may not do. They prescribe how a law is to be enacted and what form it must take, but they do not prescribe the content of any law. One term of the contract, however, is quite definitely, if not notoriously, substantive—the term that concerns the civil creed. Though Rousseau speaks of it as a law and therefore not a part of the contract, it will be seen later that it makes no sense if it is not taken as a part of the contract. Assuming this for the moment, the next clause becomes:

17. All must profess the civil creed, but, beyond that, religious toleration is accorded every dogma not subversive of the peace or morals of the community (*SC* 4. 8).

There would seem to be yet another substantive clause, if only implicit. Procedural rules are all well and good, but they are of little effect unless they are directed toward some antecedently agreed upon end or ends. Suppose a group came together and unanimously agreed to abide by the majority's will. Suppose further that the first order of business was to decide the purpose of the association. Suppose finally that the majority decides that the association should devote itself to the systematic destruction of all philosophers. In what reasonable sense could a dissenting minority be obligated? The point is that it is impossible to alienate one's will to a community or to an association as a whole before a community or an association exists. The minority in the above example is not obligated because, prior to unanimously agreed upon ends, what exists is a mere aggregation, not an association. Or, to put the matter somewhat differently, legitimate alienation presupposes an already-existent general will. Why this is so will be explained in chapter 4. Because the *Social Contract* is concerned with the principles of right as they apply to all societies, it would have been a mistake had Rousseau monogamously wedded them to a particular, concretely articulated society. The legislator of book 2, chapter 7, does his work *before* his people contract, and he may be taken as a response to the need for social substance as a complement to merely formal procedural agreements. As these points will be expanded later, let it here be assumed that there is an eighteenth clause spelling out some combination of socioeconomic goals to which all members commit themselves.

With regard to the original contract, original both fundamentally and chronologically, there is no problem of determining citizenship: anyone who consents to the contract in its entirety is thereby a citizen. But what about posterity? If the contract is silent with respect to the future, then the sovereign has authority to define conditions of citizenship. This, however, is a dangerous authority, and its abuse could defeat the whole purpose of the contract. Accordingly, I am postulating a nineteenth clause, which limits sovereign competence in matters of citizenship.

There are perhaps other clauses that I have overlooked, but the above should be enough to demonstrate that the *Social Contract* was aptly titled and that the contract plays a greater role in the determination of the subtitle, *Principles of Political Right*, than is generally appreciated. A check on the references for the various clauses, ranging from book 1, chapter 6 to book 4, chapter 8 of the *Social Contract*, also suggests that the work is poorly organized and that this lack of organization may be Rousseau's major contribution to the many incompatible interpretations of his work.

Once the terms of the contract have been enumerated, it is easier to understand what Rousseau meant by the sovereignty of the people. Strictly speaking, the contract is not operative until the people legislate in accordance with the provisions of the contract and reflect the law by their behavior. The sovereignty of the people, then, is not some mysterious, intangible, metaphysical property, or an abstraction. On the contrary, it is a phrase that describes a concrete process, namely, an assembly of people legislating in a prescribed manner. The terminus of this process is law—sovereign law. A law is morally obligatory if and only if it is a sovereign law, and in principle, though not always in practice, it is possible to establish objectively whether a law is sovereign. Was the assembly that ordained it duly authorized? Does it meet the formal conditions of a law? Did it have majority approval? Is it being conscientiously enforced? Is it an expression of the general will or merely a dictate of particular wills? This last question may in certain circumstances be difficult to answer, but it is a question that must be asked, because there comes a time when the social bond begins to loosen and laws can be easily recognized as not sovereign; they are pseudolaws, "iniquitous decrees whose only purpose is to further private interests" (*SC* 4. 1).

A political obligation that is at the same time a moral obligation must fulfill two conditions: it must indeed be a sovereign law, and it must enlist the consent of him whom it binds. Only if this latter condition is met will a person, in obeying the law obey "no one but himself, and remain as free as before" (*SC* 1. 6). How a dissenting minority can be said to obey itself is not a problem that can be fully solved at this stage of my analysis of Rousseau's political thought. A complete solution must await a consideration of various types of freedom and an understanding of what a general will is. However, it is possible to give the outline of a solution. When people speak of consent without an accompanying and limiting adjective, they invariably mean psychological consent: that is, a positive, direct willingness and inclination to accept what is at issue. This consent is proclaimed by an individual's self-regarding, particular will. It is man's natural will, the will with which he is endowed in the state of nature. To say that an individual gives his consent to the contract is to say that he psychologically consents to all its clauses. With regard to the contract this is the only relevant meaning of consent, because when he consents he has, as it were, at least one foot in the state of nature.

But note what he has psychologically consented to. The thirteenth clause requires that henceforth in his political capacity each citizen forgo his particular will and vote according to his estimate of the common good. And he has also agreed to abide by what is presumably the impersonal will of the majority. Because there is no guarantee that common good and private interest will always coincide, it may well be the case that a man's particular will conflicts with his impersonal or general will. This conflict, however, is not really to the point. So long as he continues to will the contract, he is accurately described as obeying himself, that is, his general will, even though psychologically he opposes the law in question. The more difficult case where an individual's general will conflicts with society's general will will be examined in chapter 4.

Sovereign law imposes a moral obligation because it is a product of the contract, and the contract is itself a long and complicated definition of what is to count as a moral obligation. It is often maintained that he who consents to the end consents to the necessary means. In a sense, Rousseau reverses this: he who consents to the means (the social contract as a process) consents to the end (the morally obligatory force of law). Any man who psychologically agrees to this process, at the same time morally obligates himself to its terminus, no matter what his personal desires. The social contract, therefore, is not a gimmick that is invoked to get civil society going and then quietly pushed into the background. On the contrary, more than a generative principle, it is the ongoing constitutive moral principle of society. Only insofar as it endures can laws be sovereign. Or, to put it another way, laws are sovereign only to the extent that they embody the social contract.[10]

Rousseau's contract, at least on the face of it, has accomplished what it set out to do: it has instituted a moral community where previously there was no such community; it has established a legitimate authority (the sovereign) whose will as law is morally obligatory. Conceding that a new, nonprudential obligation is created, it may and certainly will be objected that whatever this new type of obligation is, it isn't a moral obligation. It seems inevitable that any believer in a transcendent morality will reject Rousseau's account of morality as a convention. But I beg such readers to be patient. The general will is in no sense pure will; it has a cognitive dimension, and therefore there is no immediate reason to conclude that a general will is incompatible with transcendent standards of morality. On the contrary, as I will argue in chapter 8, Rousseau's conventional view of morality is quite peculiar and in the last analysis is not so very much at odds with nonconventional ethical theories.

For the present, however, we must concentrate on the conventional side of the social contract. Because the contract gives rise to moral obligations, it is logically prior to these obligations. This means that the contract itself is not obligatory, not before consent and not after consent. The question of obligation first arises with respect to the law and not with respect to the contract. The law is obligatory because it conforms to the contract. To ask further what makes the contract obligatory is to miss Rousseau's fundamental point: the contract itself is not obligatory; it is a definition of what is meant by a moral obligation. In a language community where words have fairly settled meanings, it can be asked whether a given word has been used correctly, and the issue can be referred to a dictionary. It does not make sense, however, to ask further whether the definition is correct. One could, of course, question the definition on other grounds—for example, its utility in ordering experience—but its correctness is, as it were, self-certifying. It is what it ought to be by the very fact that it is.

This analogy is not perfect, because Rousseau believed the contract to be unique, the only alternative to a state of nature. One must either accept morality as defined by the contract or live the amoral life of nature. This option not only antedates the contract, it is a continuing option both for individuals and peoples.[11] The contract is binding only insofar as it is psychologically accepted.[12] By the nature of the case, the contract cannot possibly contain a clause to the effect that consent once given can never be withdrawn. The contract contains substantive beliefs (namely, the civil creed and social ends), and it is unreasonable to expect anyone to promise that his present beliefs will never change. This is a good reason to deny that the contract is irrevocable, but the fundamental reason why consent can be withdrawn by an individual, and therefore by the people as a whole, is technical. If a person promises something and subsequently reneges, he is morally culpable. But the consent that activates the contract cannot be a promise because 'promise' is a moral term and takes on meaning only after the contract is in effect. Given Rousseau's approach, a person can consent to be a moral being, but this consent is not itself a moral act.

This formulation cannot but sound strange to readers all of whom have grown up in a moral community and have been socialized to believe they are, willy-nilly, subjects of moral imputation. But it is not so very eccentric if one starts with Rousseau's state of nature as a premise and correlates different types of consent with different types of freedom. Finally, one must always bear in mind Rousseau's claim that the convention giving rise to moral obligations is unique.[13]

If a people as a whole decide to revoke the contract, and they can (SC 1. 7), a state of nature is reinstituted in its entirety, and the only obligations that remain are purely prudential. The case of an individual who refuses to consent or who withdraws consent is somewhat different. If this individual remains in a territory inhabited by a moral community and disobeys the law, the government is morally obliged by the terms of the contract to exert force. What arises is an asymmetrical relation. The force exerted by the government, since it is presumably authorized by the people, is legitimate, but from the point of view of the individual it is merely natural force. The point to be emphasized is that the culprit has no grounds for complaint. He cannot, for example, argue that it is unfair or unjust or wrong that he be forced to obey or be punished for violating a law to which he has not consented. What he has not consented to is a standard that gives meaning to words like 'unfair', 'unjust', and 'wrong.' He is a man without a country because he is a man without a moral lexicon. The only thing he has is his natural freedom, and this cannot, strictly speaking, ever be said to be abridged in a state of nature.

Chapter 2

Freedom, Law, and the Citizen

Freedom: Three Kinds

The problem of legitimacy as Rousseau stated it is to find a form of association wherein each individual, while joining with the rest, nevertheless "obeys no one but himself, and remains as free as before" (*SC* 1. 6). The terms of the association are the multiple clauses of the social contract. But where in these clauses do we find a guarantee that men will obey only themselves and remain as free as before? In the previous chapter we sketched a distinction between psychological and moral consent. In order to understand how a man in obeying the laws obeys only himself, it is necessary to retrace our steps and proceed with more detail.

A state of nature is negatively related to the idea of a moral community. Conceptually speaking, it is the condition of men who are completely devoid of duties, either political or moral. In this condition there is only one rule for resolving conflicts should they occur: the rule of superior force. Since by its nature superior force determines fact, there is no basis for distinguishing what is and what ought to be the case. Freedom or right or liberty in this state is coterminous with power. Thus a man's natural freedom is simply his ability to effect his desires. This type of freedom has no moral significance. It establishes a right, but a kind of right for which there is no correlative duty. It is the right of the stronger to command and the obligation, but not the duty, of the weaker to submit or withdraw.

Though Rousseau speaks of man as giving up his natural freedom when he enters the civil state, this cession is not in practice complete. He cedes only as much as "the community needs for its own use" (*SC* 2. 4). In any society there are areas of behavior unbound by law or other regulatory devices. Within this private sphere it is useful to distinguish two sectors, one competitive and the other not. There are ways in which an individual can exercise his natural freedom without loss to anyone else—for example, taking a walk in the woods. In most societies there are also areas of legitimate competition. These are, as it were, miniature states of nature, restricted and structured by laws and regulations. In these areas competitors exercise their natural freedom within the rules, and it is 'might' or superior talent and ability that legitimately determine the distribution of goods. This is true whether the competition is a boxing match, a foot race, economic competition, or anything else. In these areas of lawful competition, the natural rights of competitors do not correlate with any duties. A man's right to win first place does not impose a duty on the other contestants to let him win.

There are two ways of looking at a man's natural freedom: absolutely and relatively. Man's absolute natural freedom is defined by physical laws. A man might want to walk on air, but the fact that gravity frustrates this desire cannot be viewed as a kind of tyranny abridging man's natural freedom. The absolute scope of natural freedom lies within the limits set by physical laws. As obvious as this is, it is worth stressing because it is Rousseau's paradigm for another type of freedom. It would be unusual, though not meaningless, to say that a man is free insofar as he obeys the physical laws of nature. He who would defy the law is not a free man but in many cases a dead man. In any case, obedience to the law is not a constraint on freedom, though it is a constraint on one's nature. The point is that the problem of freedom is not the problem of freedom versus constraint in general, but rather the problem of freedom versus specific kinds of constraint.

The constraints of physical law determine man's natural freedom considered absolutely. But in competitive situations new constraints are introduced—namely, the opposing interests of a second party. The actual freedom a man has at any given time is his absolute power less the resistant forces he encounters. Relative natural freedom in competitive encounters can be considerably less than absolute natural freedom. In fact it can amount to none at all when a desire is completely thwarted by a superior counterforce. Relative natural freedom is the same thing as effective natural freedom. When Hobbes describes his state of nature as the war of all against all, what he is describing is a condition where the effective natural right of all men approaches zero. It is necessary to distinguish absolute and relative freedom in order to avoid verbal inconsistencies. The civil state may require a limitation of natural liberty, but of which type? Though Rousseau gives two different accounts of the human predicament just prior to association, they agree in this: there was little effective freedom. In fact, the contract was motivated by the need to organize a collective force once the obstacles to self-preservation could not be overcome on an individual basis.[1] The contract, then, was designed not to diminish but to enhance effective natural freedom. In what otherwise would be a paradox, the contract seeks to heighten freedom (relative or effective) by limiting freedom (absolute).[2]

From an outsider's point of view the relative freedom of any given individual is seen as a variable depending on circumstances: In some circumstances he can effect his will; in other circumstances he is powerless. In a state of nature, however, it is not quite accurate to describe an individual's effective freedom as being abridged by some superior counterforce; relative freedom in any given context is simply what as a matter of fact it is. If we strip from the term 'inequality' all moral overtones, it is quite proper to speak of natural inequalities in a state of nature: the inequality that holds between the strong and the weak. What Rousseau denies is that there is a natural *moral* inequality that supposedly rests upon natural authorities.

In the state of nature the distribution of effective freedom is no more nor less a fact than the distribution of natural freedom considered absolutely. There is, however, a difference between the two facts. Since man is free, the harm that men do one another is a contingent fact, whereas gravity is an unavoidable fact. It is within man's power to create a different world, an artificial world with rules to resolve conflicts on a basis other than superior force. The aim of the contract is to substitute "moral and legal equality for such physical inequalities as nature may have created among men; and different as they may be in physical or intellectual powers, they all become equal by convention and the eyes of the law" (*SC* 2. 9).

The contract gives rise to a new type of obligation, an obligation that is foreign to the state of nature, namely, an obligation that is at the same time a duty. Though duties abridge natural freedom considered absolutely, Rousseau nevertheless claims that man in entering the civil state remains as free as before. His previous effective freedom is not what is at issue, because presumably the contract augments relative natural freedom. The 'before' Rousseau must be referring to is the first stage of the state of nature, where in the absence of competition a man's absolute and relative natural freedom coincided. Original man, though subject to physical laws, was said to be free, because he was not subject to personal constraints. As the state of nature evolved and competition arose, personal constraints in the form of superior might increased, and man's effective freedom decreased. The contract can be said to restore freedom to the extent that it eradicates personal dependencies.

Freedom, for Rousseau, is not incompatible with constraint or dependence in general but only with personal dependence.

There are two kinds of dependence: dependence on things, which is the work of nature; and dependence on men, which is the work of society. Dependence on things, being non-moral, does no injury to liberty . . . ; dependence on men, . . . gives rise to every kind of vice. . . . If there is a cure for this social evil, it is to be found in the substitution of law for the individual; in arming the general will with a real strength beyond the power of any individual will. If the laws of nations, like the laws of nature, could never be broken by any human power, dependence on men would become dependence on things.[3]

Personal dependence equates with inequality, whereas impersonal dependence insures equality. Physical laws are the models of impersonal dependence because they operate without exception and without regard to social distinctions such as status and wealth. Physical laws do not limit natural freedom; they simply define the natural scope of that freedom.

The contract entitles the assembly to legislate on its own behalf. A law creates a new form of obligation, a moral obligation or a duty. This obligation restricts man's natural freedom considered absolutely, but such restrictions are a priori necessities if one is going to speak a language of freedom and obligation with terms other than those that pertain exclusively to a state of nature. One may wish to question the merits of any given obligation, but to question the very meaning of political obligation is, for Rousseau, to choose the anarchy of the state of nature.

Political obligations or laws are analogous to physical laws. Just as natural freedom consists in doing what you want to and can do within the limits of physical laws, political or civil liberty consists in doing what you will within the limits of physical and coauthorized laws. Just as there are two ways of looking at the relation between freedom and physical necessity, so there are two ways of looking at the relation between freedom and duty. Because a man's natural freedom is not abridged by physical necessity, he is free both in obeying nature's laws and also in exercising his natural freedom. Similarly, because laws define and therefore do not abridge man's political freedom, he is free both in obeying these laws and also in exercising such legitimate natural freedom as remains. Political freedom is like the rules of a game. Rules circumscribe behavior, but they cannot be said in some pejorative sense to limit the freedom of a voluntary participant.

Rousseau sums up natural and political freedom and adds yet a third type.

Let us draw up the balance sheet in terms readily capable of comparison. What man loses by the social contract is his natural liberty, and an unlimited right to everything he wants and is capable of getting; what he gains is civil liberty, and the ownership of all he possesses. In order to make no mistake as to the balance of profit and loss, we must clearly distinguish between natural liberty, which has no other limit than the might of the individual, and civil liberty, which is limited by the general will. . . .

To the foregoing we might add that, along with the civil state, man acquires moral liberty, which alone makes him truly master of himself; for the impulse of mere appetite is slavery, and obedience to self-imposed law is liberty. [*SC* 1. 8]

Because all three types of liberty are in a sense self-imposed, Leo Strauss argues that Rousseau intentionally blurred the distinctions, because for Rousseau "the primary moral phenomenon is the freedom of the state of nature."[4] But are the distinctions really blurred? The exercise of one's natural liberty in a state of nature is always a case of self-authorization. The same is true of legitimate natural freedom, that is, the natural freedom that is not proscribed by law. If I am not otherwise obligated and I want to read a book, I'll read a book. I do not have to justify my decision before any tribunal other than my own desire. *My* desire, then, authorizes my behavior. Because selves differ, there is nothing in the idea of natural freedom that guarantees a noble or praiseworthy life. On the contrary, natural freedom is easily associated with a vulgar form of hedonism, with the slavery that results from "the impulse of mere appetite."

Laws are in a sense self-imposed, but in a very restricted sense. As long as a man consents to the contract, he may be said to consent to the law and thus self-impose it. But the consent that pertains to law is far different from the self-authorization that pertains to the state of nature: a man's consent to the law is measured by a tribunal other than particular desire. Above all, self-imposition with regard to law is *never* self-authorization. Rousseau is quite explicit: a law is that which binds all, but "that which any man . . . ordains on his own authority is not a law at all" (*SC* 2. 6). No individual or group less than the whole can authorize a law without introducing a relation of personal dependence, the very danger the idea of law seeks to obviate. At the very most a citizen coauthorizes a law, but his coauthority derives from the contract and not from his particular will.

Moral imperatives are even less a case of self-authorization than legal imperatives, for, as it will be argued later, the *content* of some moral obligations is not even capable of being coauthorized. Aside from this, what, in Rousseau's mind, demands the distinction between political and moral freedom? The difference is one of motivation. Obedience to law is not only a necessary condition of political freedom, it is a sufficient condition. Men often violate laws that in general they approve. The mere fact of a violation is no proof that the violator has ceased to accept the legislative process that created the law. An impatient motorist who jumps a red light need not be viewed as a revolutionary subversive. If a police car had happened to be behind him, certainly our impatient motorist would not have violated the law; his obedience would have been wholly prudential. But the fact that his obedience was forced does not mean that his political freedom was abridged. Political freedom is obedience to the law regardless of the motive of obedience. One would not be tempted to think a man's natural freedom was abridged because he did not like the law of gravity. Political obligations are moral obligations, and they are enforceable without prejudice to political freedom.

Moral freedom is, from a political point of view, a counsel of perfection and not a political obligation. It is, in Kantian terms, obedience to the law and for the sake of the law. A person who obeys the law despite the contrary promptings of private interest and even though he can disobey with impunity is morally free. This is what Rousseau means by moral freedom when he speaks of it as obedience to self-imposed laws. It is a higher type of freedom than political freedom, because it comprehends political freedom and adds the new dimension of self-mastery. In later terminology, the morally free man is the autonomous man. But a word of caution. 'Autonomy' is an ambiguous term. As applied to a political group, it signifies a competence to authorize laws; as applied to an individual, it signifies a voluntary, nonprudential acceptance of the law even against inclination. Self-imposition must never be confused with self-authorization.

Political freedom has two sides. First, a man is politically free when he obeys the law for whatever reason. Second, he may be described as politically free when he exercises his warranted natural freedom. Warranted natural freedom has its being within the interstices of the law. It is the first meaning that reconciles force and freedom. Rousseau, in a famous passage that many consider either nefarious or meaningless, argues "that anyone who refuses to obey the general will shall be forced to do so by the whole body; which means nothing more or less than that he will be forced to be free." [5] What Rousseau has in mind is the reluctant citizen. Anarchists aside, there is nothing particularly odd about an appeal to force on behalf of the law. Nevertheless, some commentators see something sinister in this conjunction of force and freedom.[6] At first sight this conjunction may seem paradoxical, but only if freedom is defined without qualification as an absence of constraint. But given Rousseau's tripartite division of freedom, the paradox disappears.

Since Rousseau distinguishes three types of freedom, one must ask what type of freedom force on behalf of the law guarantees. It seems evident that force cannot establish an individual's natural freedom: a citizen is naturally free when he does what he desires to do. And a reluctance overcome by force is hardly a reliable index of desire. It is equally evident that force and moral freedom are incompatible: the essential characteristic of moral freedom is that the obligation it acquits is self-imposed and unforced.[7] Thus, by elimination, the only freedom that might not be abridged by force is political freedom. Political freedom, it will be recalled, is maintained by de facto obedience to the law, independent of motivation. If force is necessary to insure compliance, then so be it. In any case, where legal compliance defines political freedom, force on behalf of compliance is indeed force on behalf of one kind of freedom.

Though this argument seems theoretically unassailable, it may still fail to convince, because the equation rests on a conception of political freedom that to many people may seem forced. But there is another way to express this equation between force and freedom that may appear less paradoxical.

For Rousseau, one cannot separate political freedom and equality, because both are defined as an absence of personal dependence. A good legislative system is one that secures both; it secures "liberty (political freedom), because any form of private dependence is that much force subtracted from the body of the state; equality, because liberty cannot subsist without it" (*SC* 2. 11). A citizen who would shirk his duty is seeking a personal exemption from an impersonal obligation; he is seeking to establish a relationship of inequality between himself and law-abiding citizens. A force that guarantees that duties are acquitted is a force that insures that strict equality obtains between all citizens. Had Rousseau argued that a reluctant citizen must be forced to be equal, few eyebrows would have been raised. But logically, though not rhetorically, 'forced to be equal' and 'forced to be free' are equivalent.

Law: Several Kinds

It should be obvious from the above discussion that the only type of freedom the contract can guarantee is political freedom. Civil society by its very nature limits natural freedom considered absolutely. Though political obligations are moral obligations, a man remains free no matter what his motives for acquitting them. The contract cannot contain a clause to the effect that all laws must be obeyed, and obeyed for the sake of duty. It cannot contain such a clause because the clause is not a necessary condition for the ends of the contract, and if the contract is, as claimed, a unique convention, all of its terms must be necessary conditions. One end of the contract is to guarantee freedom from personal dependence, and this is secured wherever the laws are faithfully obeyed, regardless of motivation. The motives for Smith's obeying the law neither add to nor subtract from the freedom Jones enjoys as a result of this obedience.

Freedom is obedience to law. But what is the nature of this law? We already know that this law must be a sovereign law, that it has standing only insofar as it meets the procedural requirements of the contract. A law may meet the formal dictates to be analyzed immediately below, but if it is promulgated by the government, it is not a binding sovereign law. Law is also an expression of the general will. This, however, is not very helpful, because an understanding of what a general will is depends upon a prior understanding of the nature of law.

Law cannot pertain to the particular. "Even that which the sovereign ordains with regard to a particular object is no longer a law, but a decree; nor is it an act of sovereignty, but of magistracy" (*SC* 2. 6). Sovereign authority, like law, is limited to the general: "sovereign power, absolute, sacred and inviolable as it is, does not and cannot go beyond the limits of general conventions, . . . hence the sovereign never has a right to burden one subject more than another, for that would be a particular question to which its competence no longer extends" (*SC* 2. 4). This apposition between general and particular is paralleled by the related appositions between sovereign and government, impersonal and personal, general and particular wills, law and decree.

But what is the nature of this generality that is the necessary, though not the sufficient, condition of law? The most obvious difficulty that surrounds any idea of generality is logical, a difficulty Rousseau bequeathed Kant and his many commentators. Consider the following propositions: (*a*) "No man may lie." (*b*) "No man with red hair may lie." (*c*) "No man with red hair over thirty may lie." (*d*) "No man with red hair over thirty born on the far side of the tracks may lie." And so on, right down to a proposition, general in form, that in fact singles out an individual. It follows that mere logical generality cannot suffice to define law, for were that the case there would be nothing to distinguish a law from a decree. What must also be considered is the extension or scope of the law: how many are bound by its prescriptions? It will be argued that for Rousseau law must embody a principle of universality. That is, it must be so framed that it applies either actually or potentially to every citizen without exception.

That Rousseau believed in a principle of universality can be supported by a variety of evidence. In the first place there are two other types of enactments which he calls laws: moral law and physical law. Though moral law is not held to be binding in the absence of assured sanction (*SC* 2. 6), its form is such as to embrace all men without distinction or discrimination. The Stoic corollary of this universality is the idea of a single human community. The proscription "Thou shalt not kill" was not limited to this or that nation, this or that group within a nation; it was conceived to apply to any being who instanced the class (man) and not to some subclass (say, rich man or poor man).

The case of physical law is even more instructive. Though moral laws may be broken, physical laws cannot. Physical laws are self-enforcing, and they comprehend everyone without distinctions. They are Rousseau's model of impersonal law. It is their impersonal force that reconciles constraint and freedom by defining the outer limits of natural freedom. For a law to qualify as impersonal in Rousseau's sense, two conditions must be satisfied: (*a*) it must regulate everyone either actually or potentially, and (*b*) its operation must not lead to inequality. It is important to bear this latter condition in mind, so as not to confuse his usage with that of those who speak of the impersonal laws that govern a market economy. This type of impersonal coercion is not what Rousseau had in mind, because its effect necessarily leads to great inequalities. For impersonal coercion to be legitimate it must affect all in the same way. As ever, equality is the touchstone.

In a more direct vein, we have Rousseau's own words: "But when the whole people legislates for the *whole people*, it considers itself only; and if a relationship is then established, it is between the *whole object* seen from a certain point of view, and the *whole object* seen from another point of view, with no division of the whole."[8]

The constant emphasis on unity and wholeness is not accidental. The social contract and subsequent laws transform a mere aggregate of individuals into a people, an artificial whole with its own personality and will. Each individual has a dual role. As a citizen he is an active participant in the sovereign process; as a subject he owes perfect obedience to the law. Subject and citizen-sovereign are correlatives.[9] Sovereignty does not pertain to an individual in any absolute sense; it pertains to an individual only in relation to other individuals similarly and mutually engaged in the legislative process. Correlatively, an individual is not a subject qua individual, but only insofar as all others are equally bound by the law. Because of this correlativity there cannot be, save indirectly, a law that subjects but a part of the citizenry.[10]

This isomorphism between the citizen as sovereign and the citizen as subject can only be maintained if laws embody a principle of universality. "All may prescribe what all must do; but no one has the right to require another to do anything he does not do himself" (*SC* 3. 16). Since law bears upon the citizen as subject and since citizenship pertains to the individual only through the mediation of the whole, it follows that no regulation of a part of the whole, say the subclass of plumbers, can count as law. Sovereignty, law, and one meaning of the general will are inseparable and for most purposes indistinguishable. Rousseau is quite explicit in asserting the interrelatedness of his secular trinity: "The sovereign, having no other force than the legislative power, acts only through laws; and since the laws are nothing but authentic acts of the general will, the sovereign can only act when the people is assembled" (*SC* 3. 12).

Rousseau is not at all hesitant in drawing the implications of this principle of universality: there can be no such thing as international law. This follows because a particular object can be outside as well as inside a state. "If it is outside, a will which is foreign to that object is not general with reference to it."[11] It also follows because between states there is no common superior, that is, there is no sovereign, and where there is no sovereign there is no law. International relations, therefore, are prudential arrangements made between governments. If a declaration of war is to be made, it must be made by the government.[12]

On the face of it, criminal law would seem to be the paradigmatic embodiment of Rousseau's conception of law. "Thou shalt not steal" places the same obligation on each and every citizen. The universality of the law suffices to insure impersonality, because by encompassing all, it does not single out an individual or a group of individuals. If all laws were of this type there would be no theoretical difficulties,[13] but the area of sovereign competence would also be severely circumscribed. As a matter of fact, Rousseau accepts as laws enactments of a different type. The sovereign, for example, can legislative privileges (*SC* 2. 6).

Conceivably, a law might assign a privilege to all citizens. Were this the case the impersonality of criminal law would be maintained. Such a status law differs from criminal law only in modality: the 'all must' or 'no one may' modality is changed to an 'all may' modality. Laws that enable citizens to make wills and marry are examples. But with the possible exception of citizenship, which will be considered below, a law conferring a universal privilege is of little theoretical interest. More interesting is the case of a privilege that is in scarce supply, a right of the relatively few.

It is obvious that such a law would be of a type different from criminal law. Not only is there a change of modality from duty to right, but, unlike the universal scope of duty, the ensuing distribution of right is only partial. If it is to count as law, therefore, the criteria of distribution must be impersonal: it cannot antecedently name an individual or a group. By the nature of the case this impersonality can only be achieved negatively: the criteria must be such as to debar no citizen from acquiring the privilege. The criteria, in other words, must insure that all citizens are potential candidates for the privilege. The sovereign, for example, may say that the citizen who contributes the most voluntary labor on public lands over a specified period of time is entitled to wear a wooden medal. But it cannot say that the plumber who repairs the most public lavatories is entitled to a badge of distinction, unless, of course, all citizens happen to be plumbers. To repeat, law pertains to the citizen; this is the highest political generality and therefore the most universal term. A privilege can relate only to man the citizen, and not to man the member of some lesser association.

This type of legislation may be used to articulate society, but it does not disturb equality as understood by Rousseau. Though it is not the case that all citizens will be equally privileged, it is the case antecedently that any citizen may be so privileged. After the fact, some and only some are rewarded, but never in such a way that their individual wills are permitted an area of personal authority over others. As long as no citizen stands in a relation of personal dependence on others, all citizens are equal.

There is yet another form of law which combines characteristics of criminal and privilege laws and adds a new one. A limited distribution of public honors is not necessarily a burden on the unprivileged. However, there are cases where an unequal distribution of social burdens may be necessitated. If such a distribution is to be made according to law, its universality must be like that of privileges. That is, if it is not the case that all citizens are burdened, it must be the case that any citizen antecedently was liable to be burdened. But since it is a question of a social burden, the modality must be that of criminal law. An individual citizen need not aspire to public honors, but, if impersonally chosen, he must acquit such public responsibilities as the sovereign may order.

Let us assume that a lawful state requires an army for defense. In a state of nature each man is the proper judge of threats to his life, and he has the right to act according to his judgment even if his judgment advises flight. But once he contracts, "his life is no longer a simple boon of nature, but a conditional gift of the state" (*SC* 2. 5). The sovereign might call for universal military training for all citizens for a period of two years. Such a law might seem to be subsumable under the form of criminal law; its extension is universal and its modality is that of obligation. However, there is a difference. Whereas criminal law creates obligations for all *at the same time*, a draft law imposes obligations on all citizens *at one time or another*.

This new qualification is hardly a theoretical threat to equality of obligations. But suppose the sovereign decides that its interests may be secured with a far smaller army; it may decide to draft only one-half of an age group each year. Then it would not be the case that all citizens are equally obliged one time or another. To guarantee impersonality, a draft law must embody something of the logical form of privilege legislation. Its universality cannot be of the 'every citizen' variety but rather must be of the 'any citizen' type. Whereas privileges are a matter of personal effort, less-than-universal obligations ought to be a consequence of chance. A lottery containing the names of all citizens of a certain age group assures impersonality in somewhat the same way as germs impersonally and randomly affect some people rather than others.[14]

Though a draft can be impersonal, an army requires personal decisions in the assignment of risks. Depending upon the tactical situation, some individuals may be called upon to risk more than others. "Now the citizen is no longer judge of the dangers to which the law wishes him to expose himself, and if the prince has told him: 'It is expedient for the state that you should die,' he ought to die; since it is on this condition only that he has lived in security up to that moment" (*SC* 2. 5). Note that it is the prince (that is, the government or some governmental agency) that makes the specific, individual application of the law, and not the sovereign.

For Rousseau, criminal law is not so much a distinct species of law as the sanction for all other types of law (*SC* 2. 12). By broadening the usual concept of criminal law, he is able to add to the laws a measure of flexibility they would not otherwise have. A good example of this may be found in his approach to a certain type of taxation.

In a nonmonied economy or one in which the distribution of wealth was practically equal, tax policy could easily be left to the sovereign. The proposition "All citizens shall contribute so much labor on public fields" meets all the logical requirements of an acceptable form of law: it embraces all citizens, it imposes equal burdens, and the obligation obtains either at the same time or one time or another. But as differentials increase, an equal tax bears unequally on rich and poor. Luxury, the presence of great differentials, was of course Rousseau's great bête noire. For many reasons that are not relevant here, he believed that sovereignty and luxury could not long coexist. Hence, the question of laws (that is, expressions of sovereignty regulating luxury) may be somewhat academic. Nevertheless, the treatment of luxury taxes in his *Political Economy* is of theoretical interest for the light it sheds on his conviction that without universality there can be no law.[15] The difficulty is that where there are de facto discrepancies in wealth, a tax that applies exclusively or differentially to one sector of society is, on the face of it, discriminatory and thus not a law. In *Emile* Rousseau argued that the sovereign could confiscate the property of all citizens but could not abolish private debts, since this would discriminate the less-than-general class of creditors (*Emile*, p. 425).

By the same right, the sovereign may set limits to personal accumulation, provided the limits are the same for all. However, there may be situations where public opinion is not sufficiently strong to discourage individual pursuit of luxury. Where this is the case, absolute sumptuary legislation may not be wise on pragmatic grounds. Alternatively, a progressive tax might be incorporated as part of the criminal code. We are accustomed to such legal forms as "No man may steal," "If any man steals a hundred dollars he will be sentenced to six months in jail; if a thousand dollars, a year's imprisonment," and so on. This form meets the requirements of the principle of universality.

Since it is within the sovereign's right to ban luxury absolutely, it is a fortiori within the sovereign's right to control luxury, provided the controls can be expressed in the form of a law. Using the above form, the sovereign can proclaim, "No man may accumulate property beyond so much. Any man who does so shall be fined (taxed) so much for each additional increment." On this view a tax is a fine that compensates in some measure for the abuse it censures.[16] Though this form of social control does not involve a new form of law, it is important to note that it can be used to regulate areas of behavior that would not ordinarily be described as criminal.

If the social contract itself were a law, as Rousseau seems to believe (*SC* 1. 7; 3. 18; 4. 2), then it would constitute yet another species of the genus law. Though it has characteristics in common with law—impersonality, equality of right, and equality of obligation—there are compelling analytic reasons to regard it as something distinct from law. Rousseau himself recognizes its uniqueness in that it is the only law that requires unanimous consent. Again, though all laws are by sovereign right subject to modification or change, "the clauses of this contract are so completely determined by the nature of the act that the slightest modification would render them null and void" (*SC* 1. 6). Any given law may be annulled without thus annulling all other laws, but if the social contract is annulled, and this is permissible (*SC* 3. 18), all other laws are by that very fact annulled.

This follows because the morally obligatory character of law is based on the contract, and 'obligation', other than prudential, has meaning only in reference to the contract. To cancel the contract is to render obligation meaningless and thus to destroy the very essence of law. It makes sense to say that the contract justifies the obligations imposed by law. It does not make sense to say that the obligatory character of the contract is justified by the contract itself. Were this the case, there would be no legitimate grounds for abrogating the contract: it would be obligatory in perpetuity. It is not the sovereign people who create the contract, but rather the contract creates a sovereign body out of a mere aggregate of individuals.

Though all the clauses of the social contract could be expressed in some recognizable form of law, for the reasons given above it is best not to consider them laws. But a new problem arises. If law cannot create law, can it create an institution to enforce itself?

This is really two questions: Can law institute a government? and, If so, is constitutional law a new species of law? With respect to the first question a distinction must be made. Though the sovereign may legislate the form of government, it cannot, as sovereign, elect individuals to staff the government. Election is a particular act, and thus is not within the sovereign's competence (*SC* 3. 12).

There is no doubt that Rousseau believed that constitutional law, which establishes a government to mediate between the people as sovereign and the people as subject, is law in his sense of the term. Since the sovereign is the sole source of any kind of legislation, Rousseau cannot and does not distinguish, as we do, statutory and fundamental law (*SC* 2. 12). Sociological considerations might dictate one form of government rather than another, for the sake of insuring a measure of permanence. But such a government would be 'fundamental' only in an extralegal sense. All laws are one in the sense of being obligatory and subject to change by the sovereign, but not all laws assume the same form.

It is not necessary to introduce a new logical type to account for constitutional law. Constitutional law may be received as a condensed version of a complex of laws that accord privileges and impose obligations on those who will eventually be chosen to fill various governmental berths. This reductive process may be complex, inelegant, and cumbersome, but its possibility is proof that something as fundamental and important as a constitution is a part of sovereign right. As a simple illustration of a reduction, one can envisage the establishment of a monarchy by the following formula: "any man chosen by lot or designated by a majority vote shall have the following privileges and obligations: 1, 2, 3, . . . , *n*," where the numbers spell out regal duties and rights. The reduction of more complicated polities would proceed along similar lines. The sovereign has great flexibility in setting eligibility standards. There may be none; there may be age limits; there may be prior service qualifications. The only proviso is that, in principle at least, no citizen is by the nature of the law automatically excluded from participation in government for all time.

Thus far laws have been analyzed exclusively within the context of the citizen-subject relation, where the individual as citizen formulates the law and as subject obeys it. These two terms are identical in extension: there is no citizen who is not a subject and every subject is a citizen. However, in society as a whole there is a sizeable class of noncitizens, namely, women, children, and perhaps foreigners. If laws regulating their behavior are permissible, they cannot be laws reglating subjects in a technical sense. For want of a better term, such laws may be referred to as those regulating dependents or, more clinically, those regulating objects. In any case, this change of relationship would seem to imply a new type of law.

All societies have laws that bear upon noncitizens or nonvoting citizens. This class includes an area of legislation that was of prime interest to Rousseau and that he explicitly considered. If sovereignty is to be maintained over a period of time, there must be an assured source of new citizens. In his advice to Poland, Rousseau says that "it is education that must give souls a national formation, and direct their opinions and tastes in such a way that they will be patriotic by inclination, by passion, by necessity." So essential is education that "the *law* ought to regulate the content, the order and the form of studies." [17]

From the point of view of the sovereign, the character formation of future citizens is undoubtedly a common concern, and to that extent it falls within its sphere. But the difficulty is that non-subjects are involved: a potential citizen is simply not a citizen. Thus the problem is to see if the sovereign has a language capable of addressing someone other than itself—whether the sovereign can speak to foreigners.

A simple solution would be to dismiss the problem and maintain that Rousseau used the term 'law' carelessly when referring to education. But this won't do, because he had a singular preoccupation with education, and if education is not a sovereign concern it would have to fall within the authority of either parents or government. The public and uniform character of the education Rousseau preached rules out the former possibility, and two general reasons preclude the latter. There is an ever-active tendency on the part of government to usurp sovereignty. To assign it control over education would be the same as insuring it the loyalty of a future generation. In the second place it must be realized that the government's language, and therefore authority, when it addresses others is highly circumscribed. It can speak only in particulars, and these particulars must be instances of some universal or law. If there is a law forbidding murder, the government can detain, prosecute, and execute an individual who commits homicide. But if there is no law against drinking, it can have nothing to say about drunkards. Without a corresponding law there can be no intelligible (that is, legitimate) decree.[18]

A program of education might be so framed as to mirror some of the traits of law. It might, for example, be truly uniform, and it might impose equal obligations on an entire class at one time or another. But the form of legislation is not what is in question; no matter how it is expressed, it is ultimately concerned with objects, not subjects. If Rousseau's conception of sovereignty is to be effectual, there must be some way of justifying this form of law, since it is difficult, if not impossible, to conceive a society lacking regulations of this type. Whether Rousseau was aware of the difficulty I do not know. As far as I know he never explicitly raised the question. I think, however, there is a way to analyze this species of law without departing from any of his principles or assuming new ones.[19]

Suppose a state possesses public lands and cattle. In order to support its government the sovereign might rule that taxes be paid by labor on these lands and by the slaughter and preparation of so many cattle per month. A law to this effect would seem to be a simple tax law. But note that in the execution of their duty the citizens are imposing their wills on entities that have not consented to this manipulation. This, it may be charged, is a facetious use of 'nonconsent,' since earth, cows, and the like are under no circumstances subjects of moral imputation. This, of course, is true, but that very fact is part of the justification of such a law. It is not the land that is obliged by the laws but the citizen. It just happens in this case that, in the course of acquitting his obligation to the sovereign, the citizen finds himself in a second relation with purely natural objects. Vis-à-vis an object, he is in a state of nature, where the only rule is that of superior force.

A child, unlike a chicken, is assigned a certain moral status because of his potential. But there is an age before which he is not deemed morally culpable and usually a later age before which he is not considered capable of participation in the political process. As a political adolescent he falls within the class of dependent objects; he is in a virtual state of nature, where he can only relate to others in terms of natural right.[20] Since he has not reached full moral maturity, there is no question of his nonexistent autonomy's being violated. During this period he, like the cow, is held to be incapable of giving moral consent to any law.

An educational law, then, like any law that involves objects, can be justified if it is conceded that a citizen can at the same time be the terminus of two different relations, namely, a moral relation with respect to the sovereign and a prudential relation with respect to the child. The sovereign, in the language of law, can order a citizen selected impersonally to teach pupils according to a prescribed curriculum. The moral obligation that is an implicit part of all laws falls on the citizen-teacher, not on the pupils. On the same grounds, the authority of the teacher is not, strictly speaking, in relation to his students, but in relation to citizens who have not been similarly burdened or honored. Rousseau, it would seem, remarkably anticipated a contemporary phenomenon by placing student-faculty relations in a state of nature.[21]

The Citizen: One Kind

Once it is conceded that Rousseau's theory of law allows for the sovereign's regulation of 'objects', including human noncitizens, ominous questions suggest themselves. Who determines the class of citizens, and are there any limitations on the kinds of qualifications that constitute citizenship? These certainly must be considered among the most fundamental questions that ought to be asked of the *Social Contract*. For, depending upon the answers, all the forms of law considered above either promote Rousseau's ideals of liberty and equality or lead to a most noxious form of despotism.

This may seem an exaggerated claim, and all the more so since Rousseau himself was apparently unaware of the implications of the questions, and, as far as I know, they have not been asked or analyzed by any major commentator. There have been analyses of what a citizen is or ought to be, but no analyses of what constitutes citizenship as such. The term 'citizen' so pervades Rousseau's writing that, like the letter on the open desk, its theoretical implications are apt to lie hidden.

Initially all contracting adults are citizens, and all accept each "as an indivisible part of the whole" (*SC* 1. 6). This would seem to say that there could be no subsequent disenfranchisement of the original contractors, but it does not say anything about subsequent generations.[22] On the face of it, it might seem that it is within the sovereign's competence to determine citizenship requirements for all newcomers. But if the sovereign has the right to make citizens, by the nature of law it has the right to unmake them. With the authority to enfranchise and disenfranchise, interest blocs could combine to vote a new citizenship law that effects a contraction of sovereignty by excluding some who have hitherto been citizens and thus increasing the class of noncitizens. In theory, each succeeding assembly could result in further reductions, and one can hypothesize a case where the sovereign becomes identical with two individuals or even one. At such a point the sovereign could transform itself into a 'democracy', that is, rule by all the citizens. The general will thus becomes identical with the government's will, and there are no longer theoretical bars to any kind of substantive legislation. There is a perfect coincidence of general, governmental, and particular wills, a possibility Rousseau obviously would not approve.[23]

Rousseau not only envisaged but expected the usurpation of sovereignty by government. As he saw it, this would always be illegitimate. But the above possibility shows that the same end can, in principle, be achieved by a succession of steps, each one of which is formally legal. Legal, that is, if the sovereign has the right to determine the franchise. Though Rousseau undoubtedly would condemn this type of sovereign contraction, the question is whether he explicitly provided theoretical checks to such a process or whether checks can be deduced from other explicit principles. Paradoxically, if restraints on sovereignty cannot be discovered in this context, the whole idea of sovereignty as conceived by Rousseau becomes meaningless: any theory that justifies indifferently any sort of sovereign-government-society relationship is sterile. It cannot establish legitimacy. Rousseau spoke without elaboration of the sovereign's right to create several classes of citizens (*SC* 2. 6). This probably means no more than the sovereign's right to confer specialized privileges or duties according to forms of law discussed above. Such class stratification is not relevant to the problem at hand, provided it is assumed that, once the citizenry are assembled to express the general will, all distinctions are suspended and all citizens meet on common grounds, free and equal.

In his *Considerations on the Government of Poland*, Rousseau's proposals envisage what is essentially an aristocracy, with "the total exclusion of all traders, artisans, and labourers from political power, the ruthless denial of the most elementary civil rights to the serfs."[24] This "illiberalism," according to Vaughan, is due to Montesquieu's growing influence on Rousseau's thought. The point is that, given certain socioeconomic conditions, the social contract simply cannot be realized. Since the present problem is one of a pure theory of legitimacy, Rousseau's recommendations for Poland are of little help in determining his theoretical stance.[25]

His advice to Corsica, however, cannot be so easily dismissed. Rousseau explicitly said that Corsica was the one country of Europe still capable of supporting legislation (*SC* 2. 10). An analysis of his recommendations, moreover, shows that he intended to implement fully all the principles of political right as he understood them. For these reasons it is necessary to consider his plan to divide Corsican society into three classes, two of which are composed of noncitizens.

Public education of minors has as its end the creation of citizenlike wills, wills which look to the common good. But this is too abstract. Civil associations are not formed without a prior sense of direction; they are formed with an eye toward instituting, maintaining, or furthering certain moral and social ideals. In general, what is conducive to these ends in a given set of circumstances ought to be encouraged in the name of the public good, and what tends to undermine them ought to be prohibited or discouraged. This is the approach Rousseau took when outlining a constitution for Corsica.

Without going into his reasoning process, his conclusions can be briefly summarized. Corsicans can retain their freedom only if their economy is exclusively agricultural, consisting of a public domain and a series of more or less self-sufficient family farms. Toward these ends Rousseau proposes to encourage strong family ties and to attract men to the soil by making family structure and ownership of land the basis of rights and status. And this, he holds, can best be done by dividing the nation into three classes. Initially all twenty-year-old Corsican males who swear an oath of loyalty shall be accounted citizens without distinction. This is a right their bravery in achieving independence has earned them. Subsequently, constitutional law is to provide for a tripartite division. At the bottom of the hierarchy are the aspirants, a residual class of those who have not met the conditions that define the patriot class. A patriot is a legally married male with property of his own. When he becomes the father of two living children and has his own house and land sufficient to support his family, he becomes a citizen.[26]

It is clear that these several requirements would promote the envisioned society. It is equally clear that the class of noncitizens contains any number of mature men who are morally and politically disenfranchised: in Rousseau's theory, citizenship is a necessary condition of moral and political obligation. Where his theory is concerned, it is irrelevant that the aspirants and patriots personally consent to their status. Being denied participation in the assembly, they cannot be said to have consented to a law of their own choosing. Some aspirants, and certainly all patriots, have reached the age of moral independence, and yet, lacking the franchise, their only relation to law is that which treats them as dependent objects. Unlike the case of cows or minors, this seems to be a clear-cut case of political oppression.

The question comes down to this: can the sovereign in defining 'citizen' set up standards that exclude morally responsible residents against their will?[27] If the Corsican constitution is taken as final, Rousseau's answer would have to be understood as yes. But if one is to view the *Social Contract* as an instrument of freedom, I think his recommendations for class divisions must be dismissed as a mistake. Rousseau, I believe, would have conceded this had he realized all the theoretical implications such a division entails. Aside from the anomaly of a law that has the effect of preventing a moral agent from assuming moral obligations,[28] there are other peculiarities about a law that restricts the franchise. Criminal law distinguishes between the citizen as such and the citizen as thief, for example. A citizenship law can never make a comparable distinction. Since such a law defines a citizen, it would be a contradiction in terms to say that a citizen has failed to live up to the conditions of citizenship. Analytically speaking, it is not a law that a citizen could either break or fulfill. It is not a law that expresses either a moral 'must', as in the case of the criminal code, or an enabling 'may', as in the case of privilege legislation. In a word, it is not a prescriptive law; being a definition, it is better classified as descriptive. The class of citizens may vary numerically, but if such a law is permissible it will always be the trivial case that those and only those who meet the requirements are in fact citizens.

If citizenship restrictions can be defined by the sovereign, a serious ambiguity emerges. Sovereign law aims at the common good. So long as the franchise is universal there is little, if any, possible conflict between the common good of the sovereign and the common good of society as a whole. However, where the sovereign contracts, a conflict is highly probable. And since sovereignty declares the common good, it is equally possible that law will become an exploitative device serving the interests of a minority. Those who believe that Rousseau would condemn this outcome must question the sovereign's right to define citizenship.

The argument from silence strongly suggests that Rousseau never foresaw the possibility of a legitimate contraction of sovereignty. His attention seems to have been exclusively focused on governmental usurpation of sovereignty, a usurpation as inevitable as it is deplorable. Nevertheless, in his analysis of the government's will to power, he explicitly considers a de facto case of sovereign contraction. This occurs when the only will that prevails is the general will of the government. This, however, is not legitimate; when it occurs the state is dissolved, "and within it is

formed another composed exclusively of members of the government; and this new state, in relation to the rest of the people, is no
longer anything more than a master and a tyrant" (*SC* 3. 10).
Since there is little pragmatic difference between governmental
usurpation and legal contraction of sovereignty through control of
the franchise, it may be argued that Rousseau's denunciation of
the former would have extended to the latter had he been aware
of it as a possibility within his theory.

The class division proposed for Corsica is all the more unfortunate because the laudable ends sought could probably have been
attained just as well without restricting the franchise. In the first
place there are educational laws designed to predispose young
minds toward internalization of the social ideals. Then again,
there might have been privilege laws, laws conferring status on
the basis of family size and amount of cultivated land. Another
possibility would have been to incorporate the relevant ideals
within Rousseau's broadened conception of criminal law. There
might, for example, have been a law that required all citizens to
cultivate land and have families. The attached penalties for different degrees of noncompliance might have involved varying
amounts of labor on public lands. As a matter of fact, Rousseau
did recommend something like this. Since aspirants, by definition, lack land of their own, they cannot pay taxes with produce.
Accordingly, it is just that they "should pay with their own labor"
(*Corsica*, p. 319). In our society this general type of tax is the lot of
bachelors, and it is a matter of economic indifference whether it is
described as a penalty, a fine, or a tax. None of these possibilities,
singly or in combination, deny a moral agent the status of citizen.

Even though it might be conceded that Rousseau would not
have approved an initial restriction of the franchise, another question may be asked. Under what conditions, if any, can the sovereign divest an individual of his citizenship? A criminal code is
meaningless unless violations are accompanied by sanctions. Are
there any theoretical limits to the punishment the sovereign can
assign a crime? This is equivalent to asking if all proposed penalties can be expressed in some valid form of law. It seems obvious
that most penalties can be so expressed. "Any citizen duly convicted of walking on the grass shall be (*a*) fined fifty cents, or (*b*)

jailed for ten years, or (c) hanged," and so forth. It is difficult to imagine a formal device that could effectively limit sovereign assignment of punishments.

Rousseau has remarkably little to say on this subject. He does, however, allow the death penalty and therefore, by implication, all lesser penalties. But what is most interesting is that his justification of capital punishment proceeds along two different lines.

(a) A citizen may judge murder to be a crime serious enough to warrant hanging, and vote accordingly. "It is in order not to fall victim to a murder that we consent to die if we ourselves commit murder" (SC 2. 5). Since a general will cannot exempt individuals, a guilty citizen can be said to consent to his own execution no matter what the disposition of his particular will on the day of execution. The point to note is that though an individual has broken a law, he may still maintain his consent to the social contract that grounds it. Where this is the case, it is a *citizen* who is executed. This may seem an irrelevant nuance when the death penalty is involved, but the principle is clear enough in lesser offenses. The ordinary driver who runs a stop sign is not likely to interpret his guilt as prima-facie evidence that he has renounced his consent to the constitution.

(b) But there may be cases where a person's behavior does constitute sufficient evidence that he no longer holds himself obligated by the terms of the contract. Such a person has violated not only individual laws but the fundamental contract itself. "He must be cut off from it [the state] by exile as a violator of the compact, or by death as a public enemy. For an enemy of this sort is not an artificial person, but an individual man, and in such cases the right of war is to kill the vanquished."[29] The point is that a citizen is an artificial person, not a man in a state of nature. In this case, accordingly, the government executes a mere individual, not a citizen.

This distinction between subjects of punishment, between a citizen and a natural man, is of no pragmatic significance in the case of death or exile. But it is important to bear in mind, lest it be thought that every breach of law is necessarily a renunciation of the social contract itself and therefore automatically warrants loss of citizenship. This distinction also suggests a major limitation on the sovereign's right to punish. If, as argued above, Rousseau would not have accorded sovereignty an absolute power of enfranchisement or disenfranchisement, it hardly seems likely that he would allow these powers to slip in the back door in the guise of criminal law.

The question of citizenship is fundamental to his whole political theory, because the formal characteristics of all the types of law discussed above are substantively mute without some indication of the permissible ratio between citizenry and society as a whole. It is therefore frustrating to find Rousseau so careless by omission in his treatment of this key subject. What follows is a somewhat speculative reconstruction of the proper relationship between crime and citizenship. It may not reflect Rousseau's conscious position, but it falls within the limits of his explicit principles and deductions therefrom.

There is a very important and fundamental sense in which no sovereign law can transform an individual into a citizen. This becomes clear when it is asked, "Who created the original citizens?" Since the sovereign is coextensive with the class of all citizens, to say that the sovereign creates citizens is to mistake logical priorities. Conversely, it is to be guilty of the same mistake to say that citizens create the sovereign. They only constitute it. Prior to the sovereign and the citizen there are only two relevant entities: individuals in a state of nature and a proposal for a very special contract, the slightest change in which abrogates it. It is each individual's act of consent that creates the citizen, and sovereignty is the totality acting in a prescribed manner. Those who do not consent remain in a state of nature; they are foreigners in a new civil state (*SC* 4. 2).

Just as an individual is under no obligation to give an initial consent to the contract and thus become a citizen, so, with a few reservations, he can withdraw his consent and thereby cease to be a citizen. In the last analysis, whether a person does consent to the contract is a question of fact. It may be a complicated and not easily ascertainable fact, but it is still a fact independent of mere verbalization. Thus a man might plead guilty to a crime, swear allegiance to the state, and nevertheless both be punished for the crime and declared a noncitizen by the government.[30] It must be stressed that in this case the government has not stripped an individual of his citizenship rights. It has merely declared the fact that the culprit has voluntarily withdrawn his consent to the contract and thus divested himself of such rights and duties. As in all human enterprises, of course, mistakes may be made and injustices worked.

There is a peculiar relationship between consent and citizenship in Rousseau's thought. To say that a person consents to a given law is not necessarily to say that he likes it, that it has the blessings of his particular will. It is to say that the person here and now consents to the principles of the social contract that justifies the law. Conversely, one cannot use psychological acceptance of a law or laws as evidence for consent in Rousseau's restricted sense of that term. One can easily imagine a total revolutionary consenting to laws protecting his life, liberty, and property. But more to the point, if one is not a citizen he cannot consent, save psychologically, to any laws whatever, because he cannot consent to the contract. He may like the terms of the contract; he might willingly assume its burdens if permitted. Given Rousseau's meaning of 'consent', no one can consent to a contract that requires his active participation in the assembly and that at the same time authorizes his involuntary disfranchisement.

The point is that consent and citizenship are two sides of the proverbial coin: a nonconsenting citizen or a noncitizen's consent are simple contradictions.[31] This is yet another reason to suspect that if Rousseau personally would have allowed franchise restrictions, he did not correctly read the implications of his original contract. The *Social Contract* enumerates a series of obligations and rights. But nowhere is there to be found mention of initial nonvoluntary exclusions. The only condition of citizenship is consent, and this consent is not only a necessary condition of citizenship, it is also a sufficient condition. Citizenship laws, purportedly justified by the contract, would in effect repeal the nonexclusivity of the original contract and thus render it null and void. Again, it seems highly unlikely that Rousseau would present his contract as the basis on which a man may live morally in a moral society and at the same time empower it to exclude moral agents from a full moral life.

Given the specialized meaning of 'consent', it follows that, just as a man cannot consent to a social contract that excludes him, he cannot, as a citizen, conceivably consent to a law that at some future time might disenfranchise him. He can, of course, unilaterally renounce the contract and thereby voluntarily give up his citizenship. But he cannot, without contradiction, will the contract and also possible loss of citizenship, since to will the contract necessarily is to will citizenship. Theoretically, if not psychologically, a person can will the contract and any form of punishment, even death, that does not entail a loss of the franchise.[32] Because of the nature of the general will, a person cannot legitimately will one thing for himself and something else for others. It follows, therefore, that if no citizen can consent to his own disenfranchisement, the sovereign simply has no language capable of expressing a franchise law, not even through the medium of criminal law.

The same conclusion is reached when one analyzes similar limitations in the language of government. The government can certify the *fact* that a criminal is no longer a citizen; it cannot as punishment divest him of something he no longer possesses. Given appropriate legislation, the courts can call a citizen a thief or a drunkard, but how is it logically or verbally possible to call a citizen a noncitizen? The government can say, "This citizen is a thief." It cannot say, "This citizen is not a citizen." Just as a citizen qua citizen cannot consent to disenfranchisement, so a government cannot without contradiction punish a citizen qua citizen with a loss of citizenship.

If neither the sovereign nor the government has a language sufficient to formulate a law restricting the vote, even as a form of punishment, it seems to follow that the franchise lies outside their spheres of authority and is wholly a function of the original contract. Any restrictive franchise law is an abridgement of the social contract and therefore not a law, since all law depends upon the contract. The nineteenth clause of the social contract might read, "Any adult male resident who publicly proclaims his loyalty to the social contract automatically becomes a citizen and remains a citizen so long as his consent continues."[33]

Chapter 3

Government

As far as the social contract is concerned there is very little that needs to be said about government. Having no legislative authority, it is magistracy rather than government as ordinarily conceived. It is wholly dependent on the sovereign both as to its form and its membership. Between sovereign and prince there is a complete separation of powers without even a microinch of overlap: the government's power "is made up exclusively of particular acts, which are not within the province of law, and not, therefore, within that of the sovereign, whose acts can never be anything but laws" (*SC* 3. 1). The initiative of the government is stringently limited by the scope of the law. Whatever can be expressed in the form of a law is the exclusive and sole prerogative of the sovereign. Individual applications of the law are the exclusive and sole prerogative of the prince. No other form of social regulation is permitted to either. How the membership of a government is selected need not detain us, save to note that the conceptual subtlety to which Rousseau resorts shows how emphatic and consistent was his claim that the sovereign must never involve itself with particular acts (*SC* 3. 17).

Rousseau rejected all contract theories that accorded legislative authority to government because that would involve an improper alienation of will to a determinate part of society. Once the terms of the social contract have been spelled out, it becomes obvious why there cannot even be a contract between the sovereign and a government without legislative powers. Such a contract would limit the sovereign's right to change its mind and dismiss the prince whenever the sovereign so desires. Moreover, in order to effect such a contract the sovereign would have to treat with particular individuals, and particular acts are expressly and repeatedly declared to be beyond the sovereign's competence. That is why "there is only one contract in the state, the contract of association, and that in itself precludes all others" (*SC* 3. 16). Because the government is so completely dependent on the sovereign, Rousseau has no need of that nebulous concept, a morally sanctioned right of revolution. Should a government usurp sovereignty, everyone is automatically back in the state of nature, where force is its own justification. And because of the strict separation of powers decreed by the contract, there cannot be the slightest doubt as to when sovereignty is usurped.

There is equally little to be said about the appropriate form of government. Though theoretically the sovereign's choice is wide, of the forms of government discussed by Rousseau only one is compatible with the social contract in all respects. The care taken to isolate sovereign and prince suggests that a pure democracy is inadvisable. When the same citizens constitute both the government and the sovereign, the desired separation of functions becomes very difficult to maintain, and particular judgments are easily mistaken for laws. As for a more restricted democracy, "it is against the order of nature for the majority to govern and for the minority to be governed" (*SC* 3. 4). Monarchy for Rousseau bears a special meaning and will be seen below to be completely inappropriate.

This leaves aristocracy. Aristocracy is a likely candidate because the natural preconditions of aristocracy coincide with the natural preconditions of sovereignty. Aristocracy is suitable to a state that is neither too expansive nor too small and to a state where there is no unbridgeable gulf separating rich and poor. Though there are two types of aristocracy, hereditary aristocracy is ruled out by the social contract itself. The sovereign can create privileges but it cannot create hereditary privileges. On strict theoretical grounds this would be impossible, because with respect to future generations the members of the aristocracy would be antecedently, and therefore personally, defined. The corollary to this is that the offspring of nonaristocratic parents would, contrary to the nature of law, be automatically ineligible for the privilege in question.[1] By elimination only elective aristocracy remains, and this Rousseau describes as the best form of government (*SC* 3. 5). The corporate will of an elective aristocracy mediates the amorphous will of a democracy and the overly concentrated will of a monarchy (*SC* 3. 2).

There is not much more that can profitably be said about government insofar as it relates to the social contract. Why then does Rousseau pursue the subject at so much greater length? With a nice sense of organization, he supplies the answer after he has discussed in some detail the different forms of government: "All the governments of the world, once the public force is in their hands, sooner or later usurp the sovereign authority" (*SC* 3. 18). This is a rather mystifying observation. Taken literally, it implies that all present governments can be traced back historically to a point when their respective peoples were sovereign. This, on the face of it, is incredible. Alternatively, Rousseau may be simply saying that government, any government, is by nature an enemy of sovereignty. It is not the case that governments usurp a preexisting sovereignty, but rather they prevent its establishment in the first place. On some theoretical plane government exists without legislative power; in the real world governments always legislate. This, it seems to me, is Rousseau's version of catch-22: without the executive force of government, sovereignty is in vain, but once this power is concentrated, sovereignty is necessarily preempted. Power may be restrained by power, but seldom, if ever, does it bow to authority. Granting this pessimistic conclusion, one must suspect that in analyzing government Rousseau is, for the most part, concerned not with magistracy but with government as normally understood, that is, as including legislative powers.

In chapter 5 I offer three examples of what a legitimate society might be like. It will there be seen that the role of government is extremely limited, so limited in fact that it scarcely merits attention. Not surprisingly, Rousseau manages to obscure this point completely with his digressions on the internal structures of governments and on the conditions appropriate to each form. Though some of what he says can be related to an analysis of legitimate government, or magistracies, most of his observations make sense

only as applied to governments with legislative force. This is
most unfortunate, because the ambiguity that attaches to the term
'government' is easily overlooked and the unwary reader might
understandably conclude that a legitimate government would be
a far more powerful force in society than would actually be the
case. As in other contexts, Rousseau has substituted points of reference without alerting his readers. Book 3 of the *Social Contract*
only incidentally bears on the problem of legitimacy; the main
thrust of its argument is a thoroughly subversive attack on monarchy. In his own disordered manner, and with the aid of assumptions imported from *Emile*, Rousseau, if I read him correctly, is
trying to establish three propositions: monarchy is an intrinsically
illegitimate form of government; it is the worst form of government; it is, in its present circumstances, an unnatural form of
government.

Monarchy: An Intrinsically Despotic Government

Rousseau categorically states that hereditary aristocracy is the
worst form of government and elective aristocracy the best (*SC* 3.
5). But then he goes on to argue that no one form is suitable to all
countries (*SC* 3. 8). It is evident that two different standards are
being invoked. I would suggest that elective aristocracy is best in
the limited sense that it is the best form of magistracy, the best of
all possible *legitimate* governments.[2] But if legitimacy is not at issue, it does not follow that an elective aristocracy is the most appropriate response to ambient conditions such as the size of the
state, the level of economic development, and the character of the
people. The relationship seems to be this: a government cannot
be or continue to be legitimate if it is not suitably attuned to its
environment, but it can be in harmony with its surroundings and
yet not be legitimate.

There are good reasons why elective aristocracy is the best
form of government, but why is hereditary aristocracy the worst?
Rousseau dismisses democracy as a government fit only for the
gods (*SC* 3. 4), and the bill of particulars that indicts monarchy is
impressive indeed. A monarch cares naught for public happiness.

His subjects are kept weak and wretched. He transmits his will through an overstaffed and rapacious bureaucracy. Appointees to high office are invariably incompetent. There is no balance between the size of a country and the talents of its ruler. Elective monarchies are necessarily corrupt, because the incumbent seeks to compensate himself for his electoral expenses. A hereditary monarchy is often in the hands of children and idiots. There is little continuity of policy, because new ministers invariably reverse that of their predecessors. And so on.

No matter how bad a hereditary aristocracy might be, in every respect it is better than monarchy as so acerbically and biliously described by Rousseau. It turns out that hereditary aristocracy is not absolutely the worst form of government; it is "the worst of all *legitimate* administrations" (*SC* 3. 10, note 1; italics added). This observation occurs in a context where Rousseau is discussing one of the ways in which a government degenerates. The process is one of contraction, wherein a democracy becomes an aristocracy, which in turn becomes a monarchy. Monarchy, therefore, and not aristocracy, is the last stage in the degeneration of governments. But the last stage in the degeneration of any vital institution is death itself; monarchy, as described by Rousseau, is simply not a form of government, where government is understood to be an executive agency subordinate to an independent and separate sovereign. Monarchy is a form of government, but only in the traditional sense of including legislative competence.

Rousseau's definitive attitude reveals itself in the way he expresses the essential difference between free states and monarchies: "In the former everything is used for the common welfare; in the latter, public and private resources stand in inverse relation, the former increasing at the expense of the latter. Finally, instead of governing the subjects in order to make them happy, *despotism* makes them wretched in order to govern them" (*SC* 3. 8; italics added).

This substitution of 'despotism' for 'monarchy' is not accidental. It is repeated two paragraphs later: "Those [places] whose abundant and fertile soil produces much with little labour need to be governed monarchically." These conditions generally characterize the south, but even "if the whole South were covered with republics, and the whole North with despotic states," the law is no less true.

The identification of monarchy with despotism is not exactly subtle, but Rousseau at one point seems to soften the equation. He says that "to be legitimate, the government must not be identical with, but the servant of the sovereign; under these conditions, even a monarchy is a republic."[3] This, however, would seem to be no more than a harmless sop to monarchial or censorial sensibilities, because at a later point he appeals to the weight of history to undermine the possibility. Aristotle had distinguished between a tyrant and a king. The former governs in his own interest, and the latter solely for the advantage of his subjects. If this is a proper distinction, it follows "that from the beginning of time there would never yet have been a single king" (*SC* 3. 10, note 1).

Rousseau describes any government that usurps sovereignty as a despotism (*SC* 3. 10). By this strict standard all governments are despotisms. But monarchy is a despotism in a special sense. The physical conditions that call for other forms of government are not such as to immediately preclude sovereignty. As long as the territory is moderate in size, the people can in principle assemble, and as long as the available surplus is small, there is less temptation to seize power. The chances are minute, but it is at least conceivable that aristocracies might be legitimate. Democracy is really not a form of government at all, or at least it soon ceases to be. "If the sovereign tries to govern, or if the magistrate tries to make laws, . . . force and will no longer act in concert, and the state being dissolved, falls thereby either into despotism or anarchy" (*SC* 3. 1). In a democracy sovereignty and magistracy are conflated, and anarchy is the inevitable result. There is no possible way of reconciling sovereignty with the conditions that characterize monarchy. Monarchy is by its nature despotic, and the phrase 'legitimate monarchy' is self-contradictory.

It is clear that when Rousseau speaks of monarchy he does not have some abstract idea in mind. What he has primarily in mind is French monarchy. This being so, it is almost a tautology to describe monarchy as intrinsically illegitimate. But Rousseau's point was that no matter how it might be reformed it could never be legitimated. There are several reasons why monarchy in the concrete is intrinsically despotic. Monarchy is associated with a relatively large territory. The sovereign can act only when the people are assembled. Even granting the strongest will, as the distance radiating from a given point increases, the logistical problems of congregating the people multiply, until at some point inconvenience becomes impossibility. In a very large state the impracticality of even a single assembly is obvious enough, but on Rousseau's principles the situation calls for frequent meetings. Though there are no precise rules for determining the number of required assemblies, in general, "the stronger the government, the more frequently the sovereign ought to show itself" (SC 3. 13). And monarchy is the strongest government.

Representation is not a permissible alternative. "Sovereignty cannot be represented, for the same reason that it cannot be alienated" (SC 3. 15). Because there is no practical way of institutionalizing sovereignty, it inevitably follows that no large state can be a republic—that is, the monarchy suitable to such a state can never be a legitimate form of government. It is not surprising, therefore, that "the principle common to all [royal] ministers, and to nearly all kings, [is] to do in all respects the reverse of what their predecessors did" (SC 3. 6). It is not surprising because what passed as legislative authority lies in their hands and not in the sovereign's.

A large territory defeats sovereignty in an obvious way. But in Rousseau's eyes, and this was true of France, large states lack cultural homogeneity. They are really conglomerations of cultural enclaves, each with its own distinctive traditions and customs. This circumstance presents an insoluble legislative dilemma: "the same laws cannot suit so many diverse provinces with different customs, living in contrasting climates and incapable of supporting the same form of government." On the other hand, "different laws do nothing but create trouble and confusion among people who live under the same rulers and in constant intercommunication, and thus move and intermarry freely" (SC 2. 9). Under these circumstances there is no one will, however disinterested, that can transcend or bridge the differences, the divergences, the oppositions that localisms invariably produce. From this point of view monarchy does not usurp the sovereignty of the people, because it does not rule a single people. It usurps the sovereignties of several diverse peoples and unnaturally aggregates them by force alone. Monarchy, then, can never be a legitimate government, because its writ goes beyond a single people; to each locality it is a kind of foreign occupation.

The limitations of monarchy set some of the parameters of sovereignty. In a general way Rousseau's views on the nature of political association hark back to those of Plato and Aristotle. In discussing different forms of polity, and having city states in mind, both Plato and Aristotle assumed a common good, respect for which differentiated lawful and unlawful forms of government. There is a common good for Athens and a common good for Thebes; there is no single common good for both. Common interests there may be in such matters as trade or the common defense against Persia. But these are to be handled as technical rather than political problems. It is for this reason that international relations play no part in the 'political' thought of either.

There is no 'political' association without a corresponding public, and beyond certain limits of size and population a public ceases to exist for want of communication, common interests, concerns, and ideals.

> The essential questions raised by these political thinkers [Plato, Aristotle, and Rousseau] were: how far could the boundaries of political space be extended, how much dilution of numbers could the notion of citizen-participant withstand, how minor need be the "public" aspect of decisions before the political associations ceased to be political? . . . As Aristotle had remarked, it was quite possible to enclose the whole of the Peloponnese by a single wall, yet this would not create a *polis*.[4]

Monarchy as conceived by Rousseau far exceeds the boundaries of a political space that could accommodate in any meaningful way the sovereignty of the people.

Monarchy: The Worst Form of Government

The caution a reader must exercise whenever government is under discussion is especially necessary when Rousseau is exploring the signs of good government. Which meaning of government is at issue, magistracy or despotism? Oddly enough, the characteristics of good government are such that they can only be found to one degree or another in despotisms. A legitimate government might be evaluated as efficient or not, but because of its utter subservience to the sovereign, *while it remains legitimate* it is not a subject of further moral imputation. Rousseau has little to say about legitimate governments, for the simple reason that there is really very little that can be said about them. The measure of good and bad, then, is a measure of different despotisms.

Many standards have been proposed as signs of good government: public tranquillity, individual liberties, crime control, international respect, an economy where money circulates freely. These are all difficult to measure. But since the purpose of political association is the preservation and prosperity of its members, there is one infallible sign. "It is the number and increase of the population." Government under which the population increases the most without resort to artificial devices, "is infallibly the best. That under which a people declines and wastes away is the worst." 5

Why is this an infallible sign? If a reader doesn't already know, I doubt that he will find the answer in the *Social Contract*. A government is not good because its population increases. Rather, its population increases because the government is good. Similarly, a government is not bad because its population is in decline. Rather, it is losing population because it is bad. Demographic statistics are a function of causes that are not immediately apparent. When the causes are found, the ultimate measure of a government's worth is revealed. It is important to approach the problem in this fashion, because even if Rousseau is mistaken as to the effects in question, his analysis merits independent consideration.

In an economically self-sufficient state, an increase in population is possible only if there is a corresponding increase in agricultural productivity. A government that encourages agriculture as its first and almost exclusive priority is in effect one that oversees a country whose population is increasing. By uniformly distributing the human resources available, all arable land would soon come under cultivation. The strength of a state lies not in its monetary wealth, but in the richness of its population. For this reason, if a state would be strong it should encourage its people "to spread out over the whole extent of its territory, to settle there, and to cultivate it throughout." [6]

Rousseau's often-repeated insistence that a healthy state is one whose population is uniformly distributed is simply his way of arguing that good governments are those that devote their full attention to the promotion of the agricultural sector of society. Any other policy is an indication of an injudicious and false set of priorities. If census figures are hard to come by, there is a far simpler way of identifying bad governments. As a rule of thumb, it can be argued that the less uniformly dispersed a population is, the worse its government. Urban concentration thus becomes the infallible index of bad government: Englishmen disputing with Frenchmen about whether London or Paris is the more populous are really "quarreling as to which nation can claim the honour of being the worst governed." [7]

The bitter resentment against the city that infects Rousseau's whole being has perhaps its deepest roots in a physiocratic assumption: only the agricultural classes produce real wealth; "the wealth which [cities] produce is a sham wealth, there is much money and few goods." [8] Paris feeds on the provinces not only for its bread but for its money also. This might be endurable if only revenues quickly circulated throughout the state as does blood in a body. "On the other hand, no matter how little the people gives, if it never gets that little back, it is soon exhausted; . . . the people is always impoverished." Monarchies are the worst offenders: under them people bear the greatest burden with the least return (*SC* 3. 8).

The luxury and idleness that one finds in cities is possible only to the extent that the countryside is impoverished. "Remember that the walls of cities are only built from the wreckage of farm houses. Every time I see a palace being erected in the capital, I have visions of a whole countryside being reduced to living in hovels" (*SC* 3. 13). Urban populations parasitically devour the national product. General depopulation may be a sign of weakness, but as applied to cities it would represent a significant increase in the strength of the state. A subject who does not exist does not produce, but, more important, neither does he consume. Cities are rapacious nonproducers and thus constitute a wholly negative factor in the national economy (*Emile*, p. 433).

The rural sector, the chief source of population, has no motive to increase itself unless it is guaranteed the fruits of its labor. Any increase in parasitic urban numbers entails a corresponding decrease of peasant surpluses through taxation. When this exploitation reaches a point where the law of diminishing returns leaves a family with no reason to enlarge itself, it merely maintains its present size. Any added increment of taxation reduces the farmer to subsistence level or below. When it thus becomes unprofitable to work the fields, young agriculturists are forced off the land and into the cities, further augmenting the list of parasites. A vicious circle results: the more the city grows, the less agriculture produces. This is a circle that can only be broken by a decrease in population or by lowering the tax rate.

It is easy enough to fault the assumptions that underlie this argument. Nevertheless, as applied to a predominantly agrarian economy, the standard that emerges from the argument has merit independent of its economic assumptions: a good government keeps the percentage of nonproducers to a minimum and insures that the tax on the productive sector of society is expended only on necessities. As a corollary, several factors combine in various ways to measure a bad government: the excessive number of non-producers, the excessive tax burden on the working classes, and the amount of tax revenues expended on luxuries. Depopulation may or may not be the sign of bad government, but economic injustice is its fruit.

This is Rousseau's standard of economic justice. Unlike the rigid standard of legitimacy, it is a sliding scale that registers many degrees. This fact alone should convince anyone that it is a standard in its own right and goes beyond the question of legitimacy. The social contract insures that a legitimate society is a just society. But if there were not a separate and independent measure, all actual governments would fall indifferently into a single, homogeneous class, the class of illegitimate governments. There would in practice be no scale to discriminate real governments. This, however, was not what Rousseau had in mind.

When the criterion of economic justice is applied, monarchy stands apart from all other illegitimate governments. It is the prototypical incarnation of injustice, and in comparison to it all other forms of government are in varying degrees admirable.

The standard of economic justice is exclusively a measure of illegitimate governments, because in a legitimate society it is the responsibility of the sovereign and not of the prince to establish fiscal policy. A legitimate government executes but does not initiate the law. That monarchy is, in Rousseau's judgment, the worst of all illegitimate governments becomes obvious after even a cursory reading of his several works. The urbanization of society that is so characteristic of monarchies is but the measure of parasitic nonproductivity; the sorry plight of the peasantry is the index of an oppressive tax system; the splendor and idleness of the aristocracy reflect monarchy's commitment to luxury no matter what the consequent injustice.[9]

French Monarchy: An Unnatural Government

Besides being intrinsically despotic, monarchy is further revealed as flagrantly unjust. But even this encompassing assessment is not the last word Rousseau has to say in his denunciation of monarchy. All the preceding observations on regal government refer to monarchy as Rousseau knew it, which is to say, French monarchy. There are, however, other points that he makes that refer to monarchy in the abstract. "In every region . . . there are natural causes which make it possible to determine the form of government necessitated by its climate."[10] What, then, are the conditions that make monarchy feasible (and these, significantly enough, are the only conditions that Rousseau analyzes in detail)?

Places providing a small surplus are suitable for free peoples. "Those whose abundant and fertile soil produces much with little labour need to be governed monarchically."[11] The defining principle of monarchy is the life of luxury enjoyed by those surrounding the throne. Because they themselves are drones, the resources that sustain their ostentatious idleness must be extracted as surplus value from a subject labor force. To seek the conditions favorable to monarchy, then, is to seek the conditions that permit blatant injustice to perpetuate itself. There are two general conditions. Monarchy is suitable to large territories whose populations are both small and sprinkled throughout the land. Dispersion insures against conspiratorial intercommunication, and it dilutes the potential for resistance to central authority. A people's force is operative only when it is concentrated; a people dispersed is "like gunpowder scattered on the ground, which ignites grain by grain only." Even if subjects wanted to resist, their physical situation would make that impossible.

But would they necessarily want to revolt? It could hardly have escaped Rousseau's attention that the vast majority of people were indifferent whether they lived under despotisms when despotism meant any government that even minimally failed to be legitimate. The overriding concern of most people is their economic well-being. Man is an acquisitive animal, and he is far more interested in his purse than he is in discharging the demanding duties he would have to shoulder in a legitimate state (SC 3. 15). This being so, the greatest danger of revolution, religious intolerance aside, lies in economic oppression. When this becomes extreme a people becomes desperate, and it may well choose revolution as a court of last appeal.

This permanent possibility determines the second general condition that must be met if monarchy or despotism is to survive: the surplus value that is needed to maintain luxury must not impose an unendurable hardship on those from whom it is exacted. The less the burden, the less the probability of rebellion. If it is assumed that the surplus necessary to slake the greed of all monarchies is relatively the same, the consequent burden required to satisfy this need is a function of how much labor is needed to produce that surplus and, in addition, to meet the subsistence demands of labor. Two variables are involved: the amount of work required to produce the surplus and the amount required to attain a subsistence level. The latter variable is in practice a double variable, because levels of subsistence vary according to how much is essential in terms of food, clothing, and shelter.

According to Rousseau, only in the south are there to be found large territories sparsely settled and also the climatic conditions that allow of the requisite surplus and a salubrious subsistence level with little expenditure of labor. This is so because the soil there is extremely fertile, yielding optimal nourishment for the labor required, and because in hot regions a worker's food, clothing, and housing needs are minimal. Under such conditions regal avarice can be satiated without unduly burdening the monarch's subjects. Where living is easy there is enough for everyone. It makes no difference that history leaves us little evidence of the existence of European-style monarchies in the south. Whatever the facts of the case, monarchy is naturally suited only to the conditions described above, and "if the whole South were covered with republics, and the whole North with despotic states, this would not make it any the less true." History, then, may not decisively defeat Rousseau's stated conditions, but where precisely is this "south" located on the map? I do not know, and I suspect that Rousseau didn't either. It is not unlikely that he was playing a game, for if we know the conditions favorable to monarchy we know by negation those that are inimical to it. May it not be the case that the mythical south is but a veil that thinly disguises Rousseau's ultimate attack on French monarchy? [12]

How does France measure up to the conditions suitable to monarchy? It is a relatively large territory, but it is also well populated, and, as Rousseau so often lamented, its population is unevenly distributed. There are several pockets of urban concentration, and the grains of gunpowder are encased in bombs waiting to explode. Frenchmen require more calories, more clothes, and sturdier houses to accommodate seasonal changes. Unfortunately, the land that feeds them is, according to Rousseau, less than friendly and yields its nurture only after insistent demand. Subsistence level is high and is reached only with much hardship. On top of this, the French peasant has to support a ravenous aristocracy and a bloated administrative apparatus that consumes taxes while providing less-than-minimal services. Monarchy is unsuited to France not only because cities as centers of resistance dot the whole land, but more imperatively because the claims of the monarchy can only be met by exploiting its subjects beyond the limits of human tolerance.

Monarchy as embodied in France and perhaps other European

countries is a despotism unnaturally resting on a socioeconomic foundation that cannot support its weight. How is this possible? Nature is not always an infallible guide as to the momentary present: "I know that there are exceptions; but these very exceptions confirm the rule, for sooner or later they lead to revolutions which restore things to the natural order" (*SC* 3. 8). France's monarchy has prolonged its unnatural existence by expending all its energies on its own preservation at the expense of the governed, "and this is how a body which is too large for its constitution weakens and dies, crushed by its own weight" (*SC* 2. 9). French monarchy is condemned three times over. It is intrinsically a despotism that has violated the social contract in every particular. It is a bad government, an economically unjust government. Finally, it is an unnatural government, a government that is out of tune with its economic base.

It is remarkable how Rousseau's analysis of French monarchy isolated before the fact those weaknesses and abuses that historians later elaborated as collectively constituting the cause of the Revolution. He had decried the mammoth yet incompetent bureaucracy, the utterly oppressive and inequitable system of taxation that kept the peasants impoverished, the neglect of the public welfare, a patronage system blind to talent or virtue, the proliferation of judicial systems, dissimilar administrative codes, interregional rivalries, the favoring of urban interests at the expense of agricultural interests, the feudal survivals, the growing lack of identification between the king and large segments of the country, and the scandal of conspicuous luxury amidst dire poverty. This may not be a call for revolution, but it is surely a prophecy: "The crisis is approaching, and we are on the edge of a revolution. . . . In my opinion it is impossible that the great kingdoms of Europe should last much longer. Each of them has had its period of splendour, after which it must inevitably decline" (*Emile*, p. 157). Monarchy is doomed, but so too are the small republics that, according to Rousseau, are naturally suited to the Continent.

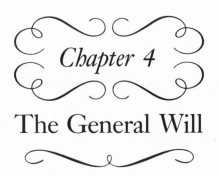

Chapter 4

The General Will

The discussion early in the last chapter of the proper relationship that ought to obtain between prince and sovereign completes, with two exceptions, the analysis of the articles of the social contract. Because the Civil Creed, as will be argued in chapter 7, is only a conditionally necessary and not a conceptually necessary condition of legitimacy, a consideration of its role in the total economy of the social contract will be postponed. What is of concern here is article 18, which details social ends and ideals.

The first sixteen articles are formal in nature—they can be univocally applied to any number of otherwise differing societies. The article here in question is substantive: its specification differs from possible society to possible society. Though Rousseau maintains that the clauses of the contract "are so completely determined by the nature of the act that the slightest modification would render them null and void" (*SC* 1. 6), this claim must be slightly modified if intelligibility is to be preserved. If one cannot conceive of two legitimate societies without at the same time conceiving of them as sharing identical social ends and ideals, then Rousseau's claim may stand unamended. If, however, two or more legitimate societies can be conceived with different social ends, then these different ideals must be reflected in the clause that specifies ends and goals. This is but a slight modification, all the more so because once this article is drawn up by a given people it cannot be changed without terminating that particular contract as a whole.

There are at least three interrelated reasons why this clause of the contract is a conceptual necessity: (*a*) Without it, Rousseau's talk about a general will is unintelligible. (*b*) Without it, it is impossible to live up to some other terms of the contract. (*c*) Without it, it is impossible to explain fully how a man in obeying the law, even if he voted against it, is in fact obeying himself. First, let us consider something of Rousseau's idea of a general will.

Sovereignty, law, and the general will are so interrelated that there are very few contexts where one is intelligible without reference to the other two. Sovereignty pertains to a people insofar as they act in a certain way. The termination of this process is law, and law is said to be an expression of the general will. The general will, then, may be regarded as a kind of mediating link between sovereignty as a process and law as its termination. As a mediating link, it plays a dual role, and this duality is a source of some confusion. When its affinity to law is stressed, problems of the general will tend to become problems concerning the ontological status of a common good that is the object of a general will. When its relationship to sovereignty is emphasized, the general will is taken as simply the equivalent of the de facto outcome of the sovereign process. Because these two aspects need not coincide, it is very easy to misunderstand Rousseau's account of the general will.

To understand what the general will is, it is first necessary to see what it is not. It is not some mystical faculty of a collectivity that exists independently of the individual wills of its members. On the contrary, it is thoroughly grounded in the individual wills of the group. An individual's will may be distinguished according to the objects of that will. A will is said to be a particular will when it seeks its own good without reference to the interests of others. A will is said to be general when it seeks a good for the group even against personal self-interest. The general will of a society, then, is a summation of the general wills of individuals. To illustrate the difference between a particular and a general will, assume that a certain level of education is recognized by all as a common good. Whenever additional taxes are required to sustain this level, bachelors are faced with a conflict. If they consult only their particular will they will find no reason to burden themselves. The particular will votes no. If they consult their general wills, they will be advised that the common good requires the sacrifice even though there is no hope of personal gain. The general will votes yes.

The general will is not the same as the will of all (*SC* 2. 3). According to Rousseau, the will of all, as distinct from the general will, is nothing but the sum of particular wills. This is difficult to understand, and I have been unable to discover a satisfactory example. The social contract is itself the product of the particular wills of all, and the contract thereafter is surely a part of the general will, if only as its necessary condition. It is possible to conceive of a case where the general will of all is mistaken and therefore at odds with the real general will. Suppose the sovereign unanimously agrees that an army of five thousand is required for the common defense. The next question is how to raise the army. Everyone agrees that whenever possible it is better to effect common goods on a voluntary basis rather than by compulsion. Because the general will has a negative as well as a positive side, it is the sovereign's right to determine what is not in the public's interest. Accordingly, some citizen asks the assembly whether the army ought to be drafted. If every citizen mistakenly believes that there will be volunteers aplenty, the will of all will frustrate the real general will, which is to provide security by whatever means necessary.

The distinction between a person's actual will and his real will can be traced back at least to Plato. What an individual does or intends is for the most part an index of his actual will. But if the unforeseen consequences of an act are or would be disastrous, it is claimed that the actual will was not the real will. It is on the basis of this distinction that forcible frustration of an actual will is sometimes justified: the man who is prevented from crossing a bridge known to be unsafe, the thirsty child whose mother snatches a bottle of poison from him, the drunk who is not allowed to drive, and so on.

It would save a lot of analytical headaches if one could simply identify a person's general will with his real will. Unfortunately this will not do, because the distinction between actual and real cuts across both particular and general wills. In the example on the military draft, it is useful to distinguish between the actual general will and the real general will. But it is equally useful to distinguish between an actual particular will and a real particular will. The actual will of the man who sought to cross an unsafe bridge was frustrated in the name of his real will, but the real will here is his real particular will; it has nothing to do with a general will.

The general will is not the will of the majority in every case. A majority will is a necessary but not a sufficient condition for establishing a general will. Where the social bonds are weak, what passes for the general will is really no more than the particular will of a majority (*SC* 4. 1). But how precisely are we to distinguish between a true general will and a particular will of a majority? It seems evident that the distinction cannot be a merely formal one, because it is not inconceivable that a particular and a general will might coincide; for example, I like being a soldier, and my being a soldier is for the common good. One cannot begin to understand what a general will is until it is seen as in conflict with a personal, particular will. And this is possible only to the extent that they seek substantively different objects. The substance of a general will is not all of one piece: it changes with the enactment of each new law. Since law presupposes sovereignty and sovereignty in turn presupposes the contract, additions to the general will also presuppose the contract.

Because laws are part of the general will and are posterior to the contract, at least some part of the general will is posterior to the contract. The question is whether the general will in toto is posterior to the contract. On the face of it this seems highly unlikely, for men do not form associations armed only with procedural rules and subsequently decide the purposes of association. Without laboring the point, it should be obvious that some degree of socialization precedes the contract: it could never have been framed or understood without a common language.

The question is whether social ideals are to be generated solely by means of procedural rules or the contract is to be viewed as an instrument for protecting, maintaining, and promoting antecedent ideals. In the former case the ideals would have to be created ex nihilo.[1] On this supposition, the general will would consist solely of procedural rules and subsequent laws passed by the assembly. By extension, over a period of time, customs, manners, and the like, provided that they could be expressed in the form of law, could, as implicit laws, also be considered part of the general will.

But the trouble with this point of view is that a purely formal procedure either can never get off the ground or, if it does, it contradicts itself. Suppose at the first assembly someone proposes that a theater be introduced. Before this can be decided it must first be decided whether the issue is one of common concern. But since on the creation hypothesis there is not yet a public (that is, a known area of common concern), there is no way to make this decision. In fact, since there are no public standards the question is meaningless. Even if we waive this difficulty, it reemerges in voting on the proposal itself. Each individual must ask himself whether a theater is a *common* good. Once again he is faced with a total lack of evidence with which to decide the issue and must stand mute. Prior to some substantive general will an individual has only his particular will; he can only judge whether he as an individual desires a theater. But if he votes this will, he has violated that term of the contract that calls for impersonality.

It may seem paradoxical in the light of Rousseau's constant insistence that particular and general wills stand in opposition, but at some stage of a general will's historical development, it is authoritatively general only insofar as it enlists the particular wills of all. Either there are literally some common goods that distributively appeal to the particular wills of all, or there are no standards by which laws can be enacted. Without such standards there is no way to determine whether a proposed law is for the common good. These standards, whatever they might be in the concrete, are spelled out in article 18 of the contract and, like the other articles, are binding only insofar as an individual maintains the consent of his particular will.

Without some such article the general will becomes some sort of a mystical entity, free floating and unanchored in anything that resembles human volition. Without this article the legislative authority of the sovereign is stillborn because there is no way for the sovereign to know what is for the common good. The contract transforms an aggregate into a people only if the contract embodies their common ideals. Strictly speaking, the contract does not so much create a people as it certifies its antecedent existence and gives it a new dimension, a legitimate political existence. This position is not simply a deduction from the nature of the contract. There is good evidence that this was Rousseau's explicit stance. His whole discussion on the legislator does not make sense unless the legislator is seen as creating a new and common way of life.[2] Whatever this entails constitutes after a period of time the general will of the people by constituting the people itself. It is this way of life that gives substance to the contract and in relation to which it can become operative.[3] Subsequent laws also are a part of the general will. The original content of the general will, or at least a part of it, may be what Rousseau refers to as a type of law, "the most important of all, which is graven not in marble or bronze, but in the hearts of the citizens; which forms the *real constitution* of the state; . . . which revives or replaces the other laws when they grow old or are extinguished, which preserves the people in the spirit of its *original institutions*. . . . I am speaking of manners, morals [*moeurs*], customs and, above all, of public opinion" (*SC* 2. 12; italics added). Manners, morals, customs, and public opinion define a people and constitute its abiding common good. It is this common good that is the object of a people's general will.

The legislator might be viewed as an individual general will that multiplies through emulation until it becomes a will of all. At this point the rest of the social contract becomes feasible as a way of maintaining this antecedent general will. The legislator is an ideal construct related to an ideal polity. But the antecedent general will he represents is taken by Rousseau to be an empirical fact that predates government. In the *Second Discourse* Rousseau argued the priority of a general will to political association: "At first society consisted only of some general conventions which all individuals pledged to observe, and regarding which the community became the guarantor for each individual . . . to say that the chiefs were chosen before the confederation was created and that the ministers of laws existed before the laws themselves is a supposition that does not permit of serious debate."[4] In the absence of a determinate government, disorders arose. The original agreement had to be extended to include a constitution: "The people having, *on the subject of social relations*, united their wills into a single one, all the articles on which this will is explicit become so many *fundamental laws* obligating all members of the State without exception" (*Second Discourse*, p. 169; italics added). The protosocial contract (that is, the general will that antedates government) has a substantive content, a unanimous agreement on 'social relations'. It is easy to miss this substantive clause of the contract because in the *Social Contract*, where the definitive contract is described, Rousseau's main concern was with procedural rules and the institution of government.[5]

An unanimously agreed upon way of life must, then, be assumed to be a part of the original general will and the social contract itself. It is a variable clause of the contract because the procedural rules are compatible with different, but by no means all, life styles. This original general will constitutes the end of association, in relation to which subsequent laws are to be judged as compatible or not. As a part of the contract, a people's way of life is a real and abiding general will.

This original general will, substantively expressed as a clause of the full contract, is, it seems to me, crucial to Rousseau's theory of obligation. Nevertheless, it is impossible to reproduce it with any specificity. One reason is that it is a variable clause depending on a people's circumstances and on whatever it is that gives them a unique identity in terms of a common way of life. There are factors that negatively limit it by excluding, for example, what would be accounted immoral societies. This follows because a legitimate general will is a moral will under the constraints of the moral law. What is more, it would seem to be limited to very few options concerning the economic organization of society. There is an overriding principle that further restricts it: no will that wills predetermine inequality can be a general will. None of the above is sufficient to dispel all ambiguity, but for the sake of continuing the analysis it is assumed that this clause defines in some broad sense the ends of society.

The social environment thus created is both limited by and constituted by these ends. Such an environment, since it can never be immoral, is by definition 'always right', always what it ought to be. It makes sense to ask what the environment is; it does not make sense to ask whether it is true. This is an important point because there are some cognitive questions that may be addressed to parts of the general will. Where ends are concerned the general will is infallible because what it wills *is* the reality. The case is different when means become problematical. Assemblies are convened, not to debate ends, but to consider matters that might be adjudged threats to these ends, or to seek means of strengthening or furthering them, or to consider proposals that might enhance the common life without threatening ends.

Unless social ends, ideals, and goals are included in the social contract, it is impossible to see how a dissenter, in obeying the law, is nevertheless obeying himself. Inclusion of ends does reduce radically the liability of minorities, and, if laws are restricted to means only, it is difficult to see how a minority conscience could be compromised. This could not be the case if ends were debatable. It cannot be emphasized strongly enough that legislation concerns means and not ends. If legislation ordained ends, the contract would be abrogated in the same way as if sovereign legislation marked off a predetermined group within society.

Anything less than unanimity on ends means a divided will, or rather at least two wills, neither one of which has moral authority over the other. Depending on the nature of the split, a few cases can be distinguished. If an individual ceases to will the ends, he has in effect withdrawn his consent to the contract and placed himself in a state of nature vis-à-vis the rest of society. If a sizeable group dissents but defines itself in terms of some new end, it has withdrawn consent from the initial contract and recovenanted. Of course, the new ends must be compatible with the other clauses of the social contract. The practicalities of the situation I will not try to imagine. Theoretically, however, the dissenting group is in a position similar to that of a subgroup of a church which breaks off from its parent and recovenants.

In practice, of course, it may not be so easy to distinguish ends and means, and all the less so if the ends are graven in hearts and not explicitly set down in the contract. Moreover, novelties may be inadvertently introduced with consequences that are destructive of ends. Rousseau was quite aware of this.[6] His distaste for novelties is in large measure explained by his perception that ends are affected and that where ends change, the contract and the general will are threatened. To repeat, the doctrine of the general will as it applies to votes in the assembly is unintelligible unless it is assumed that there is a universal consensus with regard to basic social ideals. The embodiment and maintenance of these ideals are the common good; they are what the real general will seeks. By definition, a people cannot be mistaken about these ends, but they can be mistaken about the effect of given proposals designed to support these ends.

It is in this limited context that we must judge Rousseau's contention that the minority is always mistaken vis-à-vis a well-intentioned majority and is therefore obliged by a law proclaimed by the assembly to be the general will.[7] It is at this point that the dual character of the general will creates a problem. The actual general will is the outcome of the sovereign process; it is the general will as judged by the majority, mistaken or not. The real general will is a different law that would have better supported the common good. There is no question that the minority was mistaken about the actual general will, but events may prove that it was not mistaken about the real general will. In view of this latter possibility, why is the minority always morally obliged by an actual will?

It must be stressed that in a theoretical analysis of concepts, a good many empirical assumptions must be made. In the case at hand it is assumed that the actual will is in fact a general will and not the coincidence of a majority of particular wills. Psychologically, then, there is nothing to distinguish majority and minority opinion: each is equally certain that its judgment about the common good is correct. Where intentions are equally honorable on all sides, disagreements would seem to argue the absence of some publicly verifiable test to settle the issue.

This is a major consideration because too many examples that give plausibility to the distinction between actual and real wills, and the consequent right to oppose the former in the name of the latter, are examples where the real will can be antecedently known and demonstrated: the man forcibly prevented from crossing a bridge known to be unsafe, the thirsty child whose mother snatches a bottle of poison from him, and so on. If the truth is to oblige it must be demonstrable, and this is precisely what so infrequently obtains in political decisions before the fact. In physical experimentations incompatible alternatives may be simultaneously tested, and a reasonably reliable judgment can be made. Social experimentation is an entirely different matter. Not only is it impossible to test incompatible policies at the same time without doing violence to the idea of law, the consequent failure of one policy does not, even after the fact, prove the 'truth' of the untested policy. The vagaries of human affairs are such that one is advised to suspect any theory that equates political obligation with submission to the truth. It is the present that generates obligation; *real* wills are mostly revelations of the future.

The problem of truth does not become a decisive factor in the moral equation before the event, but only after the fact. If history proves an actual general will to have been mistaken, then, again assuming universal good intentions, the sovereign is entitled to change its mind and amend its actual will along lines more in conformity with its real will as it now sees it. This change may vindicate the wisdom of the minority, but there is no conceivable way in which it can retroactively justify disobedience to the mistaken law. Rousseau's conception of law is such that, should a law prove undesirable, its disadvantages would have been suffered equally by the majority and the minority. This is a crucial point for any understanding of his treatment of minority obligation. It is one thing for a law to be substantively a mistake and quite another for it to be immoral.

To say that one is not obliged by laws from which consent has been withheld is misleading. If there were only one man in existence, or if men lived solitary lives, there could never be a moral obligation, because moral obligations can never be generated by an individual solely in reference to himself. As a sovereign, an isolated individual may change his mind, that is, relegislate to himself, at any time, and there is no person or extrapersonal standard to condemn him. This being the case, the consent that creates obligations cannot be simply a psychological acceptance of this or that law. For Rousseau, the only consent that creates obligations in a political context is consent to the terms of the social contract, the procedural rules plus social ends that give rise to specific laws both in form and content. These constitute the ultimate common good because, defining moral obligation in general, they ground the morally obligatory character of all laws in particular. Moreover, since the contract is held to be the foundation of society, in its absence there is simply no common good.

Because Rousseau believed the terms of his contract to be unique (that is, the only conceivable basis of licit authority in a given society), a dichotomy is established: either a man consents to these terms or he is in a state of nature, subject exclusively to the law of superior force. There is no third term in Rousseau's political theory; obligations are either moral or prudential. Assuming that a dissenting individual has not withdrawn his consent, his mistake as judged by the majority is not a certification that their *actual* will is the *real* will; his mistake is limited to what as a matter of fact was the actual general will.

It has been objected that if the substantive 'truth' of the law is not in question, the vote is nothing more than a vote on what the vote will be.[8] In this case a citizen would not be voting his convictions concerning the common good, but rather his estimation of the convictions of the majority. There is a passage in the *Social Contract* that might give credence to this interpretation. When a law is proposed the question is not whether one approves it, "but whether or not it is in conformity with the general will" (*SC* 4. 2). If the general will in question is the actual general will, then there would seem to be some merit to the objection. But three points can be made against this position. In the first place, it is by no means evident that the net effect of estimating the vote would significantly differ from judging the issue on its own merits. The size of the majority might be increased, but there is no reason to believe that what would otherwise have been a minority opinion would, by a simple change in the terms of the vote, become a majority opinion.

Second, if Rousseau intended the vote to be a preestimation of the majority's position, he went to great lengths to make the game difficult: "If the people were sufficiently well-informed, and if in their deliberations the citizens held no communication with one another, [the general will would emerge]. . . . If the general will is to be well expressed, therefore, it is important that there should be no partial society in the state, and that each citizen should have personal opinion only" (*SC* 2. 3). What are the people to be well informed of? If each citizen is to come into the assembly his own master and without prior consultations with other citizens, what "personal opinion" can he have with respect to the personal opinions of others? At some point the issue must be confronted substantively, and it is here and only here that good information is relevant. If in the course of deliberation there are no strong indications of what substantive position has convinced a majority, there is no reason for an individual not to vote his own estimation of the common good. Finally, Rousseau restates the question in less ambiguous terms. A citizen is mistaken if he changes the terms of the question, if "instead of saying with his vote, 'It is advantageous to the state,' he says, 'It is advantageous to a certain individual or to a certain party that a certain proposal should be enacted.'"[9] Clearly, the question posed here concerns a personal estimation of the objective referent of the general will, namely, the common good, and not a prediction of the outcome of the vote.

In any case, an actual general will has been declared. Subsequent events may prove it mistaken, but the 'truth' of the proposal is not relevant to the problem of moral obligation. In Rousseau's system, granting the contract, there is simply no such thing as a right to disobey, whether it be claimed by an individual, by a minority, or, for that matter, by the majority. The whole idea of law as conceived by Rousseau is that it lays an equal onus on all. To claim the right to disobey is in effect to claim an exemption, and this constitutes an assault on equality.

If the essence of the general will, social ends and ideals, is already included in the social contract, it is difficult to see how the will of a subject who continues to consent to the contract can be morally compromised. The particular will is involved only with respect to the contract itself; it has absolutely no moral standing with respect to subsequent laws. The only possible conflict between subject and sovereign is when their respective general wills differ. But given Rousseau's theory, general wills can only differ with respect to means. If ends were at issue, one or the other would be recommending a change in the contract, which is the same as abrogating it. It cannot be repeated too often that an individual or a group always retains the right to withdraw from the contract, but at the cost of forfeiting his or their moral status vis-à-vis those who remain faithful to the contract. A dissenter, on this hypothesis, is no longer morally obliged, but he is prudentially obliged. If the conflict is over means, a dissenter cannot without contradiction claim a moral right of disobedience and still affirm the contract, because the contract defines the sovereign as a legitimate authority. It follows, then, that even a dissenting general will is free when it submits to the sovereign. The freedom in question is, of course, political freedom. So long as a subject consents to the contract he is free in obeying the law, no matter what the disposition of his particular or general will.[10]

An individual who still affirms the social contract has no way to justify disobedience, because disobedience entails a rejection of majority rule, and majority rule is mandated by the contract. Of course an individual may selfishly disobey a law without rejecting the contract. But in this case he has consented to his own punishment should he be prosecuted.

In this and the preceding chapters, eighteen separate clauses or articles of the social contract have been analyzed. Leaving aside for the moment the article concerning the Civil Creed, these eighteen clauses, as far as I can see, comprehensively define Rousseau's social contract. The question now is whether this contract solves the problem of legitimacy as defined. Recall the parameters of Rousseau's projected solution. A polity is legitimate if (*a*) no subject stands in a relationship of personal dependence, and (*b*) each subject in obeying the law obeys only himself. Recall also that Rousseau claims that his solution is unique, that the problem cannot be solved in any other manner. In order to test these claims it must be asked whether each clause is a necessary condition in relation to the parameters and whether conjointly they constitute a sufficient condition for obviating personal dependence and insuring self-obedience. An article is a necessary condition if its absence can invite personal dependence or frustrate self-obedience. Collectively the articles are a sufficient condition if no further necessary conditions need be conceived.

In chapter 1 it was explained that an individual must totally alienate his personal will to the group as a whole. The group as a whole is in this way invested with sovereign legislative authority. All members of the group assume the duty of participating in the legislative process (article 1). If one is not a part of the legislative process, one cannot be said to obey oneself when obeying the law. Sovereignty is inalienable (article 2) and, as a specification of this, it is indivisible (article 3). Were sovereignty alienable, the resulting will would be a will of less than the whole and therefore a personal will. A sovereign's will is free, that is, a sovereign can never bind itself; it may rightfully change its mind (article 4). Were this not so, the citizens might in time be subject to a will that is presently not their own.

Since individual alienation must be total, there can be no reserved rights. Probably with Hobbes and Locke in mind, Rousseau explicitly denies an individual's right to put his own life above all other considerations (article 9) and also denies the inalienability of property (article 15).

The sovereign cannot legislate with regard to a part of its membership, because with respect to that discriminated part, legislation would be particular and that part would be personally dependent. A sovereign will must be a general will. Thus, sovereign law must be essentially general, impersonal (article 12; cf. chapter 2), and confined to matters of common concern (article 11). In order to insure this, citizens must vote their estimation of the common good and not their personal interests (article 13).

Because a legislative will is ineffective unless executed, a government (executive and judiciary) must be instituted. The sovereign alone determines the form of government (article 6), and government's authority rests completely on sovereign sufferance (article 8). If it were otherwise, a particular will would have authority over a general will, i.e., the sovereign would not be a sovereign. It follows that the government has no legislative authority; its writ is limited to particularistic applications of sovereign law (article 10). The government must enforce the law without exceptions (article 16), for otherwise discriminations would occur, and discrimination is the antithesis of a general will.

Unless the sovereign is assembled it cannot express its will, and it may be the case that the citizens are subject to a will that is not presently the will of the sovereign. Therefore the social contract must mandate periodic assemblies (article 7). The sovereign will is determined by the majority (article 5). There must be some procedural rule if the sovereign is to have a voice. The sovereign has no authority to exclude an otherwise eligible individual from citizenship or to disenfranchise a citizen (article 19). An individual who is subject to but not a member of the sovereign is subject to an alien, and therefore to a personal, will.

All the above articles directly or indirectly are necessary conditions, without which a measure of personal dependence becomes inevitable. Because I cannot think of any further necessary safeguards, I would judge that collectively these articles constitute the sufficient condition for preventing personal dependence among citizens. If this is so, then Rousseau has solved a part of his problem of legitimacy. He has so arranged it that, at least conceptually speaking, no citizen need stand in a relationship of personal dependence. But two problems remain.

Though an unconditional right of self-preservation is incompatible with total individual alienation, the sovereign can never alienate its right to preserve itself and still remain sovereign. Nevertheless, when the very life of the sovereign is in jeopardy, *salus populi est suprema lex*; the people may save themselves any way they can. Rousseau argues that under such perilous conditions sovereignty may be suspended and a dictatorship established (article 14). Whatever the specifics of this article, it is evident that where dictatorship exists and a particular will is regnant, sovereignty is inoperative. No matter how pragmatically necessary a dictatorship might be, it can never, except in some Pickwickian sense, be construed as an a priori condition of legitimacy. Why this article is a part of the contract I can only guess. Perhaps what Rousseau is saying is that sovereignty is such a precious value that individuals, when necessary, ought to risk their lives to preserve it. But it is not so precious that it is worth the extinction of the group or the subjection of the group to an alien power.

There is a final problem. If a person is subject only to impersonal laws, in a formal sense he may be said to be free from personal dependence. But I cannot see how it necessarily follows that in obeying the law he is obeying himself, even if he participated in the legislative process. Earlier in this chapter, I argued that one must distinguish legislative goals and legislative means, and that legislative goals cannot themselves be the product of law but are presuppositions of all laws. As presuppositions of all legislation, they must engage the consent of all members of the association, and thus must be an integral part of the social contract (article 18).

It is one thing to dispute means and something quite different to contest ends. Suppose there is a group that has peacefully occupied a territory for centuries. Within that group a majority party arises whose basic goal is to violently expand the state at the expense of its neighbors. Suppose further that the minority are pacifists. The minority may vote against foreign adventures, but in what intelligible sense can they be said to obey themselves when forced to participate in violence? When fundamental principles are in conflict, a minority can never be said to be free, because there is no general will that can reconcile such differences.

It should be obvious that tremendous difficulties, perhaps insurmountable, would be encountered if one were to attempt to draft this article. In general, the difficulties vary directly with the complexities of a given society: the more complex a society is, the less probability there is of attaining unanimity with respect to ultimate values. Nevertheless, it is only to the extent that such a consensus can be attained and incorporated in the social contract that Rousseau can be said to have solved the problem of legitimacy. Sixteen articles suffice to guarantee impersonality, but article 18 is further required to satisfy the claim that in obeying the law a person is obeying himself.

In one sense a purely conceptual analysis of Rousseau's approach to the problem of legitimacy is complete. If you view his complicated argument from a high level of abstraction where all assumptions can be granted, I think you will find that he has indeed *conceptually* solved his problem. But this is hardly satisfactory. What we have is a disembodied spirit; what we need to supply is some corporeal substance.

Chapter 5

Property and the Division of Labor

In the preceding chapters I have tried to systematize Rousseau's principles of right. Rather than interrupt the flow of the argument I have for the most part waived questions of practicality and postponed discussions of the socioeconomic implications of the social contract. And there are definite socioeconomic implications. The most obvious one is that the contract can be valid only for a very, very small state. Population and territorial size cannot exceed those limits beyond which periodic assemblies of the people become impossible. Moreover, there appears to be an inverse relation between size and the purity of a general will. One of Rousseau's objections to monarchy was that its rule encircled diverse local wills that could not be synthesized into a general rule. The contract requires not only smallness but also relative homogeneity of minds and wills.

But the biggest limitation imposed by the contract is to be found in Rousseau's strict interpretation of law. Because legitimacy permits only impersonal dependence, the sovereign must limit itself to what affects all either potentially or actually. It should be evident that a very large percentage of what today passes for law does not square with Rousseau's literal interpretation of impersonality. Because of our elaborately articulated division of labor, social order requires that the various parts of the whole be closely regulated. Our laws may be impersonal with respect to the members of a group, but, since no group is coextensive with the whole, group obligations are not obligations assumed by society as a whole. Statutes regulating railroads do not regulate shipping; statutes regulating prices in one area of the economy are silent with regard to other areas. Examples could be multiplied indefinitely, but the point, I think, is clear: the voice of Rousseau's sovereign must stand mute in a very large variety of contemporary circumstances.[1]

For Rousseau there are only three voices to be heard in society: the sovereign's, the government's, and an individual's or a group's. Where one cannot speak, the tendency is to assume that another voice is empowered to fill the vacuum. Thus, a limitation of sovereignty might be viewed as a corresponding increase in the authority of government. But this would be improper. If the sovereign is unable to say "plumber" or "carpenter" or "engineer," the government has no authority in these areas. Governmental propositions differ from sovereign propositions only in quantification. They otherwise share an identical vocabulary of nouns and verbs.

Rousseau does allow individual initiative outside the public realm: "it can be seen that the sovereign power . . . does not and cannot go beyond the limits of general conventions, and that each individual can freely dispose of whatever goods and liberties these conventions have left to him" (*SC* 2. 4). The silence of the laws gives rise to an area of competitive freedom. There is nothing in the formal requirements of law that determines the scope of sovereignty. In theory the sovereign could, at one extreme, all but stifle competitive freedom, and, at the other extreme, take an extreme laissez-faire position and remove just about all restraints.

Purely formal considerations cannot decide what is the proper scope of competitive freedom. If in the exercise of that freedom no significant inequality arises, it would seem to be quite proper to enlarge the competitive arena. But the sovereign does have the responsibility to bar personal dependencies, and on an economic level that means the sovereign must see to it that no man is rich enough to buy another's labor or poor enough to be forced to sell his own (*SC* 2. 11). There is, moreover, another consideration that determines, at least negatively, how much individual freedom the sovereign ought to permit. The social contract is unworkable unless the sovereign is composed of citizens of a special kind. The demands of citizenship require that individuals repress their particular wills on behalf of a selfless general will. If too much competitive freedom is permitted, the particular will becomes inflamed and the general will is enervated: competitors are not apt to have brotherly concern for one another.

The principles of right ought not to be viewed in a vacuum. They presuppose a special type of man, and, as Rousseau well knew, man is in large measure a product of his social environment. What he further knew was that social environments have a logic of their own. Not every institutional pattern attains stability. Where laws run contrary to the nature of a society, "the state will never cease being troubled until it is destroyed or altered, and invincible nature has resumed its sway" (*SC* 2. 11). Unnatural states exist, but sooner or later they lead to revolutions.

Rousseau, the protosociologist, saw that there are strict limits to institutional coexistence: institutions possible by themselves are not necessarily possible together. Since institutions both reflect and mold attitudes and beliefs, some institutional possibilities are incompatible with certain sets of beliefs and desired attitudes. Though Rousseau sometimes gives the impression that social causality is unilinear after the fashion of mechanical causality, his real model is organic causality, a dialectical interplay between the several dimensions of society.[2] For Rousseau there is simply no part of society that exists as an independent variable; change the value of one variable and all the other variables must in time be respecified if the social equation is to balance. In a society in equilibrium man is free to resist change, but once change occurs there is a social logic that runs its course independently of human will.

Rousseau's functionalist approach to society was far from disinterested; it was Rousseau the moralist that guided Rousseau the sociologist's every step. Whenever he criticized social phenomena he did so because he believed that they could only thrive in an environment that was hostile to certain moral ideals. Similarly, his praise of other societal patterns cannot be adequately explained as products of personal eccentricity. Rousseau's love of the simple life can perhaps be linked with a type of romantic sensibility, but it has its theoretical roots in the sociological exigencies of his system of political right.

Rousseau's attack on the arts, for example, is not unconditional. If it were, it is difficult to see why he would bother to distinguish, as he does, between good and bad artists. What he is fundamentally attacking is the type of society in which the arts flourish. True talent is a rare commodity limited to a small elite. Truly great works are too few in number to meet the voracious appetite of a culture-obsessed society. As a result all kinds of lesser artists spring up seeking novelty for its own sake. In order to be successful they must at once pander to and corrupt the taste of their patrons. This market for culture dialectically corrupts both artist and patron, and it puts virtue and talent in opposition one to another. "And if, by chance, among the men distinguished by their talents, there is one who has firmness in his soul and refuses to yield to the spirit of the times and disgrace himself by childish work, woe to him. He will die in poverty and oblivion" (*First Discourse*, p. 53).

Aesthetics aside, Rousseau's fundamental criticism of the arts is that they thrive only in a luxury society, and a luxury society is synonymous with immorality, a lack of virtue, and inequality. "Thus the dissolution of morals, a necessary consequence of luxury, leads in turn to the corruption of taste" (*First Discourse*, p. 53). And "what brings about all these abuses [of the arts] if not the disastrous inequality introduced among men by the distinction of talents and the debasement of virtues?" (*First Discourse*, p. 58). Since a luxury society is one in which there is a sharp division between working poor and idle rich, it is necessary to seek out the economic roots from which luxury grows. Though the arts may further the corruption of society, they cannot be the ultimate cause of that corruption.

The most obvious fact about a luxury society is that it depends upon a money economy. Money of itself is not for Rousseau the root of all evil but it is a very great evil.[3] If Poland wishes to become powerful and make a big splash on the international scene, Rousseau recommends that it have an economy based on money and that it "encourage material luxury, and the luxury of spirit which is inseparable from it. In this way [Poland] will create a scheming, ardent, avid, ambitious, servile and knavish people, like all the rest [of Europe]; one given to the two extremes of opulence and misery, . . . with nothing in between" (*Poland*, p. 224). But if the goal is freedom, among other things money must be made to appear contemptible. "In short, of all the incentives known to me money is at once the weakest and most useless for the purpose of driving the political mechanism toward its goal, and the strongest and most reliable for the purpose of deflecting it from its course. [Men can be made to act only out of self-interest], but pecuniary interest is the worst, the basest and the most corrupting of all" (*Poland*, p. 227). A money economy depersonalizes the role of citizen and in so doing weakens his dependence on the state. "As soon as public service ceases to be the main business of citizens, and they prefer to serve with their purses rather than with their persons, the state is already on the brink of ruin" (*SC* 3. 15). They hire mercenaries rather than fight themselves. They appoint deputies and stay at home. Preoccupied with commerce, profits, and comfort, they "convert personal services into money payments. People give up a part of their profits in order that they may have more leisure to increase them. . . . *Public finance* is a slavish word unknown to *republics*. In a *truly free country*, the citizens do everything with their own hands, nothing with money." [4]

There are other ways of meeting public expenses. They can be met, for example, by corvées, payment by personal labor on public projects. Officials can be paid directly with food and the like. Admittedly, a barter economy is inconvenient and inefficient, "but the evil is slight in comparison with the host of evils it prevents! . . . Look at every country, every government, every part of the world; nowhere will you find a great evil in morals and politics where money is not involved" (*Poland*, p. 228).

Similar prescriptions are to be found in Rousseau's project for Corsica. Agriculture is to be encouraged, and commerce, because it requires a money economy, is to be avoided. Where money flourishes everything becomes an article of trade. "I am so fully convinced that any system of commerce is destructive to agriculture that I do not even make an exception for trade in agricultural products" (*Corsica*, p. 303). Necessary internal transactions can be made by barter. Rousseau's horror of money seems somewhat overwrought until one realizes that the ultimate culprit is the institution that makes money necessary. The key is to be found in the *Second Discourse*, and it is echoed and reechoed in subsequent works. As long as men were individually self-sufficient, they remained free and happy. "But from the moment one man needed the help of another, as soon as they observed that it was useful for a single person to have provisions for two, *equality disappeared*, property was introduced, labor became necessary" (*Second Discourse*, p. 151; italics added). When men turned to agriculture for their subsistence, a division of labor was introduced. "Metallurgy and agriculture were the two arts whose invention produced this great revolution" (*Second Discourse*, p. 152). The invention of other arts followed, necessitating a surplus food supply to support those specializing in these new arts. Small differences in talent and industry led to inequality in wealth. Then followed a quasi–state of war between rich and poor that was terminated by the institution of government.

The economic ideal is the self-sufficiency of a Robinson Crusoe. But

the exercise of the natural arts, which can be carried on by one man alone, leads on to the industrial arts which call for the cooperation of many hands. The former may be carried on by hermits, by savages, but the others can only arise in society, and *they make society necessary*. So long as only bodily needs are recognized man is self-sufficing; with *superfluity* comes the need for *division and distribution of labor*, for though one man working alone can earn a man's living, one hundred men working together can earn the living of two hundred. As soon as some men are idle, others must work to make up for their idleness.[5]

The moral apparently is that the less efficient an economy is, the less room there is for the idle rich.

That Rousseau strongly objected to a division of labor is clear enough. His distaste can be seen by way of contrast to a type of life he praised, and in the economic organization of a society he recommended. He has words of high praise for one stage of Swiss history. Because of a demanding climate the Swiss were forced to work so hard that they had little leisure to develop passions. Snowbound half the year, each family was thrown back on its own resources. "Each in his own household practiced all the necessary arts and crafts; all were masons, carpenters, cabinet makers, wheelwrights . . . being well off on what he had, he desired nothing further. Since needs and interests did not conflict, and no one depended on anyone else, their only relations with one another were those of benevolence and friendship." Such men could not properly be called virtuous because, being independent, they had no vices to overcome. "It cost them nothing to do good; and they were good and just without ever knowing what justice and virtue were" (*Corsica*, pp. 295–96).

The independent man is a happy man because there is within him a perfect balance between desire and power of satisfaction. This type of man embodies qualities that serve as standards for Rousseau: he is happy; he has few desires; he is a jack-of-all-trades in the sense that he himself is capable of all needful economic functions. Within the group there is a variety of these functions, but there is no division of labor based on specialization. And where there is no specialized division of labor, no man is personally dependent on another. All men of the group are equal.

Though there is definitely nothing illegitimate about a group of independent men, this sort of group can hardly serve as a complete paradigm of proper political association. The independent man, being in a sense a law unto himself, is something quite different from Rousseau's conception of the citizen. Ideally the relationship between citizen and citizen ought to be as weak as possible and that between citizen and sovereign as strong as possible, "in order that each citizen may be perfectly independent of the rest, and extremely dependent on the city" (*SC* 2. 12). Individual economic independence facilitates the first condition, but it completely frustrates the second. In order for a citizen to be dependent, though impersonally, he must be a member of a state where he has duties that implicate others.

The details of how such a state might be organized can be

found in Rousseau's constitutional recommendations for Poland and, more specifically, for Corsica. Roughly, the economic ideal is an agrarian economy made up of individually self-sufficient farms. Unavoidable transactions are to be made by barter, not by money. Rousseau acknowledges that an agricultural division of labor would be more efficient, "but this consideration for all its importance is only secondary. It is better for the land to produce a little less and for the inhabitants to lead better regulated lives" (*Corsica*, p. 309; cf. letter to M. d'Alembert, *Politics and the Arts*, pp. 60–61). This combination of no specialized division of labor and barter is not accidental. For where there is a fairly extensive and articulated division of labor, the economy requires money to set the value of the various specialities. Such discriminations could not be made by any form of law. Thus, a specialized division of labor is incompatible with the sovereignty of the people in an area of fundamental concern like the economy.

Rousseau's war against all forms of inequality is not a pre-Marxist version of the classless society. Quite the contrary. He would be as hostile to a humanized communism as he would be to any form of capitalism. His quarrel is not with property as such but with property as defined within an economic structure that entails a specialized division of labor. It is this structure that is the basic evil and the root of all consequent evils. He would undoubtedly accept much, if not all, of Marx's critique of the exploitative character of capitalism, but since contemporary Marxists do not repudiate a division of labor, Rousseau would reject them also.[6] In Rousseau's view exploitation is possible under all circumstances, but it is inevitable and irreversible whenever a division of labor reaches a certain level of complication. People may choose a division of labor in the name of other values such as wealth, status, and comfort, but the price they pay is liberty and equality. The price of liberty is not only eternal vigilance but also a primitive economy.

Rousseau's primitiveness is not an accident. An advanced economy would have to be based on money, and with respect to labor it would be a wage economy. But when one man is forced to sell his labor to another, a relation of personal dependence arises between them. It is irrelevant whether this relationship is between individuals, as in pure capitalism, or between an individual and his government, as in socialism, for in both cases the superior is less than the whole body politic. The only way to avoid this is to arrange the economy so that "no citizen is rich enough to be able to buy another and none so poor as to be forced to sell himself" (*SC* 2. 11). It is only in this way that equality may be preserved, and equality is a necessary condition of liberty. But universal personal independence is possible only where economic relations are extremely simple and free from the regimented discipline so necessary for an articulated division of labor.

There is another objection to a division of labor that must be mentioned. The more complex it is, the more it fragments both the individual and society. An individual's being is in large measure reduced to his specialized roles and, because society is so complex, a person is seldom able to grasp his significance in relation to the whole. Hence arise various forms of alienation. And as the number of roles multiply, group wills are formed, leaving little room for a general will. Each division of labor generates its own particular interests with the result that "we have physicists, geometers, chemists, astronomers, poets, musicians, painters; we no longer have citizens" (*First Discourse*, p. 59). The same may be said of carpenters, masons, commercial men, and so on. The point to note is that for Rousseau, 'citizen' is more than a political category. It suggests an individual who can identify with every aspect of his society, an individual who is at one with himself because his society is at one with itself. He stands in contrast to the fragmented man who reflects the fragmentations of his society.

In view of his fear of a specialized division of labor, it is understandable why he would prefer an economy consisting of a multitude of atomic, self-sufficient farms cultivated by individual families. There is no reason I can think of that might demonstrate the incompatibility of such an economy and any of the principles of right. However, though Corsica and Poland are to be structured in such a way that individuals are far more answerable to the state than the independent Swiss, this dependence does not measure up to the theoretical maximum so long as the economy is basically in private hands. It is to be hoped that the absence of both money and a specialized division of labor will guard against personal exploitation, but it is nonetheless true that to the extent that each family is economically self-sufficient, its dependence on the state is lessened. No matter how one wishes to view Rousseau's recommendations for Corsica and Poland, they do not add up to collectivism in an economic sense. This really is not surprising, for Rousseau the sociologist was perforce Rousseau the conservative, always fearful lest a radical change in one area of society entail unwanted changes in other areas. "Worthy Poles, beware! Beware lest, in your eagerness to improve, you may worsen your condition. In thinking of what you wish to gain, do not forget what you may lose. Correct, if possible, the abuses of your constitution; but do not despise that constitution which has made you what you are" (*Poland*, pp. 160–61). Serfdom is surely a great abuse, but given the realities of Poland's situation it must be endured—at least temporarily.

These same realities may have counseled private agriculture, but it is of prime importance to understand that there is absolutely nothing in Rousseau's abstract theory that necessarily calls for anything resembling private property as we know it. To appreciate this, consider his theory of property. When he speaks of property Rousseau primarily has agricultural land in mind, because his modified labor theory does not make too much sense when applied to a pastoral people and even less when applied to a hunting society.[7] On the face of it his theory is quite simple. At the moment of covenanting each member gives up all that as a matter of fact he possesses (*SC* 1. 9). More accurately, he waives any personal claim he might have for his possessions. The nature of these claims is of theoretical significance because there is no new or emergent claim that might justify collective sovereign possession vis-à-vis other states.

What, then, beyond the mere fact of possession, gives warrant to a personal claim in the state of nature? Abstractly considered, in a state of nature claims are measured by force alone and have 'validity' only to the extent that they are self-executing. But man's situation immediately preceding the contract must be imagined in more concrete terms. There are any number of conceivable scenarios of the precontract period, including Hobbes's state of universal war. But none of them would make sense unless one assumes that in the last stages of the alleged state of nature men are already to some degree socialized. Were this not the case, they would lack, for example, a common language with which to contract. Now even a minimal society implies some rules of conflict resolution other than sheer force. The emergence of an embryonic morality is, according to Rousseau, one of the features that distinguish the pure natural man from man in nascent society (*Second Discourse*, p. 150). To Rousseau's mind one such rule was or ought to have been the recognition of the right of the first occupant, but with several reservations. Nevertheless, he emphasizes that this right, "though more real than that of the strongest, does not become a true right until after the establishment of the right of property" (*SC* 1. 9). That is, possession becomes property only after it is sanctioned by the sovereign and guaranteed by public force. It is difficult to give a name or locate ontologically this prior right of possession, which is something more than the right of superior force and something less than a full-fledged legal right. It would seem to fall within Rousseau's idea of natural law as conditional, an idea that will be analyzed later, because it is really a corollary of the generally conceded right to life itself: in certain circumstances the fruits of cultivation are essential for survival.

But a right justified as a condition of survival cannot go beyond what survival requires. A man may take what land he needs to sustain himself and his family, but no more. Having this land, he has no further rights in other fields. The exigencies of life initially give a man the right to use land, but "it is labor alone which, giving the cultivator a right to the product of the land he has tilled, gives him a right to the soil as a consequence, at least until the harvest, and thus from year to year; which creating continuous possession, is easily transformed into property" (*Second Discourse*, p. 154). Labor for Rousseau is necessary, not only to justify a claim, but also to conserve it: untilled land reverts to the common. But, more important, there can be no 'natural' justification for claims to surplus accumulations: prior to civil society a man is at most entitled to the necessities of life, provided he works for them; he is not entitled to superfluities. This is a significant reservation. For if superfluous property is justified by natural law, then so also is the inequality that inevitably arises when the surplus of one becomes the insufficiency of another.

A man may as a matter of fact, possess more than he needs, and this surplus may be respected either out of fear or even by prescription. But it must be understood just how limited are the theoretical rights Rousseau allows man with respect to land. This is of consequence because the social contract transforms individual possession into collective possession, but it does not in any way change the moral status of what is collectively possessed. This has international implications, because if there are limits to what an individual may rightfully possess, there are corresponding limits to collective possession, and exorbitant territorial claims, whether made by an individual or by a state, have no justification save that supplied by force. Within a given state the contract through the laws can transform surplus accumulations into legal rights, but these are rights only within the contracting community; vis-à-vis other communities the contract changes nothing.

It is easy enough to summarize Rousseau's theory of property in the abstract, but then the question of variable perspectives creates difficulties. In the *Second Discourse* the origin of the state and the establishment of property rights is viewed as a devious plot of the rich to secure by collective force those possessions they at best could only precariously maintain as individuals (*Second Discourse*, pp. 158–60). Rousseau clearly understands the advantage of collective possession. "But just as the might of the city is incomparably greater than that of an individual, so also is public possession in fact stronger and more irrevocable than private possession, without being more legitimate, at least from the point of view of foreigners" (*SC* 1. 9). But then there is another perspective. He had earlier assumed that men would leave the state of nature only when they had "reached the point where the obstacles to their self-preservation in the state of nature [were] too great to be overcome by the forces each individual [was] capable of exerting to maintain himself in that state" (*SC* 1. 6). This would lead one to believe that the state is a product of economic necessity: individuals cannot eke out an existence without the cooperation of others. From this point of view the alternatives were to unite or to perish.

The choice of perspectives is pivotal because the probability of the social contract is a function of antecedent 'property' relations. If there is inequality of wealth, what compelling motive would the rich have to surrender their resources to collective control? Or if the rich are to receive them back, what motive would the poor have to guarantee in perpetuity this inequality? Rousseau was not unaware of this problem. He notes that "the social state is advantageous to men only in so far as they all have something, and no one has any more than he needs." Where inequality does exist, it is perpetuated by bad governments enforcing laws that are "always useful to those who have property, and harmful to those who have nothing" (*SC* 1. 9, note 1).

The choice of perspective is pivotal in yet another way. Since the contract initially transforms all individual possession into collective possession, the problem of redistribution presents itself. Rousseau does seem to suggest that what a person possessed prior to the contract will be returned to him, but now in the form of property guaranteed by public force. "The singular feature of this alienation is that the community, far from despoiling individuals of the possessions it accepts from them, does no more than confirm them in legitimate possession, changing usurpation into a genuine right, and use into property" (*SC* 1. 9). But why would people contract simply to duplicate their antecedent economic situation? Peaceful and secure possession might seem a reasonable answer, but in whose interest is this? If antecedent possessions were unequally divided, as the *Second Discourse* suggests, it seems unlikely that the dispossessed poor would agree to legitimate their inferior estate. If, on the other hand, as the *Social Contract* suggests, the motive was impoverishment and economic necessity, it is difficult to see how the same distribution under another name solves any problems.[8]

Practical difficulties aside, it must be emphasized that even if the sovereign were to allow private property, this right is something less than might be expected. "The right of each individual over his own property is always subordinate to the right of the community over all; otherwise there would be no substance to the social bond nor any real force in the exercise of sovereignty."[9] It is of the very nature of sovereignty that it has the right to change its will, to take back, in an equitable manner, what it had previously bestowed. That is a theoretical point, but on a practical level anything approaching absolute private property in an agrarian economy threatens much of the spirit of the contract. This would be to exclude the sovereign from an area that bears upon a man's most fundamental interest: his subsistence. And no matter what the initial distribution of property, the *Second Discourse* argues that in the course of time inequality of talents and ambitions would result in greater and greater economic inequality (*Second Discourse*, pp. 154–55), and at some point the poor would be forced to sell their liberty for bread.

But there is another side to the coin. The more a man is unconditionally secure in his property or the more he is dependent for his livelihood on private individuals, the fewer are the ties that bind him to the community as a whole. Independent men and personally dependent wage slaves have at least this in common: neither class makes good citizens. This is the very reverse of the ideal political relationship that would minimize personal and maximize communal dependence. The wage slave is maximally dependent on persons, and the independent man is minimally dependent on the community.

There is another point to be made. What precisely would be involved should the sovereign decide to convert individual possessions into private property? Initially all it can do is guarantee an individual's antecedent 'natural' rights with public force. But at this stage property has only a minimal meaning. Property is not simply something tangible such as land; it is that something plus an attached right or set of rights. It is idle to scan some Platonic heaven in search of the one true meaning of property. Rights in the face of sovereignty are always conventional. Property can only mean what the sovereign says it means. The sovereign might say that property includes the following: the right of use or non-use; the right of indefinite accumulation; the right of bequeathing property; the right of contracting with it—even the right of destroying it. Or it might say that property includes only one or two of these rights.

The point is that Rousseau's labor theory as applied to the state of nature at most grants to an individual the right to that amount of the product of his labor that is necessary for subsistence, that and no more. If the sovereign chooses to reaffirm this 'natural' right once the contract has established sovereignty, the resulting economy might be said to be an economy based on private property, but it would certainly not be a capitalist economy.[10]

The sovereign can of course redefine this minimal meaning of property by sanctioning additional rights. But there is nothing in the nature of the contract that demands this. In fact an entirely different script is possible. "It may also happen that men begin to unite before they have any possessions, subsequently acquiring a territory sufficient for all, and either *use it in common* or else divide it between them or in proportions fixed by the sovereign" (*SC* 1. 9; italics added). Since private property tends to frustrate the social ideal, the logic of the contract would seem to demand that it be restricted as much as possible. The idea of communal ownership seems far more promising. And this is exactly what in another context Rousseau takes to be the ideal.

> Far from wanting the state to be poor, I should like on the contrary, for it to own everything, . . . my idea . . . is not to destroy private property absolutely, since this is impossible, but to confine it within the narrowest possible limits; to give it a measure, a rule, a rein which will contain, direct and subjugate it, and keep it ever subordinate to the public good. In short, I want the property of the state to be as large and strong, that of citizens as small and weak, as possible. [*Corsica*, p. 317]

The less economic power an individual possesses the more dependent he is. If economic power is in the hands of some individuals, this dependence becomes personal dependence contrary to the aims of the contract. If, however, economic power is centered in the community as a whole, individual dependence is impersonal.

It will be recalled that Rousseau's problem of social organization involves two parameters: minimal personal dependence and maximal communal dependence. In the abstract, communal control of the means of production would insure the latter, but since society for Rousseau is all of one piece it remains to be seen what sort of a collective economy might harmonize with the many other things he holds essential to legitimacy and to the absence of personal dependence. Up to a point it is possible to construct such an ideal society in Rousseau's own words: there would be no specialized division of labor, no money, no luxury, and so on. Unfortunately, Rousseau nowhere joins these with a description of a collective economy. It is necessary, then, if the social contract is to retain credibility, to supply the missing pieces. Rousseau would be the first to concede that his principles of right are meaningless unless they can be embodied, if only ideally, in the flesh and blood of a concrete society. In a weak sense he has left us a model, but because it involves a private economy, it does not exhaust the collectivist potential of his ideal parameters. A more suitable model is conceivable, and, surprisingly, it is not as ideal or utopian as one might expect. In fact, it can be constructed by combining elements drawn from historical descriptions of several peasant societies.

In his rather remarkable book *Mutual Aid*, Pëtr Kropotkin tells of the many cooperative enterprises man has engaged in over the centuries. Pieced together, they form a picture of a society that Rousseau might have enthusiastically applauded.[11] Conceive first of all a society where just about all the land, including fields, forests, orchards, vineyards, peat bogs, and quarries, is communally owned. The young men spend a few days in the forest felling timber, and the wood is later divided among all the households for fuel. The vineyards are cared for on a communal basis and, similarly, herds of cows. Milk, butter, and wine are supplied each family from communal stores. Private homes are made of wood and stone from the communal forests and quarries. Both private and public buildings are erected by collective labor, and no money is ever exchanged.

The peasants have their small plots of land, but should any suffer a bad harvest, he is sustained from communal stores and thus is never forced to sell his fields or eventually himself. Plowing, planting, and harvesting are common enterprises, as are the celebrations that signal the end of a project well done. Hardly anything is a purely private affair. A young girl's dowry is supplied by her female neighbors. Even where cattle are privately owned, they graze on public lands and are collectively cared for by their owners on a rotating basis. The bulls, as ultimate means of production, are of course communal property.

There are any number of problems that require public attention. When the cemetery wall has to be raised, the work of carrying sand and water, making mortar, and serving as masons is done by volunteers. The same holds true when the roads are in need of repair or when a public fountain is to be built. Expensive equipment such as wine presses is kept by the commune. Should a private house be destroyed by fire, the family is lodged free with neighbors till the community can build and furnish a new home.

Irrigation canals must be built and maintained, forests cleared, trees planted, marshes drained. All these are cooperative projects. Though certain decisions require unanimity, so closely knit is the community that this is no obstacle to decision making. There are associations which dispense free medical aid. When a man is ill his work is assumed by his neighbors. No one is jeopardized because of ill fortune. The sick, the infirm, widows, and orphans are supported by public charities.

One could go on and on, but the above should suffice to make a few relevant points. All individuals in this model are extremely dependent, since little of what supports and sustains them is their own property or the exclusive product of their own labor. On the other hand, because this dependence is universal it is also mutual and symmetrical: in the ordinary course of events A depends upon B in the same way B depends on A. Services on behalf of other individuals, such as home building, or for the common good, such as road repair, are decreed by custom or by law. From a legal point of view the obligations so decreed may be said to be impersonal: they do not pertain to this or that individual but to any individual in this or that position where *all* individuals may be in that position. That is, the obligations could be expressed in such a way as to meet the formal requirements of law. But this meaning of impersonality is strictly formal; the manner in which social obligations are acquitted is thoroughly personal, for only neighbors, not strangers, build one another's houses.

Moreover, though the economy consists of distinguishable operations—planting, harvesting, road repair, dam building, wine making, shepherding, and so forth—these tasks are not the exclusive concerns of specialized subsections of society. On the contrary, they are for the most part just so many different roles played alternately by all citizens. The cohesion of society in this model is not the organic solidarity of Durkheim's division of labor, which holds society together because of the mutual interdependence of skills that are only found in *different* areas of society. Our model is not a case of distinguishable subsections, but rather a case where each individual depends upon all other individuals and in exactly the same way. To put it another way, there is a near-perfect symmetry between individual and society. Because the potential roles of a given individual practically exhaust the totality of social roles, he is related to society as a microcosm to a macrocosm. This is in contrast to Plato's idea of a division of labor. His state is not really man writ large, or at least not all men. An artisan's individuality, for example, is no more than the small writing that describes the productive sector of society; a man who works does not rule. In this context one can better understand Rousseau's strictures against associations. Despots disparage associations because isolated atoms of men offer less resistance than men united. But this is not Rousseau's main point. Associations, as we know them, respond to an articulated division of labor, and because they express the corporate will of some subclass of society, they threaten the general will. If society, on the other hand, is so structured that there is no specialized division of labor, if everybody does everything at one time or another, then no one exhaustively identifies himself with a given role. If a man is both a mason and a farmer, it is not in his mason-interest to subvert his farmer-interest. The rise of associations signals on the public side an end of common goods; on the private side, the beginning of the fragmented individual. When this occurs, the more associations the better, because this at least minimizes concentrations of power.

In this model of a self-sufficient community there is no need to evaluate, hierarchically, different social roles. Since all citizens play all roles, there is no need to mark them off in terms of money or title. Where social roles are self-executing without invidious comparisons, there is no need of money at all. Where private property is minimal, where the community guarantees each his subsistence and where there is no money to accumulate, there can be little distinction between rich and poor. A necessary condition of equality is thus insured.

This society is self-sufficient only in the relative sense that it has all that it wants. Its wealth is not to be found in money or luxury, but in Rousseau's sense of happiness: its powers and desires are in balance. If it were to want more than it could produce communally, it would have to change its economic base, institute a specialized division of labor, and introduce money as a measure of value. Such an economic change would initiate fundamental changes in society as a whole. On Rousseau's principles, vanity, luxury, and a proliferation of needs would all interact to destroy the cooperative spirit on which the common good had rested.

But until this occurs there is little need of a formal educational system for the transmission of technical knowledge, and no reason to encourage the sciences. Most of what passed for education in the eighteenth century would be irrelevant. However, the continuity of society does depend upon a different type of education, namely, the transmission of values and a sense of group loyalty. But this need not take the form of strident indoctrination. "How then is it possible to move the hearts of men, and to make them love the fatherland and its laws? Dare I say it? Through children's games; through institutions which seem idle and frivolous to superficial men, but which form cherished habits and invincible attachments" (*Poland*, p. 162).

Whatever the means, the goal of education is to have the individual completely identify himself with the community. The ego's frame of reference is enlarged; it is expanded beyond the 'I' stage until it embraces the 'we'. Loyalty and a spirit of cooperation are the highest civic virtues. In such a society the individual, at least in principle, can be perfectly socialized, because his society is homogeneous and thus can be internalized as a whole and without remainder. Save for a partial division of labor based on sex, there is no part of society an individual cannot identify with, because there are no social roles he is not potentially destined to play. Under these circumstances there is an intersubjective general will, whether in the form of law, custom, or tradition, permeating every aspect of social existence.

On a socioeconomic level such a community responds to the exigencies of the social contract. There is a known and pervasive common good to give substance to the general will; there is universal equality; no individual is or need be subject to the personal will of another; all individuals are completely, and in the same ways, dependent on the community as a whole. If one wishes to call this a conformist society, it must be remembered that it is a conformity that unites friends and not something imposed on strangers.

With regard to this model the question is not whether Rousseau had it in mind but whether it incorporates in a reasonably unified way the socioeconomic conditions he sees as preconditions for his abstract principles of right. It seems that it does. There is no money, no cultivation of the arts and science, no industry or commerce, no luxury, no extremes of rich and poor, no dependence on private wills, yet complete dependence on the community. There is inculcation of civic loyalty, an agrarian economy, communal recreation and games, minimal private property, equality. And above all this society is so structured that in a literal sense it is every citizen writ large. Because society and the individual mutually reflect one another, there is not only an objective common good in almost every aspect of society, there is subjectively a near coincidence of particular and general wills. The subjectively felt good of the individual is by design almost always the same as the objective common good. In such a society children grow up in an environment where a cooperative spirit and primary regard for the community are as much needs of the psyche as food and water are of the body. Eccentricity, selfishness, and personal vanity would simply be maladaptive traits, and individuals so possessed would find little to nourish them in such an environment.

The point to be reemphasized is that, given this context, a general will would be the 'natural' will of the individual. The objective side of the coin is that there are literally common goods. By contrast, in a society where interests are fragmented and incompatible, it is the particular will that is natural. This is not simply a matter of subjective selfishness; there is, as always, an objective side. It is not enough for a person to desire to will the common good. There must be a specific common good to will, and such goods progressively become less and less as society becomes fragmented by an evolving specialized division of labor. There are common goods for this area of society and common goods for other areas. But there are fewer and fewer common goods for all areas. Or, to put this same thought differently, the possibility of a general will decreases as the area that can be regulated by the formal conditions of law contracts in relation to the totality of society. It is necessary to distinguish the selfishness of a man who lives in a society where common goods abound from that of a man living in a society where objective common goods are few. In the former case the man might have willed generally; in the latter there is little that might be willed generally.

The *Social Contract* makes much of a general will, but there can be no general will in the concrete unless objectively there is a common good to will. And that is why, as Rousseau well knew, the social contract is meaningless save in relation to a very few types of society. A communal society similar to that depicted above would seem ideally suited to the needs of the contract, but, though Rousseau does emphasize the communal in most other areas of society, he has little to say about it when the economy is at issue. This rather strange silence may be simply a practical response to conditions as he found them, as in the case of Poland and Corsica. Or it may be due to theoretical reasons he saw limiting man's sense of community.

According to Kropotkin a communal way of life was incompatible with the nation-state's thirst for centralized power. In various ways it sought to break up communal land and redistribute it to individuals. But the cooperative spirit of peasant communities resisted such attempts, "and wherever the peasants had retaken possession of part of their lands they kept them undivided."[12] In the long run the state triumphed and private property with its attendant individualism became the rule. In Kropotkin's eyes the desire to cooperate is a natural impulse that can only be stifled by extraneous forces. If his reading of human nature is even roughly correct, then a Rousseauan society cannot be dismissed out of hand on purely psychological grounds. But the question is whether Rousseau's account of human nature can accommodate a cooperative spirit sufficient to ground a thoroughly communal society.

Rousseau's continued insistence that man is naturally good is not very helpful. In fact it has very pessimistic overtones. As applied to man in a state of nature it has no moral significance at all; solitary, primitive man is only rarely and momentarily involved in conflict situations, and the sole relevant rule of resolution is natural right, that is, power. It is true that Rousseau also characterizes some men in society, including himself, as naturally good in the sense that by disposition they have no inclination to do harm to others. But this type of goodness seems to be limited to those who are not active participants in society's affairs. Like Rousseau they live on the fringes of society and, while not harming others, they avoid situations that involve duties. In any case, such men are too exceptional to constitute a norm or even an ideal when it is a question of politics with its many duties. Rousseau normally pictures social man as a creature forever tempted to stray from the straight and narrow, forever seeking to enhance his condition at the expense of others.

For Kropotkin society is natural because man is spontaneously a cooperative being. It is on this point that the two part company. Both might agree about what society ought to be, but whereas Kropotkin sees the idea frustrated by external and artificial forces, Rousseau views it as possible only under the most artificial conditions, and even if these conditions are realized, he anticipates a 'natural' degeneration into the normal condition where particular wills dominate. At first glance this pessimism seems gratuitous in a man who assigns such a major role to society in the formation of individual character. Why cannot a certain type of society induce or cultivate the cooperative spirit necessary to sustain the social contract? The answer to this depends upon Rousseau's conception of human nature as detailed in the *Second Discourse*.

Chapter 6

The Search for Human Nature

Any contract theory of political association proceeds on the assumption that man is not by nature a political animal. Rousseau's claim is more radical: man is not by nature a social animal. His conclusion is well known, but there seems to be little understanding of how he went about justifying it. To be sure, attention may be directed to the fine parade of empirical data he passes in review in the *Second Discourse*. But it should be obvious that there was no available evidence that could conclusively support this conclusion. At the very most, the evidence Rousseau adduces harmonizes with, but does not necessitate, his conclusion. The truth is that his conclusion is predetermined on other grounds, and it is the conclusion that selects the evidence and not the evidence that decides the conclusion. The problem is to identify these other grounds.

Rousseau claims that the method underlying the *Second Discourse* is the conditional reasoning that scientists employ, which is "better suited to clarify the nature of things than to show their true origins, like those our physicists make every day concerning the formation of the world" (*Second Discourse*, p. 103). At first this may sound strange coming from an author who is purportedly dealing with origins. A little reflection, however, shows that in the absence of facts this was inevitable. How do the cosmogonists referred to by Rousseau overcome a similar scarcity of facts? The case of Descartes is, at least methodologically, typical. A century earlier, he had exercised his speculative talents by constructing a cosmogony that pictured the present articulated universe as the terminus of a long evolutionary process that started with an unarticulated, uniform distribution of matter. This kind of speculative enterprise cannot get off the ground unless the cosmogonist comes equipped with an apparatus he judges to be reliable independently of his speculative conclusion. It need hardly be added that the credibility of his conclusions is a function of the trustworthiness of his apparatus. Descartes's apparatus was his physics, and that did not prove very reliable. But the point is that Rousseau is quite mistaken in believing that the conditional reasoning of cosmogonists clarifies the nature of things. On the contrary, the nature of things must be known before the game can get underway.[1]

What does Rousseau bring to his game? His answer is, from one point of view, really startling. "I have tried to set forth the origin and progress of inequality, the establishment and abuse of political societies, insofar as these can be *deduced from the nature of man*" (*Second Discourse*, p. 180; italics added). In the Aristotelian tradition the essence or nature of a thing was associated with the perfection of that thing and could only be determined after it reached an optimal stage of development. Given only a baby or an acorn, the nature of man or oak trees would forever remain hidden. Ostensibly Rousseau sought to identify human nature by identifying man's original condition. But this is impossible, because history has long since erased this condition from human memory. Man's original condition, then, does not provide the clue to human nature; on the contrary, human nature provides the clue to man's original condition.

How, then, does Rousseau arrive at his conception of human nature? He cannot arrive at it by a historical reconstruction, and, given his definitive picture of human nature, it is evident that he is operating on non-Aristotelian lines. He does have a method, but one will look in vain for an explicit exposition of it in the *Second Discourse*. The *Second Discourse* is an application of this method, and it is this method that Rousseau brings to his speculative game, much as Descartes's cosmogony was a special application of his physics. To discover this method one must look to *Emile*, a later work, where Rousseau through the vicar explains how the nature of matter is disclosed:

I see it [matter] sometimes in motion, sometimes at rest, hence I infer that neither motion nor rest is essential to it, but motion, being an action, is the result of a cause of which rest is only the absence. When, therefore, there is nothing acting upon matter it does not move, and for the very reason that rest and motion are indifferent to it, its natural state is a state of rest. . . .

. . . But it is not true that motion is of the essence of matter, if matter may be conceived of as at rest. . . .

. . . For my own part, I feel myself so thoroughly convinced that the natural state of matter is a state of rest. . . . The first causes of motion are not to be found in matter; matter receives and transmits motion, but does not produce it. . . .

. . . Is it not plain that if motion is essential to matter it would be inseparable from it, it would always be present in it in the same degree, always present in every particle of matter, always the same in each particle of matter, it would not be capable of transmission, it could neither increase nor diminish, nor could we ever conceive of matter at rest. When you tell me that motion is not essential to matter but necessary to it, you try to cheat me with words.[2]

The surprising revelation that Rousseau was apparently unaware of the principle of inertia is not yet the point at issue. The important things to note are the criteria he uses to distinguish essential and nonessential properties and to determine a thing's natural state. An essential property is, first of all, a property which cannot be conceived to exist apart from the thing in question and, second, which manifests itself in an invariant way. Provisionally, the natural state of a thing is the condition of that thing when it is not acted upon by external forces.[3] It is well to get clearly in mind what the second criterion demands. Even if matter were always in motion and never perceived at rest, motion would still not be an essential property because bodies move with varying velocities. An essential property, according to Rousseau, must characterize all the members of a class in exactly the same, determinate way. Any property that does not invariantly pertain to all members is an accidental determination.

The only possible use this criterion can have is negative: if something is not invariantly present, it does not belong to the nature of that thing. Try to conceive of any property that pertains to all the members of a species in this invariant manner and you will fail. Rousseau would concede that men are animals, but no two men are animals in exactly the same determinate way. As unrealistic as this criterion is, it justifies Rousseau's first step beyond recorded history. By the nature of the case, history gives us nothing but men in society. Look where you will, as an empiricist you will find nothing but organized societies. How in the face of this massive and uncontradicted evidence is it possible to conclude that man is not naturally social? Simple. If men were naturally social, their sociality would manifest itself in roughly the same determinate way, just as the behavior of animals belonging to the same species falls roughly within the same pattern. But the staggering variety of human societies proves that there is no similar natural pattern that marks off human society. Therefore, man is not naturally social. Q.E.D.

But Rousseau has another criterion, the criterion of conceivability: a property is essential if and only if its absence is inconceivable. This is a less restrictive criterion because it does not by itself require invariance. A property is essential provided that the thing cannot be conceived without some possible variations of that property. A specific shape, for example, is an accidental property of a piece of wax, but some shape (that is, shape indeterminately conceived) is essential, because by this criterion a shapeless finite body is inconceivable. There is another side to this criterion. If a thing can be conceived as possessing a certain property, the contradictory of that property cannot be itself an essential property. Because a body can be conceived at rest, its contradictory, motion, cannot be an essential property. Similarly, because a body can be conceived in motion, rest is not essential. If body is indeterminate with respect to rest and motion, then a body at rest will forever remain at rest unless acted upon by external forces. There is nothing in the nature of body that can immanently account for motion. Rousseau at least got half the principle of inertia correct.

Motion and rest are here viewed as external relations, because bodies are essentially the same whether in motion or at rest. They must be distinguished from certain intrinsic accidents. These accidents are characterized by two things: (*a*) they admit of variations, and (*b*) the substance in question cannot be conceived minus all these variations. Shape is such an accident. A body may assume various shapes, but it cannot be conceived as shapeless. The variations are related to one another as *contraries*, and it does not make any sense to ask which of an indefinite number of contraries is the natural state of the substance in question. The case of rest and motion is different because they are related as *contradictories*: a body is either in motion or at rest; there is no third term. Because of his pre-Newtonian physics, Rousseau felt compelled to ask which of the two constitutes a body's natural state. Since a body cannot be conceived as neither at rest nor in motion, an option is forced.

Rousseau chose rest as a body's natural state because it was not a caused phenomenon, whereas motion depended upon the continuous influence of an external force. There was, however, another reason why he preferred rest. Rest is a homogeneous, uniform condition. It does not admit of contraries; a body either is at rest or it is not. Motion, on the other hand, does admit of contraries. There is only one rest but an indefinite number of motions differing in direction and velocity. If Rousseau had chosen motion as body's natural state, according to the criterion of invariance he would have had to choose a specific velocity and direction, and this is clearly inane.

Rousseau speaks of the conceivable and inconceivable as indices of the essential. This warrants a little more attention. If a body can be both in motion and at rest, then the corresponding idea of body must be indeterminate with respect to both. It is not particularly clear what the positive content of this idea is. For the sake of argument let us say that ultimate bodies are inert, solid atoms. Is it possible to conceive of these inert atoms as lacking all dynamical potentialities, to conceive atoms that are not only at rest but that are incapable of being moved? Given Rousseau's rather imprecise idea of conceivability, I can see no reason why this is not a conceptual possibility. But since he does allow for motion, he cannot conceive of body as lacking dynamic possibilities. Any given motion may be an accident, but the enduring potentiality of motion is of the very essence of matter.

One can understand why Rousseau's idea of matter is indeterminate with respect to both motion and rest: empirical data satisfied him that bodies are indeed sometimes in motion and sometimes at rest. His idea had to accommodate what he took to be the facts. I can conceive a body in motion or at rest because my idea already provides for this option. If I start with an idea of a body lacking all dynamic potentialities, then I cannot conceive that body in motion. I know that men can be social animals because I have the empirical evidence that as a matter of fact they do live in societies. Can I conceive of them as originally living solitary, nonsocial lives? Yes, but only if I start with an idea of man that is already indeterminate with respect to these contradictory descriptions. The point is that Rousseau's method of discovering natures is in part circular. There is no way to determine whether a thing can be conceived without a given property unless that thing is observed without the property in question or unless the definition of the thing is such as to permit or forbid the conception. His criterion, thus, is not really a conceptual test at all, it is decision by imagination. For Rousseau the imaginable determines the conceivable.

The trouble with allowing the imagination to arbitrate possible reality, however, is that ordinarily imagination is limited to the visual and therefore to the superficies of things. While it is true that the denotation of most general, universal, or class terms is learned on the basis of how their members superficially appear, the relevant sciences must probe far deeper to find a fruitful connotation. Anyone can imagine pears issuing from what in all other picturable respects is an apple tree, but no respectable pomologist would accept this picture as an index of possibility. The imaginable of itself is not an acceptable indication of either fact or possibility, and one must beware whenever Rousseau implicitly makes appeal to it.

The search for human nature must begin with an agreed-upon denotation of the term 'man'. For Rousseau this is no problem: 'man' denotes any animal that any eighteenth-century physician would recognize as a man. The *Second Discourse* is not a treatise on somatic evolution. The next step is to play a game of subtraction. How much can be subtracted from the contemporary man without endangering the survival of the species? What can thus be subtracted is not a part of human nature for the same reason that motion is not an essential property of matter: man can be conceived without what has been subtracted. Thus, it is not true that the family as we know it is natural, because we can conceive otherwise. And the reasoning is similar for all the other subtractions that leave us with Rousseau's version of primitive man.

But note once again, this is not really a game of conceiving, for if it were, it would be over before it started. If something can be validly stripped from contemporary man without doing violence to human nature, then Rousseau has come forearmed with an essential definition of what constitutes human nature, and all the rest is a self-indulgent display of erudition. To put it quite bluntly, whatever plausibility Rousseau's idea of natural man enjoys is because of the imagination. Can you imagine a man minus all social attributes, including language and reason, surviving in a state of nature? The tautological answer is, "Yes, provided you give him the physical capacity and sufficient animal sense to survive." Multiply this version, being careful to add female counterparts, and you have a well-known picture.

Let us conclude that wandering the forests, without industry, without speech, without domicile, without war and without liaisons, with no need of his fellowmen, likewise with no desire to harm them, perhaps never even recognizing anyone individually, savage man subject to few passions and self-sufficient, had only the sentiments and intellect suited to that state; he felt only his true needs, saw only what he believed he had an interest to see; and his intelligence made no more progress than his vanity. [*Second Discourse*, p. 137]

However, you cannot play the game successfully if all you do is subtract, because in this type of abstraction the relation between beginning and end is not symmetrical. One can, for example, abstract a genus from several species, but the genus, then, is indeterminate with respect to any given species. That is, you cannot deduce a species from a generic idea. So at a minimum a player must make at least one addition. In order to bridge the enormous gap between natural and social man, you have to provide a principle that will allow for the return trip. This is the principle of perfection or perfectibility, which is simply an unexplained principle whose theoretical burden is to span every nonbiological change from what man originally was, according to Rousseau, to what he now is. All that it says is that natural man had the potential for becoming man as we now know him. It should be noted that perfectibility is added to Rousseau's concept of human animality for the same methodological reason that mobility, the potentiality to be moved and in turn to move another, is added to a 'static' concept of matter. Matter may be naturally at rest, but the fact of motion demands a correlative potentiality. Exactly how perfectibility is related to free will is not clear. Though natural man, like any other animal, can be imagined without free will, Rousseau had to attribute it to human nature either as a separate faculty or as included in the blanket concept of perfectibilty. Unless man is in some sense free it is idle to distinguish a general and a particular will.

Let us for the sake of further analysis concede that Rousseau is able to conceive (imagine) natural man. Note what, according to his method of determining natures, this concession entails. It automatically follows that man is not by nature a social animal. Because matter can be conceived both at rest and in motion, neither motion nor rest is a determinate part of its nature. Similarly, because man can be conceived both as a social and a nonsocial animal, he is by nature neither a social nor a nonsocial animal.

Because Rousseau was unaware of the principles of inertia, he held that rest rather than motion was matter's natural state. Now it is absolutely essential to understand this distinction between a nature and a natural state. What belongs to a nature belongs of necessity. If a thing loses a natural property it ceases to be itself. But matter is no less matter whether it is at rest or in motion. Therefore, neither can be said to be a natural property. Motion, however, pertains to a body, not solely because of its nature but because of an external force, namely, another moving body. In the absence of this external influence, the nature of the body by itself completely determines a state of rest.[4] Rousseau must make a similar choice between man as social and man as nonsocial. Neither is a natural property, but, because they are contradictories, one and only one is descriptive of man's natural state. Given his methodology Rousseau's choice was inevitable: if human nature had not been subject to external and nonhuman forces, man would have remained naturally at rest as a solitary, self-sufficient animal.

The solitary life was the obvious choice for at least two methodological reasons: (*a*) Like rest, the lives of primitive men as described by Rousseau were pretty much all of one piece because they were so limited. By contrast, the lives of social men are as variable as the degrees of motion (*Second Discourse*, p. 138). (*b*) Because there are so many social patterns it would be impossible to select one determinate pattern rather than another as man's natural state.

Just as matter at rest can never spontaneously move itself but requires, in the last analysis, a will, so also natural men would never have spontaneously associated. Given the fact of association, continuing socialization is due to those men already socialized, just as matter once set in motion continuously transmits motion. As for the origin of the socializing process, Rousseau argues that man's social potentials "could never develop by themselves, that in order to develop they needed the chance combination of several foreign causes which might never have arisen and without which he would have remained eternally in his primitive condition." The events that led man out of the state of nature could have happened in several ways. Rousseau's choice of these events is conjectural, but that is quite proper, because "the conclusions I want to *deduce* from mine [Rousseau's scenario] will not thereby be conjectural, since on the principles I have established, one could not conceive of any other system that would not provide me with the same results, and from which I could not draw the same conclusions."[5] Rousseau is quite right. Historical accuracy is not important, because no matter how natural man became socialized he was doomed to corruption.

As close as the parallel is between Rousseau's analyses of the nature of matter and of man, there is one momentous difference. Though rest may be matter's natural state, it hardly seems appropriate to describe motion as unnatural and artificial. Even if it is viewed as a kind of violence done to nature, it is done by a divine will, and besides, matter does not appear any the worse for it. Indeed, motion "gives life to nature" (*Emile*, p. 236), and that certainly is better than an unarticulated expanse of inert matter. The case of human nature is far different. Though perfectibility is an essential part of human nature, it seems that for the most part it produces artificiality, unnaturalness, and evil. In the case of man, unlike the case of matter, Rousseau seems to assume that what is not in its natural state is antinatural, that social man is unnatural. What is it about human nature that it carries within itself the seeds of its own destruction?

Not all of Rousseau's observations on human nature are inextricably linked with his conception of primitive man. His phenomenologically fundamental point that man is unique in a way no other species is unique, for example, stands on its own feet. Even if man never lived a solitary life, it would still be the case that social man is an exceptional creature. He is unique because he is related to his environment in a way no other animal is.

Though we know today that there has occurred an evolution of species, at any given time an animal is approximately in a state of equilibrium with its environment. Heredity has programmed into an animal a set of fixed needs and behavior patterns designed to satisfy those needs. But survival also depends upon a suitable environment; any protracted imbalance between organism and environment results in the death of the individual and perhaps the extinction of the species itself. The pattern of adaptive behavior is rigid and limited. "An animal is at the end of a few months what it will be all its life: and its species is at the end of a thousand years what it was the first year of that thousand." An animal is ruled by instinct: "nature commands every animal and the beast obeys." So imperious is nature's rule that an animal cannot deviate from its program even when from a different point of view it would seem advantageous to do so. "Thus a pigeon would die of hunger near a basin filled with the best meats, and a cat upon heaps of fruit or grain" (*Second Discourse*, pp. 113–15).

The reason for this is that meat as nourishment is no more a part of a pigeon's environment than fruit is a part of a cat's environment. In a strict sense, an environment is not the sum total of physical objects that are found in a given area; it is something peculiar to each species and is limited to what hinders or abets satisfaction of those needs that define the organism. Each species is, as it were, tuned into nature on its own private frequency and responds only to what it hears on that frequency. Its environment is that small part of nature which is of concern to its well-being. In this sense, though different species share the same territory, their environments are by no means identical. For the most part an animal is unable to alter its environment. And even where in a limited way it can, it does so only to the extent of providing satisfaction for the limited and changeless set of needs that heredity has bequeathed it. It is these needs that define a suitable environment, and it is not the environment that determines the needs. Discounting evolutionary transitions, an animal and its specific environment are near-changeless constants. Outside of death or dying, there are no needs that are left unsatisfied, and there are no environmental factors that induce new needs.[6]

By way of contrast man is a free agent, which in this context simply means that he is not, for the most part, instinctively tied to a predefined environment. Nature alone and infallibly rules animals but does not so rule man. "Thus dissolute men abandon themselves to excesses which cause fever and death, because the mind depraves the senses and because the will still speaks when nature is silent" (*Second Discourse*, p. 114). Natural man, as described by Rousseau, was little more than an animal. His needs were purely physical, few and easily satisfied; his imagination was dormant; his knowledge was limited to that which pertained to survival, and since survival was there for the asking, he had neither foresight nor curiosity; having no language, his mind was incapable of wonder, science, philosophy, or religion. In a word, he lived in an environment as narrowly circumscribed as that of any other animal.

In this environment men coexisted as equals. Even granting there were innate differences in potential, "what advantage would the most favored draw from them to the prejudice of others in a state of things which permitted almost no sort of relationship among them? Where there is no love, of what use is beauty? What is the use of wit for people who do not speak, and ruse for those who have no dealings?" (*Second Discourse*, pp. 138–39). Historical accuracy aside, there is implicit in Rousseau's description of natural man a regulative idea that serves him in other contexts: the more limited the environment, the less the likelihood of inequality and, as will be seen, of unhappiness. The limited environment is also relatively natural in one of the many meanings of that term. Unknown circumstances and the faculty of self-perfection drew men out of this state of innocence, and society was born. Regardless of what one makes of Rousseau's account of this transition, there are parts of it which are integral to his social thought and are worthy of independent attention. Though all men are potentially rational, there are certain preconditions for reason's substantive development. The most obvious precondition is a language, for without it there is nothing to mark off classes, express relations, or solidify knowledge. Language is above all the medium through which reality is filtered and given a structure: "minds are formed by language, thoughts take their colour from its ideas" (*Emile*, p. 73). With a developed language, man is able to create a new type of environment, a symbolic universe. Rousseau is certain that language is essential to thought, but the question of origins leaves him puzzled, "for if men needed speech in order to learn to think, they had even greater need of knowing how to think in order to discover the art of speech" (*Second Discourse*, pp. 121–22).

Then there is a second precondition. A language is something shared, and even in a rudimentary form it presupposes some social intercourse. But once again the question of origins leaves Rousseau undecided. "Which was most necessary, previously formed society for the institution of languages, or previously invented languages for the establishment of society?" (*Second Discourse*, p. 126).

After the fact, one can see the close connections that link reason, language, and society, but something further must be added to account for their mutual development. Rousseau gives different accounts of the origin of society, but, once associated, men's affective lives undergo a change. A new order of needs arises. Collectively, these novel needs have their origin in vanity, the desire to shine before others. This mutual need to make invidious comparisons is one of the ties that hold people together. These new passions dialectically interact with reason: "human understanding owes much to the passions, which by common agreement also owe much to it. It is by their activity that our reason is perfected; we seek to know only because we desire to have pleasure. . . . The passions in turn derive their progress from our knowledge" (*Second Discourse*, p. 116).

What Rousseau has in effect given us is an embryonic theory of the social origin and development of mind and emotion. Reason is not simply a passive mirror of reality; it creates new realities, new social environments. With the aid of language, reason breaks the narrow circle of man's natural environment, but in the process a curious reversal occurs. No matter how animals otherwise differ, they have this in common: their needs define their environment and their needs are predetermined by nature. Social man by contrast is unique in that so many of his most deeply felt needs are determined by his environment, that is, by society itself. Even social animals are not social in this sense. It is not their society that assigns individual roles, but, rather, differently preprogrammed individuals pursuing their individual destinies automatically effect an adaptive division of labor. Man alone is subject to induced needs, and it is this that distinguishes him from all other animals.[7]

To an individual growing up in society, his acquired needs have much the same force as natural needs, and he confronts his society as his natural habitat. Precisely because he recognized the force of induced needs and attitudes, Rousseau recognized the necessity, though not the desirability, of the corresponding social environment. There was never a question of a mass return to a state of nature, because society inevitably created and transmitted needs that could never be satisfied outside of society.

To the extent that man has animal needs, he too has a natural environment. But he has other needs, and since needs correlate with an environment, these additional needs entail an enlarged environment. "The look of the other," for example, was not part of man's original environment, but once men banded together they "grew accustomed to consider different objects and make comparisons; imperceptibly they acquire ideas of merit and beauty which produce sentiments of preference. By dint of seeing one another, they can no longer do without seeing one another again" (*Second Discourse*, p. 148). This is an induced or, in Rousseau's terminology, an artificial need, but it is none the less a need and thus relates to an environment.

Over the course of history these needs proliferate, and distinctive sets of these needs mark off one society from another. Whereas natural men are hardly more distinguishable than states of rest, social man wears as many different masks as there are different velocities. Man lives on and off the earth, but his real home is the symbolic environment he has created. His beliefs, his preferences, his institutions, traditions, customs—none of these are given by nature or deducible from a genetic code. Nevertheless, they are as real as the flesh a hungry lion craves or the grass that nurtures a cow.

This social environment is the world into which a child is born, and in time this world molds his psyche almost as infallibly as nature shapes his body. No individual man is self-created. "Man makes himself" refers to a long historical process wherein successive generations, sometimes consciously, mostly not, have created a social environment which in turn creates future men. It is this environment and not nature that is the chief architect of man. The uniqueness of man is that his primary nature contributes little to the definition of his environment, whereas his self-created environment is the main determinant of his second nature. It is for this reason that the structural parallel between human nature and the nature of matter cannot be complete: motion does not transform the nature of matter, but socialization effects radical changes in man's original nature.

If an animal's needs are left unsatisfied, it dies. If a person's induced needs are left unsatisfied, he still lives, but unhappily. Why is it that man creates his own unhappiness? For Rousseau the answer is vanity, that Hobbesean principle of self-preferment. Desires rooted in vanity can never be satisfied, because their measure is always relative to other people. The ideal is not simply to be number one in any competitive arena but to be ever farther and farther in front of number two. Vanity is the spur; more and more fields of competition arise; criteria of excellence multiply; one's rank is established, "not only upon the quantity of goods and the power to serve or harm, but also upon the mind, beauty, strength or skill, upon merit or talents" (*Second Discourse*, p. 155). Because these qualities are relative, they are necessarily scarce and in short supply. Where they are lacking men are driven to counterfeit them, and thus arises the divided man.

To be and to seem to be become two altogether different things; and from this distinction came conspicuous ostentation, deceptive cunning, and all the vices that follow from them. From another point of view, having formerly been free and independent, behold man *due to a multitude of new needs*, subjected so to speak to all of nature and especially to his fellowmen, whose slave he becomes in a sense even in becoming their master; rich, he needs their service; poor, he needs their help; and mediocrity cannot enable him to do without them." [*Second Discourse*, pp 155–56; italics added]

Self-sufficiency is the key to happiness, and the paradigmatic case of the self-sufficient man is the primitive savage. "Desiring only the things he knows and knowing only those things the possession of which is in his power or easily acquired, nothing should be so tranquil as his soul and nothing so limited as his mind" (*Second Discourse*, p. 213 note k).

Though there is no turning back to a state of nature, social man's happiness depends upon a similar principle. If man is to be happy, society must be so arranged that desires and powers are in such balance that men will desire only that which individually or collectively they have the power to satisfy. This is nature's norm, and it is in relation to this norm that society in the concrete is not only artificial but unnatural in a pejorative sense. Ideally, as witness the peasant community, a society can be conceived where need and satisfaction balance and where there is no personal dependence. But in the concrete all societies sooner or later give rise to personal dependence and induce needs that cannot be satisfied.

It is almost universally conceded that Rousseau was an extremely pessimistic thinker. A psychoanalyst might trace this despair to some pathological imbalance in his psyche. It might be explained as a simple inductive generalization based on personal experience. It might be explained in any number of ways. What I wish to show now is that there is a theoretical basis for Rousseau's pessimism, and that that basis is found in his a priori account of human nature that locates man's natural self outside of society. Though Rousseau constantly distinguishes a particular and a general will, it must not be thought that he is talking about two different faculties. He is distinguishing man's *only* will according to the ends it pursues. This will is constantly torn between a desire for self-enhancement and a concern for the common good.[8] For Rousseau this clash is inevitable, because man's natural will is particular, and government arises precisely because of the need to reconcile the Hobbesean clash of particular wills.

If man is a creature of will and if his natural state is one of solitude, then there is no natural end other than his own interests to determine his will. Rousseau distinguishes between *amour de soi* and *amour-propre*, but it is problematical just how operative this distinction really is. Man is described as naturally good, and this is compatible with love of self so long as the self in question lives in a noncompetitive environment, that is, outside society, where the self's needs are limited to what can easily be satisfied without prejudice to the similar needs of other selves.

When natural man enters society he has but one will, his natural love of self. This will is not mysteriously transformed into vanity; it is the same will simply functioning in a different environment.[9] It is only a semantic nicety to say that natural man lacked vanity; what he lacked was an environment in which self-love expresses itself as vanity. Just as eyes do not see in darkness, self-love does not seek preference outside society. But given light, eyes will see, and given society, *amour de soi* becomes *amour-propre*; the change in either case is not in the faculty but in the environment.[10] The love of self is an extremely powerful will.

Though Rousseau speaks of man's free will, its efficacy is quite dubious. For the most part, Rousseau describes man as almost compulsively selfish. The only possible cure for this seems to be rigid social control and thorough indoctrination. Either device presents its own distinctive problems of freedom, but one cannot appreciate or sympathize with a recommended social cure until one appreciates the extent and seriousness of the disease. Rousseau is in a very peculiar position. On the one hand inequality is unnatural in terms of moral law; on the other, it is natural in the sense that man's natural social will relentlessly seeks to establish it. And it is this social will and the nature of social man that is at issue. Rousseau had objected that Hobbes and others had not succeeded in identifying natural man because they had stopped short of a pure state of nature and instead had described social man. But this is of little but academic interest, because, like them, Rousseau's overriding concern was with social man, and when social man is the question there is precious little to distinguish Hobbes from Rousseau.[11] Their political remedies may be different, but for both, pride or vanity is the beast that must be tamed.

Rousseau's many and various descriptions of civilized man easily compete with those of the worst detractors of human nature.[12] The human predicament is tied to a paradox, because "the vices that make social institutions necessary are the same ones that make their abuse inevitable" (*Second Discourse*, pp. 172–73). Even if there were a people fit for legislation, by the time their reason had developed to a point where they could give rational consent to the contract, it would be a prideful reason. That is, even if the people were not initially proud, the very process of socializing them to legitimacy would create a pride that defeats that end. There is simply no way out, and Rousseau admits as much. In a letter to Mirabeau (26 July 1767) he compares the central problem of the *Social Contract*—"to find a form of government which puts the law above man"—to geometers' attempts to square the circle.

If, unhappily, such a form of government is not to be found, *and I honestly confess I think it cannot be*, my opinion is that it is necessary to go to the other extreme, and put the man straightway as far above the law as possible, establish, consequently, arbitrary despotism, and the most arbitrary possible. In a word, I see no tolerable mean between the most austere democracy and the most complete Hobbism, for the conflict between men and the laws, which throws the State into continual civil war, is the worst of all political conditions. [*Letters*, p. 352; italics added]

But then he hastens to add, "But the Caligulas, the Neros, the Tiberiuses? . . . My God! . . . I fling myself writhing to earth, and groan because I am a man." Man is evil and needs a tyrant, but a tyrant is no less an evil man. It is no mere coincidence that

Rousseau considered a Hobbesian political solution, however briefly, for, natural man aside, there is little to distinguish their pessimistic views of human nature as it pertains to social man. It is important to reemphasize that Rousseau's pessimism is not ultimately rooted in empirical evidence. Though he had evidence aplenty documenting man's selfishness, he also had his historical examples of societies (for example, his beloved Sparta) where an individual's first loyalty was to the state no matter what the personal cost.[13] That selfishness is part of a social man's nature follows from his unfortunate use of a defective a priori method in the *Second Discourse* that leaves man unprepared and even unfit for society. Vanity, to repeat, is simply man's natural love of self attuned to a new environment where socially defined goods are in short supply. In this new environment natural goodness is irrelevant, because in Rousseau's system it is but a satellite of the more fundamental idea that man is not naturally social. Roughly speaking, natural goodness and nonsociality are so balanced that if you tip one side of the scale the other side is proportionately disturbed. Thus the transition from a state of nature to society is paralleled by the transformation of goodness into vice. In this sense society corrupts man. Given society, then, vice or the dominance of a self-serving particular will is man's new nature.

But if man's first nature can be transformed, why not his second nature? If society can corrupt man, why can it not also redeem him? The transition from natural to social man was mostly a case of developing natural potentials, for example, reason. The natural will was changed only in the sense that its scope was enlarged: there were new opportunities and ways of satisfying self-love. Man's second nature has a great deal of stability because induced needs prevent it from lapsing back into a pure state of nature. The decisive fact is the natural strength of the particular will. Though Rousseau accords society by far the most significant role in character formation, natural man does not enter society as a complete *tabula rasa*; there is an indelible message written on each man's slate: "Me first." Society can form or, if you will, deform natural man in an indefinite number of ways, but it can never eradicate the old Adam in him.

There are limits as to what socialization can accomplish. But it is not altogether clear what limits, in the abstract, Rousseau might assign. From one point of view, the ideal limit of socialization would be achieved when the particular will of every citizen is the same as the general will of society as a whole. Rousseau intimates such a possibility when he speaks of societies where there is justice without conscious virtue, societies based on natural goodness (*Emile*, p. 156). Were such societies possible, their members, though objectively just, would not be, strictly speaking, moral agents. On the other hand, there would be no need for morality in the sense of a conscious struggle for self-transcendence. Leaving this possibility aside as an anomaly in Rousseau's thought, every one of his major works argues that virtue is essential to any legitimate polity. And this necessity marks the upper limit beyond which socialization cannot go.

Education, or, if you will, indoctrination, can accomplish just so much. The particular will cannot be socialized out of existence, but, because man has a free will, there is a possibility that it can be transcended. It seems to me that it is impossible to get from Rousseau anything even remotely resembling a clear idea of what free will is and how it relates to reason, conscience, or, for that matter, the particular will itself. Man can only have one will, but it would seem that when it wills naturally, that is, particularly, it is not free, "for the impulse of mere appetite is slavery and obedience to self-imposed law is liberty" (*SC* 1. 8). Only the moral man is free, and he is free because he sincerely consents to a law even against the contrary promptings of his particular will. The particular will looks for privileges and exemptions, whereas the very idea of law excludes them. True consent, then, implies a struggle, and because the conflict is internal, if it is resolved on the side of morality, it is self-resolved; that is, the relevant law is self-imposed.

It is necessary to emphasize that for Rousseau morality always involves a struggle, and this fact indicates the limits of socialization. John Chapman comes as close as anyone to grasping Rousseau's problem, but I think he too misses this point. He argues that Rousseauan man is so selfish that if this selfishness is not sublimated by social conditioning, political freedom is impossible. Agreed. But then he adds that the conditioning necessary to this end destroys all chance of moral freedom.[14] This assumes that conditioning or socialization can be complete. It is not self-evident to me why in theory the loss of moral freedom is truly a loss if it is replaced by the social equivalent of natural goodness. But that is not the point. What I have tried to argue is that for Rousseau socialization can never be complete, except perhaps for rare individuals, and it cannot be complete because the basic units of society are naturally nonsocial and even, if you will, antisocial.

Rousseau's theoretical analysis of human nature is sufficient evidence that moral man is engaged in protracted warfare with himself. However, the same point can be made in a different way. Rousseau's lifelong preoccupation with virtue is well known. But what is virtue? "This word 'virtue' signifies *force*. There is no virtue without combat; there is none without victory. Virtue consists not in merely being just but in being so through triumphing over one's passions, through reigning over one's heart" (*Letters*, p. 364). This, together with his conception of law, is basically the Rousseau that inspired Kant. There is ample room for morality because inclination and duty are all too often at odds. How virtue relates to all the other entities that grow in Rousseau's metaphysical garden, I do not know. But his general point is reasonably clear: there is no amount of socialization that renders self-discipline superfluous.[15]

And that is the problem. Society can stabilize a second human nature, but not a third one that could reliably support a general will. The struggle is too much for most men, and even among a moral elite there is a constant temptation to backslide. Because man has no stable third nature, the cooperative spirit that animates Kropotkin's communes would in Rousseau's view be not only unnatural but also short lived. Nature endures while the artificial perishes. And nature simply has taken no pains to unite men.

From the little care taken by nature to bring men together through mutual needs and to facilitate their use of speech, one at least sees how little it prepared their sociability, and how little it contributed to everything men have done to establish social bonds. In fact it is impossible to imagine why, in that primitive state, a man would sooner have need of another man than a monkey or a wolf of its fellow creature; nor supposing this need, what motive could induce the other to provide for it [*Second Discourse*, pp. 126–27].

The virtuous man is the most unnatural, the most artificial being in all creation. What specifically engages a man's pride or vanity may indeed be artificial, but vanity or pride as such is solidly grounded in nature-according-to-Rousseau. This is the heart of Rousseau's pessimism. There is no equality without virtue, and virtue is a commodity that is and will remain in short supply, because there is such little natural demand for it.

The *Social Contract* considered by itself has enough intrinsically self-limiting features to lead one to question its feasibility. But the real irony is that the *Second Discourse* seems to have doomed it even before it was written. The *First Discourse* had antecedently condemned vanity and all its works, but left open the question whether it was a curable disease. The *Second Discourse* is the definitive diagnosis: the disease is terminal. Selfishness is not an individual idiosyncrasy; it is a nearly invincible manifestation of a nature trying to adapt to an alien environment. Or, alternatively, because the relationship is dialectical, it is the internalization of the selfishness that necessarily characterizes any society that has developed beyond a certain level of sophistication. This irredeemable pessimism is not irreconcilable with most of Rousseau's other works. The extraordinary precautions taken to insulate Emile from society merely reflect the seriousness of the disease. Only an extreme pessimist would dare counsel a barter economy in the face of the relentless tide of western economic history. Happy endings apparently are not even credible in fiction. The authoritarian seeds that are scattered throughout Rousseau's corpus are not so much ideals as they are counsels of despair.

The *Social Contract*, however, presents special problems. It is, to say the least, a poorly organized work. But I hope that I have shown that it is possible to reconstruct a consistent theory of political right in the abstract. And there is the rub. By the eighteenth century history had long since passed beyond the socioeconomic limitations demanded by the contract. What these limitations are can be read in Rousseau's description of a people fit for legislation. Given the *Second Discourse*'s account of the interaction between reason and passion, their primitiveness—indeed, their almost primeval simplicity—should come as no surprise.[16] But where are such people to be found, and, if they can be found, where is a legislator to be found? Historical implausibilities aside, Rousseau could never escape his self-imposed dilemma: Either passions will defeat the contract or reason is insufficiently developed to understand it. Even if there were a level of psychic development where reason was strong enough to grasp the contract and passions weak enough to sustain it, that equilibrium could not long be maintained. This is a deduction from his analysis of the dynamics that society initiates, and it explains why Rousseau believed that nothing, not even a hypothetical legitimate polity, could withstand history's corrupting influence. The *Second Discourse* may not be intrinsically Rousseau's best work, but it apparently had an influence on his thinking that he was unable to overcome and that colored all his other writings. That his method was defective is not to the point; what he *believed* to be the truth of human nature was what shaped his thoughts.[17]

There are many political observations in the *Social Contract* that do not depend upon the principles of right, but they seem to me to be of dubious value for the contemporary world. That leaves, then, only an abstract theory of legitimacy. What the practical value of such a theory is I will not try to say. Absolutists may use it to condemn all governments indiscriminately. Others may use it as a regulative ideal to measure governments on a sliding scale of legitimacy. Still others may see it as a blueprint for the community's regaining local control from big government.

The *Social Contract* may be an unsatisfactory work in many respects, and it may even be irrelevant, but it is not true, as some commentators believe, that it represents a shift of Rousseau's thought from the position he took in the *Second Discourse*. This shift supposedly is from an honorific individualism to a pejorative collectivism.[18] But in fact the two works are continuous. The *Second Discourse* is by no means a paean to the individualism of social man. On the contrary, along with the *First Discourse*, it is a powerful denunciation of the excesses that derive from unbridled vanity. It is this vanity considered as a disease that demands collectivist therapy. Since, however, the prognosis is gloomy indeed,

Rousseau offers an alternative: the self-disciplined, nonhedonistic individualism of Emile.

The *Second Discourse* and the *Social Contract* are related to one another as actual disease and possible cure. In this respect they are not discontinuous analyses. Had Rousseau not introduced the chapter on the civil creed, the two would also share a common, thoroughly secular outlook. As long as the principles of right are considered in the abstract, there is no theoretical need to include the creed as one of the clauses of the social contract. But given the lugubrious conclusions of the *Second Discourse*, Rousseau must have belatedly realized that there was simply no secular cure for a disease that, infecting the contract from birth, would soon kill it. In a not so strange way, the civil creed expresses Rousseau's deepest despair: only a salutary fear of divine retribution may save man from himself. This is not to say that such a fear will save him; it is to say that without it he is certainly doomed.

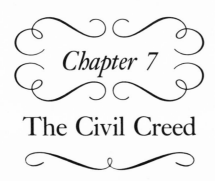

Chapter 7

The Civil Creed

With the possible exception of that most misunderstood phrase, 'forced to be free,' there is no aspect of Rousseau's political theory that is more passionately condemned than his doctrine on civil religion. Lester Crocker, for example, sees it as one more link in the chain that Rousseau forged to enslave the individual. It implies constant spying and surveillance; it leads to arrest on suspicion of wrong thinking.[1] Even otherwise friendly critics like Alfred Cobban and Charles E. Vaughan have the strongest reservations: "in the end, one cannot pretend to regard the chapter on the Civil Religion as other than unfortunate: . . . it helps us to understand why its author should have been so often regarded as the apostle of tyranny and an enemy to liberty in the state."[2] Vaughan sees the creed and its attendant penalty as an invitation to hypocrisy, since a man with no sense of duty would not scruple to commit perjury. But in any case, enlightened opinion rejects any state control of speculative opinion or belief.[3]

Perhaps the strongest condemnation of all is supplied by F. C. Green.

Rousseau in his fanatical zeal to preserve the sanctity of his social pact, was prepared to go to any extreme, at least on paper and in the heat of literary composition. Recklessly, in that fatal article of his civic profession of faith, he conceived the formula for a process of judicial mass murder which, with various refinements, was destined to form the basis of the twentieth-century totalitarian state. That a noble creation like the *Contrat social* should have been disfigured by such a monstrous appendage is one of the most baffling enigmas recorded in literature.[4]

What Green and several other critics seem to imply is that the creed is somehow not necessary to the integrity of Rousseau's argument. Vaughan, for example, while recognizing that it "represents, at least in sum and substance, the settled opinions of the author," notes that with regard to the *Social Contract* it was an afterthought.[5] But this recognition does not explain in what way the creed is related to the body of that work, for presumably it is related or Rousseau would not have seen fit to include it.

The necessary first step in any attempt to understand the role of the creed is to determine just precisely what it is. Rousseau tells us, "There is, therefore, a purely civil profession of faith whose articles the sovereign is competent to determine."[6] If the creed is, as explicitly stated, a sovereign act, then it is a law.[7] And if it is a law it is no part of the contract that establishes sovereignty. But since the sovereign is free to legislate or not, no law, not even the creed, is a necessity. On this interpretation the creed in no way compromises the contract and can be read as a momentary aberration on Rousseau's part, an unjustifiable presumption to speak in the name of a people not yet founded. In any case, on this reading it is a detachable part and not essential to his theory.

Even so, there is something strange about the creed considered as a law. Suppose a people including atheists pledged their loyalty to the terms of a contract that makes no reference to religious belief. Should the assembly propose to institute the creed, consider the plight of the atheist. He might, as was not uncommon among eighteenth-century atheists, judge that a belief in God was for the common good and vote accordingly. If his atheism was not previously known, he might continue as a member of society at the small cost of giving lip service to a formula he did not really believe. But if he is a known atheist, the very first law of the land has the effect of both disenfranchising and exiling him. As noted in the discussion on law, the spirit if not the letter of the contract forbids any such procedure. If the creed were a permissible law, any law disenfranchising a part of the original contractors, whether for ideological or for purely secular reasons, would also be permissible.

But this identification of the creed with law simply will not do, and for several reasons. If it were a law, it would be the only law that Rousseau considers in detail in the entire *Social Contract*. Again, because the creed dictates a set of beliefs, the net result is that it must be unanimously passed. Those who cannot subscribe to it are exiled. But Rousseau clearly states that only the contract itself requires unanimity. Moreover, the creed, unlike any other law, apparently cannot be repealed, for he speaks of it as though it were some sort of a priori condition of society itself. It embodies "sentiments of sociability without which it is impossible to be either a good citizen or a faithful subject" (*SC* 4. 8).

The main objection, however, against viewing the creed as a law is that as such it cannot solve the problem it is in part designed to solve. To appreciate the sense in which the creed is an afterthought, consider the status of the social contract minus the creed. It was Rousseau's firm conviction that religion was essential to society, since no state had ever been founded or conserved without it as a basis. "As soon as men live in society, they require a religion to maintain them there. Never have a people continued nor will they ever continue without religion."[8] This belief was by no means peculiar to Rousseau. In fact, the inseparable connection between religion and political stability was as close to a universally accepted axiom in the West as one can find. The inconclusiveness of interfaith warfare led to a doctrine of limited tolerance in certain places, but this tolerance seldom extended to avowed atheists. Philosophers might indulge in atheistic speculations in private, but never before servants, because few would dispute Voltaire's aphorism "If there were no God, it would be necessary to invent him." In discussing a people fit for legislation Rousseau simply assumed that they were religious, or else how understand the authority of a God-sent legislator?

But among such a people there would be no need for a civil creed. They are already religious and united by "common bonds of origin, interest or convention"; they have not yet borne the true yoke of laws, and they have no customs or deepseated prejudices (*SC* 2. 10). Their simplicity and lack of sophistication suggest religious unity. Among such a simple people atheism would be unthinkable, because atheism as a doctrine belongs to a much later stage of civilization and intellectual development. Under these circumstances the creed would be superfluous: the people already believe in God, atheists are unknown, and religious unity precludes an intragroup problem of intolerance.

In fact the creed would have been superfluous in all pre-Christian societies with which Rousseau was acquainted. These societies were not burdened with church-state conflicts. For practical purposes religion and the state were one and the same. Each city or state had its own gods, who were identified with the political system as a whole and with the laws in particular. Religion, far from being a political liability, was a powerful means of reinforcing patriotic loyalty.

The civil creed, as will be seen, is Rousseau's solution to the church-state problem. But this problem arose only with the advent of Christianity. The church, in claiming to be an indispensable instrument of salvation, effectively separated theology and politics. Because of the inevitable jurisdictional disputes that arose between priest and prince, the unity of society was in constant jeopardy. Despite contrary pressures, Christianity "has always retained, or recovered, its independence of the sovereign, and has remained without any necessary connexion with the body of the state" (*SC* 4. 8). In England and Russia the prince is the titular head of the church, but in fact he is related to the clergy as a government is to a sovereign legislature: he enforces but does not legislate dogma.

Priestly religions like Roman Catholicism bifurcate a man's loyalties. Subject to different authorities, his duties come in conflict. As a good citizen he cannot give absolute allegiance to the church; as a good Catholic, he cannot fully commit himself to the state. Such religions are politically unacceptable, because "anything which breaks the unity of society is worthless; all institutions which set man at odds with himself are worthless" (*SC* 4. 8).

The chapter on civil religion is related to the rest of the *Social Contract* as an afterthought in a very special way. In a pre-Christian context the secular version of the contract, that is, all the terms of the contract minus those supplied by the creed, would have sufficed to ground a purely secular morality. But at some undetermined moment it must have occurred to Rousseau that a "people fit for legislation" was, Corsica excepted, a thing of the dead past. So too was any hope of reviving some form of patriotic paganism. If the *Social Contract* was to have even the semblance of relevance, it would in some way have to come to grips with the contemporary scene, and this included above all the reality of Christianity. The creed is not directed to situations where religious unity prevails. In such situations the creed would be superfluous: a vocal atheist would be a foolish rarity; unanimity solves the problem of tolerance; and the positive creed adds absolutely nothing to already-cherished beliefs. The creed only becomes an issue because "now that there no longer is, nor can be, any exclusively national religion, you should tolerate all those which tolerate others insofar as their dogmas contain nothing contrary to the duties of the citizen" (*SC* 4. 8).

The creed then is relevant only in certain situations, where several churches are competing for the hearts of men. It is, in a word, Rousseau's version of a religious settlement between church and church on the one hand, and churches and state on the other. In an age of fervid faith the terms of such a settlement must be prior to contractual consent, that is, the settlement cannot be a law but must be incorporated into the original contract. No man of deep religious sensibilities is going to sign a blank check with regard to his religious future, and even less so if he finds himself a member of a religious minority. The very most a sincere believer can do is check his proselytizing zeal and tolerate, if tolerated in return, those of a different persuasion. Given the times, religious toleration was no easy matter save to atheists, whose nonbelief made them indifferent to the niceties of theological debates.

In theory Rousseau might have decided upon a complete and absolute separation of church and state. Had he done so, he would not, on that score at least, have been consigned to the contemporary liberal's hell. Why he did not choose this route will be considered below. Here it is necessary to note the exclusions entailed by the creed and to discuss them in turn. A required belief in God seems to rule out atheists. The negative dogma rules out the intolerant, which is a synonym for Rousseau's favorite target, the fanatic. There is a third class, universally overlooked, the theist who does not hold to the sanctity of the contract and its laws.

The fanatic is one who believes that he has a monopoly on

metaphysical truth, and that in virtue of this monopoly he has a right to impose it on others and to exempt himself from obligations he deems incompatible with his truth. In the eighteenth century the garden variety of fanatic was the religious zealot, but Rousseau's criticism of the fanatic applies equally well to the fanatical atheist.

Society, as conceived by Rousseau, rests on more than a set of rules: it has an affective basis. Ideally, citizens should feel for one another the love that reputedly unites brothers. On a more pedestrian level lesser ties suffice, but there are limits. The fanatic cannot live in peace with nonbelievers, for "it is impossible to live at peace with people whom you consider damned; to love them would be to hate the God who punishes them; you are bound either to save or to torment them" (*SC* 4. 8). This may be simple fact. In that case, all Rousseau is saying is that fanatics and non-fanatics will not consent to live together. However, the logic of the case is something quite different. The fanatic is not barred because of the civil creed, which only makes his exclusion explicit; he is barred because of the very nature of the social contract itself and would have been excluded even if the creed had never been written.

Because no man can meaningfully consent to a contradiction, the exclusion of the fanatic is more accurately described as a self-exclusion. A man holding a position incompatible with the terms of the social contract cannot in good faith accept that contract. But this is precisely the choice confronting the fanatic. He claims a privileged truth not certified by the sovereign and the right, or rather the duty, to force the wills of his neighbors. He cannot maintain this claim and at the same time consent to a contract that repudiates the authority of any will other than the general will. To be specific, a Roman Catholic cannot rationally give his loyalty to a church that claims independent legislative authority and at the same time affirm the unrestricted, inalienable, and indivisible sovereignty of the people. The same contradiction applies to any proponent of intolerance, for intolerance rests upon the belief that it is sometimes justifiable to enforce beliefs that are not approved by the sovereign and to which individuals have not consented. Fanaticism and intolerance are one and the same.

It is only some lapse in logic that can explain how a commentator can praise Rousseau's contract in general and question the specific that would exile the intolerant. The terms of the social contract, like the rules governing a sport, are all of one piece. No one is forced to participate, but if someone does he must consent to the rules and recognize that what is legitimate in one game is forbidden in another. If, for example, a basketball player races down the court without dribbling and scores a basket, the goal will be disallowed. His appeal that running with the ball is permissible in football is quite irrelevant. The point to note is that his rights as a basketball player have not been abridged because it is the rules that define him as a basketball player. If he is ejected it is because he does not want to play that particular game. Similarly, those who profess a faith contrary to the social contract need not be condemned out of hand—football may be preferable to basketball—but they are nonetheless excluded because they do not want to play this game. Just as it is impossible to participate in two sports at the same time, so also it is impossible to play the incompatible roles of citizen, as defined by the contract, and fanatic. The fanatical atheist, like the fanatical sectarian, is excluded, not, strictly speaking, because of the merits or demerits of his beliefs, but because these beliefs are incompatible with the secular terms of the contract.

The case of the nonfanatical atheist is different. Given the other terms of the contract, one can deduce the impossibility of including fanatics, but there are no formal conditions that imply the exclusion of atheists. This exclusion must, therefore, be mediated by a set of substantive beliefs. But first let us distinguish three cases of atheism: the fanatic, the silent atheist, and the vocal but nonfanatical atheist. The fanatical atheist has already been ruled out for nonideological reasons. As to the other types, it should be noted that, given Rousseau's image of the atheist, it is highly improbable that an honest atheist would want to enter the contract. For Rousseau, an atheist is not simply an abstraction who does not happen to believe that God exists. In the flesh he is a sophisticated intellectual, a cosmopolitan more at home abroad than in his native land. Atheists are not to be found in rural communities, because their natural habitat is the city, where vice and luxury flourish. As we have seen, there is a sociological basis to the contract that demands a way of life in every respect unlike the climate in which atheism prospers. One's imagination strains trying to picture the elegant Baron D'Holbach content with the frugal, unexciting life of a peasant. From this point of view atheists and even theists sharing a similar way of life are in effect self-exiled, not for their beliefs but for their unwillingness to accept the simple life implied by the contract. These observations obviously do not explain why Rousseau's creed excludes atheists. If they did, voluntary self-exclusion would render proscription redundant. They are given to suggest that a lot of what critics find stifling in Rousseau springs from sources other than the creed. But what if there exists an atheist who loves the simple life and in every other respect supports the contract and its laws? If he is of the silent variety, he makes for an interesting case. The creed, Rousseau tells us, is not so much a set of religious or metaphysical doctrines as it is an expression of "sentiments of sociability" (*SC* 4. 8). The sentiments the creed presumably is designed to inspire or affirm are those that prompt a man to respect and uphold the contract and its laws. If in this context this is all the creed means, what is there to distinguish belief in the creed from a similar belief inspired by a different set of metaphysical principles? The transempirical references of the creed are not offered as ends in themselves but as what Rousseau took to be necessary conditions of moral obligation. If, contrary to Rousseau's belief, an atheist could sincerely accept the other terms of the contract, he could in good faith profess the creed, because pragmatically his belief in moral obligation as it pertains to public life in this world is, by hypothesis, identical with that of the equally sincere believer.

The silent atheist is tolerable if for no other reason than that no one is aware that he is being tolerated. Even his refusal to join a church cannot count against him, because there is nothing in the creed that would debar an unaffiliated deist. It would be ironical to equate his silence with hypocrisy, because in a sense he is the only one who fully embodies Rousseau's conception of the ideal citizen, a person whose loyalties are so completely absorbed by the state that there is nothing left over. This can never be the case with those who believe in a transtemporal destiny. Whether, given the pragmatic meaning of the creed, silence is hypocrisy may be left to those purists who have deprived children of their Santa Claus and have vehemently condemned the many nonbelievers who pledged allegiance to America under an older formula.

Rousseau himself was unable to conceive of a legitimate society of atheists, but if such were possible there is nothing in the basic contract that would prevent the substitution of a purely secular pledge of allegiance for the creed as it stands. But the point is that Rousseau was quite obviously assuming that the potential contractors would be all or for the most part believers, a not unreasonable assumption for an eighteenth-century writer.

Because Rousseau's attitude toward atheism, or at least public atheism, was hardly novel, it is difficult to understand why critics, flourishing in an entirely different climate of belief, should berate him so furiously. The affective ties that hold a society together may be quite different today, but Rousseau's problem persists: can or will a society tolerate that which it deems subversive of itself? There is no such thing as absolute tolerance unless it be found in a state of nature. Every society, through its criminal codes, expresses its intolerance of certain types of behavior. For example, laws bearing on slander and libel prove that freedom of opinion and expression are judged to have their limits. The issue here is why Rousseau chose to banish avowed atheists.

It should be noted at once that contemporary tolerance in matters of religious belief comes easily because religion, occasional rhetoric to the contrary, is no longer regarded as the base on which the state is anchored. Complete separation of church and state works reasonably well because there is a similar separation in the psyches of citizens: both believer and nonbeliever for the most part isolate their religious convictions from their images of themselves as citizens. But this, of course, was not always the case, and to condemn Rousseau's mistrust of atheists is to condemn the many centuries during which religion was a vital factor in the affairs of men. Such a judgment may inflate one's sense of moral superiority, but it is a culturally parochial judgment and essentially anachronistic.

One might defend Rousseau by arguing that he is not saying that atheists ought to be excluded but that the majority of contractors, being themselves religious, would in fact not contract with nonbelievers. But this is not quite convincing in the light of Rousseau's frequent identification of atheism and unsociability. The formal terms of the contract do not bar atheists as they do fanatics. Their exclusion must therefore have been mediated by a different set of beliefs. There are at least two general clusters of belief that might have served as middle terms. The first concerns the destructive effect of atheism on the rest of society. Atheists

destroy and trample under foot all that men reverence; they rob the afflicted of their last consolation in their misery; . . . they tear from the very depths of man's heart all remorse for crime, and all hope of virtue; . . . [atheism] degrades the soul, concentrates all the passions in the basest self-interest, in the meanness of the human self; thus it saps unnoticed the very foundations of all society; for what is common to all these private interests is so small that it will never outweigh their opposing interests. [*Emile*, p. 276]

The vocal atheist must be excluded because his doctrine is destructive of public happiness and because, by questioning all foundations of moral obligation, he breaks the social bond and isolates men within the narrow, unsociable sphere of selfish private interests.

The same conclusion is reached by a slightly different route, emphasizing not the atheist's effect on society but what might be termed his ideological inability to be a good citizen. The good citizen must be virtuous because virtue alone enables a person to overcome his natural selfishness and to subordinate his personal will to the general will. But the atheist, lacking religion, is incapable of self-transcendence: "I do not mean by this that one can be virtuous without religion; I held this erroneous opinion for a long time, but now I am only too disabused" (*Letter to M. d'Alembert*, p. 97). The atheist lacks a motive strong enough to inspire virtue: "if there is no God, the wicked is right and the good man is nothing but a fool" (*Emile*, p. 255).

The formal terms of the contract define the good citizen. But they also set forth in secular terms the meaning of a moral agent.

Thus the good citizen is automatically the good man. However, Rousseau despaired of a purely secular morality. In a letter to M. Moulton, 14 February 1769, he wrote, "You are too good a reasoner not to see that the instant you reject the First Clause . . . you take all morality from human life" (*Letters*, p. 367). The atheist is excluded, then, not because of his beliefs as such, but because he is incapable of assuming moral responsibilities, and this is a necessary condition of good citizenship, without which the contract is in vain.

If this was Rousseau's sole reason for excluding atheists, then it is clear why in all other contexts he preached a doctrine of tolerance for all but fanatical atheists.[9] His sole political objection to atheism is that it is incompatible with a sense of moral obligation. In any but a legitimate society as defined by the contract, moral sensibility is politically irrelevant, because outside these limits only prudential obligations obtain with respect to governmental decrees. And in matters of mere prudence there is nothing that especially distinguishes atheists from believers.

But if the atheist can be tolerated outside the contract, the fanatic cannot. Fanaticism is the one unforgivable sin. The fanatic feels himself under a divine mandate to persecute all he cannot convert. It is this sense of destiny that makes him an enemy of public peace, and peace is a desideratum in any type of society. An atheist on purely prudential grounds can live in peace with his neighbors, but not so the fanatic: "even the angels could not live at peace with men whom they regarded as the enemies of God" (*Emile*, p. 273 note 1). The intolerance of the fanatic is not simply an ideological intolerance. "Those who distinguish between civil and theological intolerance are, in my opinion, mistaken. These two forms of intolerance are inseparable. . . . Wherever theological intolerance is allowed, it cannot fail to have civil consequences; and as soon as it does, the sovereign is no longer sovereign, even in temporal matters" (*SC* 4. 8). This, of course, was almost a commonplace in an age when organized churches like the Roman Catholic Church had ready access to the seats of government and did in fact have administrative authority in areas such as marriage. Today, for the most part, the religious fanatic puts little strain on our tolerance;[10] ours is an age of widespread religious skepticism, at least with regard to the niceties of theological elaborations. In general, the skeptic is less psychologically vulnerable to the defamations of the dogmatist than vice versa, and claims on behalf of an exclusive supernatural truth are more apt to evoke a knowing smile than pained resentment. If Rousseau had lived in a period where fanaticism had no hope of success, he might even have tolerated the fanatic, because his concern with beliefs as they pertained to politics was limited to their practical consequences.

The civil creed not only exiles atheists and fanatics, it also separates state and organized religion. Beyond a profession of the few simple and uninterpreted dogmas of the creed, each citizen is free to believe and worship as he pleases. Rousseau might have explicitly barred atheists, announced a complete separation of church and state, and let it go at that. Instead, he chose to invest the state with a quasi-religious aura. This did no violence to the consciences of the various contractors because, no matter how the various sects differed they all shared a common faith, namely, the positive dogmas of the creed and a belief in the central significance of religion. They also believed that there was a transcendent source of morality. If at the time a person had been asked why he was or ought to be moral, the answer would inevitably have included some reference to God's will and the hope or fear of heaven and hell. The clash of dogmas never in the slightest affected the universal belief that morality was grounded in a religious faith. Under the circumstances how could Rousseau reconcile this theory of morality, which he also shared, with his conception of a wholly secular society with purely temporal ends, if not by incorporating a quasi-religious creed as a condition of membership? A common profession of a minimal faith cannot reconcile dogmatic differences, but it is at least a first step toward social cohesion.

Let it be emphasized that the situation confronting Rousseau was not of his making. He did not create doctrinal conflicts; he abhorred them. He did not originate the near-universal conviction that without God morality is vain; he merely shared it. Above all he neither instituted nor encouraged the view that social solidarity depended upon a religious orientation. On the contrary, his personal religion was a solitary, private affair, and he sought to achieve solidarity by encouraging a type of emotional patriotism best exemplified by Sparta. Religious divisiveness, he prophetically realized, could only be transcended by engendering deep enthusiasm for an exclusively temporal goal: a love of country independent of, but not necessarily contrary to, a love of God. This, Rousseau believed, would be impossible were atheists or fanatics admitted to membership. Just as men who reciprocally consign each other to hell cannot live in peace, let alone in fraternal unity, so also the believer, any believer, finds it impossible to join in happy alliance with the atheist who would rob him of his heaven, and the more so because in his eyes the atheist rejects moral obligations. Whether this is a mistaken view is irrelevant; what counts is what the vast majority believed. If this is intolerance, then it is a mass intolerance in the face of which Rousseau might be said to have capitulated in order to secure his main end, the establishment of as completely a secular society as conditions allowed.[11] If the state cannot overcome religious sensibilities, it is best advised to make use of them for its own purposes. It is not the least of Rousseau's paradoxes that he thought that a society which was at once secular and moral was possible only if all its citizens were by their faith transtemporally inspired.

If circumstances did not permit a perfect separation of state and belief, Rousseau was determined to reduce the overlap to a minimum. Only those dogmas generally thought essential to morality are included. And in order to prevent theologians from becoming constitutional lawyers, it is forbidden to elaborate or explain them; the commonweal in effect demands no more than the faith of a child. God rewards the just and punishes the wicked. No citizen can escape judgment, because God's providence looks to each individual. The benevolence of God might possibly have been included because it suggests that God's love is not restricted to a given form of worship or limited to any one theological description of the divine nature. In a word, it suggests the unsupportability of religious intolerance.[12] Finally, the social contract and the ensuing laws are to be held sacred. This last dogma is still further evidence that the creed is a part of the contract and not itself a law, for how can a law whose authority is based solely on the contract retroactively sanctify that contract?

When the creed is viewed solely in terms of its content, it becomes impossible to understand the exaggerated criticisms to which it is subjected. It proposes a liberal separation of church and state, qualified only by the exclusion of atheists, those preaching or practicing doctrines contrary to public morals, fanatics, and others who cannot meaningfully subscribe to the terms of the contract. The plain truth is that this is wholly unoriginal. In fact, it may reasonably be viewed as no more than a French translation of the negative core of Locke's views on toleration, views that are seldom, and never vehemently, censured. As for fanatics, consider Locke's assertion: "No peace and security, no, not so much as common friendship, can ever be established or preserved amongst men so long as this opinion prevails that dominion is founded in grace and that religion is to be propagated by force of arms."[13] As for opinions contrary to public morality, "no opinions contrary to human society, or to those moral rules which are necessary to the preservation of civil society, are to be tolerated by the magistrate" (p. 50). On this basis Locke would proscribe religions claiming special prerogatives such as the right not to keep faith with heretics. This prerogative implies the right of dominion and the right to dethrone princes professing a different religion. The fanatic is thus twice condemned. "I say these [who claim prerogatives on religious ground] have no right to be tolerated by the magistrate, as neither those that will not own and teach the duty of tolerating all men in matters of mere religion" (p. 51). Note that Rousseau, unlike Locke, does not demand that citizens *teach* tolerance.

Mohammedans (read "Catholics") are not to be tolerated because their ultimate allegiance is to a foreign power, that is, they cannot unreservedly swear to the terms of the civil contract. "Lastly, those are not to be tolerated who deny the being of a God. Promises, convenants, and oaths, which are the bonds of human society, can have no hold upon an atheist. The taking away of God, though but even in thought, dissolves all; besides also, those that by their atheism undermine and destroy all religion can have no pretense of religion whereupon to challenge the privilege of a toleration" (p. 52). As for all other beliefs, even false beliefs, "if they do not tend to establish domination over others, or civil impunity to the church in which they are taught, there can be no reason why they should not be tolerated" (p. 52). If an atheist is taken to be one who does not believe in God, immortality, and divine retribution, Locke's *Letter concerning Toleration* is, before the fact, no more than an expanded version of Rousseau's Civil Creed.

But if Rousseau can be seen as a proto-Hitler, why not Locke also? The answer probably has something to do with Rousseau's vivid rhetoric. If anyone, having publicly assented to the dogmas of the creed, "behaves as if he did not believe them, he should receive the death penalty; he has committed the gravest of crimes; he has lied in the presence of the law" (*SC* 4. 8). The association of a creed with any form of punishment, let alone the death penalty, is to the contemporary liberal intellectual what the bell was to Pavlov's dogs: his hackles bristle in righteous indignation. Crocker, for example, is particularly incensed by the idea that the state may infer from a person's actions or inactions his otherwise hidden beliefs, and then execute him for perjury. "What is this, if not the doctrine of arrest on suspicion of wrong thinking?"[14]

If Crocker and others are right in this interpretation, then Rousseau is doubly damned, because in a letter to Voltaire, 18 August 1756, he held that in matters of religion a man cannot control what he believes or disbelieves.[15] In this letter Rousseau first argues the desirability of a civil creed, but he does so without reference to a belief in God. Atheists may be banished, but only if, like their religious counterparts, they are fanatics, that is, if they try to force nonbelief on others.[16]

Under these restricted terms of exclusion neither the silent atheist nor, if such is possible, the silent religious fanatic is a threat to society, and both can accordingly be tolerated. The issue cannot be what is silently believed in the recesses of one's mind, because this, being hidden, is by definition beyond detection. The issue, as Rousseau explicitly states, is overt behavior. The death penalty is reserved for the person who "behaves as if he did not believe them [the dogmas]" (*SC* 4. 8).

This chapter on civil religion does not spell out what Rousseau took to be the precise pragmatic meaning of the creed, but in the light of his usual tolerance for thought there is no reason to hold that he did not think of the creed exclusively in pragmatic terms. If this is so, there is no need to infer hidden beliefs from overt action: the action is the belief and is punishable in its own right. Is a murderer condemned because he does not really believe homicide is wrong or because in proven fact he has killed another? Crocker apparently assumes that the evidence sufficient to prove disbelief would not otherwise warrant capital punishment. But this assumption is entirely gratuitous, and all the more so because it fails to accommodate other aspects of Rousseau's thought.

The creed is related to the other terms of the contract in a unique way. Though in a substantive way it limits the sovereign's competence in matters of religion, the distinctive spirit of the creed in relation to the rest of the contract is really nonsubstantive. It does not add anything further to the contract but, given the special conditions of the time, simply supplies a quasi-religious reinforcement to the contract as a whole. From this point of view the pragmatic meaning of disbelief is the same as the pragmatic meaning of disbelieving or rejecting the secular version of the contract. What suffices as evidence of the one suffices as evidence of the other.

Had the creed been omitted, it is highly doubtful that commentators would have read into the work an implicit call for boards of inquisition. And yet the secular contract in its own way constitutes an orthodoxy, a set of right beliefs. The positive dogmas of the creed are presumably factual assertions: all other terms of the contract have the character of 'ought' statements: "No citizen ought to be debarred from the assembly," "All citizens ought to vote according to the common good," and so forth. Why would a person who had silently withdrawn his consent to these terms be any less a public enemy than the silent atheist or fanatic? But if he is no less a liar before the laws, and if religious orthodoxy must be preserved even in the depths of a person's heart, then, if an inquisition is necessary to preserve religious orthodoxy, it is equally necessary to preserve secular orthodoxy.

The ironical side of this *pari passu* argument is that a stronger case could probably be made for a secular inquisition than for a religious one. The political importance of religion consists in this, that it makes a citizen love his duties. Obviously the duties in question are secular obligations, because you cannot without circularity or an infinite regress posit a religion to make a man love his religious duties. Aside from dogmas that might contravene public morality or the terms of the contract, the sovereign is indifferent to religious belief, "for the sovereign's competence does not extend to the next world, and thus the fate of its subjects in the life to come is none of its business, provided that they are good citizens in the present one" (*SC* 4. 8). This is clearly not a theocratic position: religion, when not purely personal, is for the sake of the state and not vice versa.

The pragmatic import of the creed, therefore, is purely and simply secular. That the creed was never intended as a religious test in the usual sense is further indicated by a closer analysis of the various dogmas. Fanatics, to repeat, are excluded not because of the creed but by the other terms of the contract. This single negative dogma could, therefore, have been omitted. This leaves the rule separating church and state plus the positive creed. However, the remaining dogmas are not symmetrically related. The Christian audience to which the *Social Contract* is addressed would readily accept the mutual interrelations that bind together beliefs in God, benevolence, providence, immortality, and divine retribution: God implies immortality implies divine justice implies God. All these form a single bundle. Belief in the sanctity of the contract is quite another matter. One can be a theist and not believe in the sacredness of any human convention. Roman Catholics and certain fanatics, for example, hold the former set of beliefs but cannot, according to Rousseau, allow the latter. But given the then-accepted meaning of 'sacred', a belief in the sanctity of the contract implies a belief in a God who sanctifies it. This is Rousseau's version of a divine right theory of political obligation. From the point of view of conceptual economy, then, he could have reduced the creed to a single dogma proclaiming the sanctity of the contract. This is the only operative dogma because it alone pertains exclusively to this life, the limits of which are the maximum limits of any temporal society: "the fate of its subjects in the life to come is none of its business."

The religious fanatic believes in God but not in the sanctity of the contract and, therefore, is ejected because he refuses to play the game. The atheist is banished not because he does not believe in an afterlife, a belief which at best is politically relevant only in a most indirect way, but because he, like the fanatic, does not consider himself morally obliged by the contract. If Rousseau is mistaken in this and if there is some atheistic analogue of the sacred, there is no further theoretical reason to exclude the atheist. But this dogma also bears on a third class, the nonfanatical theist who will not bow to the sanctity of the contract. This is by far the most interesting category. In an age of few atheists and in a society where fanatics are easily detected and exiled, the enemy of the state once formed is most likely to fall into this class. His sin is not wrong thinking—he believes in God—but wrongdoing, for there is no set of questions that could expose a theist who has abjured the contract in the silence of his heart.

It is difficult to understand why some critics so readily read the spirit of Torquemada into the creed. By nature Rousseau was strongly opposed to the inquisitorial spirit: "I am, in my religion, tolerant by principle, . . . I tolerate everything except intolerance; but any kind of inquisition is odious to me. I regard all the inquisitors as just so many satellites of the Devil. For this reason I would no more care to live at Geneva than at Goa. Only atheists could live at peace in such lands, because all the professions of faith cost nothing to him who has no faith in his heart" (*Letters*, p. 257). Rousseau's personal attitude aside, there are several reasons that strongly suggest that an inquisition was never intended. No bureau of thought control could be a part of the contract. This is a theoretical impossibility, because an inquisition, however structured, must be an agency of government, since it is concerned with the particular. And since no given form of government is entailed by the contract, neither is any particular governmental commission. Recognition of this theoretical implication completely absolves the contract, if not Rousseau, of any charge of inquisitorial illiberalism. Should an investigatory body be subsequently authorized, it would have to be as the result of a specific law passed by a specific people assembled.

But given the context that necessitated the creed in the first place, this is highly unlikely. What motive could a people, mainly religious but divided in their beliefs, have for legislating a tribunal of doctrinal purity? The creed is designedly so simple that among believers heresy could only be detected by elaborating that minimum: "You say you believe in God but deny his triune nature. Therefore, you don't really believe in God." But this sort of inquiry is precisely what the creed prohibits. In any case it is unthinkable that members of different faiths would mutually jeopardize themselves by authorizing such an inquisition: no one could be assured of a coreligionist as his judge. The silent atheist, as already noted, would forever escape detection, and the vocal atheist reveals himself. An inquisition would, therefore, either be unacceptable or powerless or superfluous.

There is yet another reason to doubt that Rousseau would have countenanced examinations for religious orthodoxy. An inquisition would have the effect of calling attention to and glorifying the dogmas of the creed. But with the exception of the sanctity of the contract, these dogmas have an otherworldly reference, and the last thing Rousseau wanted was to divert his citizens' attention from the here and now of their commnity. The creed was the maximum concession Rousseau was prepared to make when he realized that his secular version of the contract was inadequate to the task of associating a group of Christians divided over religious beliefs. Had his purpose been more religious than secular, he might have decided upon an expanded version of the creed along the lines of what he took to be the pure, simple faith of the Gospels. But because the Gospels preach the noble doctrine of the brotherhood of all men, they encourage a cosmopolitan orientation that rules out total allegiance to a specific polity. For Rousseau pure Christianity not only fails to vivify the laws, its otherworldly preoccupations tend to detach a citizen from his state. The point is clear: though this form of Christianity is both noble and true, it would be a political contradiction for a secular state to endorse it officially, because their respective ends are incompatible. The civil creed is, then, a compromise, but one that is in no way intended to depreciate the primacy of the political;[17] it is far more eloquent in what it does not include. Religious inquisitions, to repeat, would do nothing but obscure this primacy. The nonideological nature of the creed can best be seen in the case of the nonfanatical theist who is in theory capable of lying before the laws. If in lying he has committed "the gravest of crimes" (*SC* 4. 8), the greatest crime is not to be found in what he believes but in how he acts in relation to his fellow citizens. In this chapter on civil religion Rousseau does not spell out precisely what constitutes lying before the laws. However, it may be recalled that there is a counterpart to this when only the secular version was under consideration. The gravest crime considered then was the nonideological crime or set of crimes that proves a man has rejected the contract and has voluntarily placed himself in thorough opposition to society. Because the heart of the creed is to be found in the sanctity of the contract, the two situations are pragmatically identical. The man who has "lied in the presence of the law" is the same man who, "in attacking the laws of society, makes himself by his heinous crimes a rebel and a traitor to his country; he ceases to be a member of it by violating its laws; he even makes war upon it" (*SC* 2. 5). The analysis made in chapter 2 of the relation between such a man and the contract may be applied in every respect to the man who recants in silence the civil creed, because in both cases it is the nontheological aspects of the contract that are involved. Because his was a formal analysis, Rousseau could not detail the specifics that might prove social treason, but to the extent that he did treat the concept, he did so in a context that was not even vaguely related to a person's theological beliefs. And this was only proper because, his critics to the contrary, Rousseau's traitor was an enemy of the people, not for his beliefs, but for his antisocial actions.

The Civil Creed is an embarrassment not because of its purported illiberality but because it undermines Rousseau's original attempt to establish the conditions of a purely secular political morality. As an amendment to the secular contract, it really implies that there are alternative versions. The secular version is offered as a definition of moral obligation, and therefore there can be no transcendent standard of obligation in relation to which a consent once given must be maintained in perpetuity. The religious version, on the other hand, assumes, as do all religions, that there is an antecedent and transcendent source of obligation. Moreover, by sanctifying the contract the religious version in effect makes it irrevocable. The creed, then, is not simply an afterthought; it is a counterthought. It would be meaningless to argue that the contract is sacred only so long as men consent to it, for in that case sanctity adds nothing to consent.[18] Nor can it be convincingly argued that Rousseau's rhetoric momentarily got the better of his theoretical judgment, for he repeats this position much more explicitly. Called upon to write a constitution for Corsica, he proposed the following oath of allegiance: "In the name of God Almighty, and on the holy Gospels, by a sacred and *irrevocable* oath, I join myself—body, goods, will and all my powers—to the Corsican nation. . . . So may God be my help in this life and have mercy on my Soul."[19]

The creed, let it be stressed, is not an integral part of the principles of right. It is a response to two problems, one of which stems from Rousseau's estimation of human nature and the other of which derives from the specific course of Western history. Atheists must be excluded because natural man has absolutely no motive, and therefore no power, to subjugate his particular will. Unless man's will is checked by fear of divine retribution, he will never successfully extricate himself from a political state of nature. The creed from this point of view is a special legacy of the *Second Discourse*.

But faith is not enough. Faith is a passion and, like all passions, it is potentially disruptive. Or, more precisely, given the history of Christianity, religion is a positively disruptive force. The creed represents the least common denominator in the battle of the sects. From this point of view the creed is Rousseau's attempt to defuse interchurch conflict by restricting theological elaborations to the private sphere. This is hardly thought control or an invitation to the inquisitorial spirit or, least of all, a formula for judicial mass murder. Where all potential covenanters are already believers, the creed is a completely innocuous pledge of allegiance. Far from being an instrument of repression, the creed guarantees against ideological duress. The creed is part of the contract, and the sovereign cannot add unacceptable refinements or elaborations to it without abrogating the contract itself.

Nevertheless, the creed is at odds with other conditions of the contract. Rousseau, as has been noted, was not very good in keeping his various historical perspectives in order. The creed is in part a response to a problem that arose at a relatively late stage in the development of man. It is for the most part a post-Reformation problem; it is a problem that one cannot conceive of as occurring to a "people fit for legislation."

Viewed dramatically, there is something very sad about the civil creed. Up to its appearance the reader has been offered a novel theory of political obligation that is grounded in a very special type of convention. This convention celebrates the sovereignty of man; it is a convention that coerces man only to the extent that he voluntarily accepts this coercion. Suddenly and without any prior indication, Rousseau undermines the most essential principles of his theory: consent once given is now irrevocable, and it is God, not man, that sanctifies the contract. This is total surrender and he admits as much. "After *having established* the true principles of political law [*droit*], and *having tried* to establish the state on that basis, . . . [I should have done many other things]" (*SC* 4. 9; italics added). Rousseau was certain that he had indeed solved the problem of political right in the abstract. He was less sure that a state could be established on that basis. The civil creed is not a part of the principles of political right, but it is definitely a prerequisite for polities in the concrete. Once this tension is recognized there is no sense going on, and the *Social Contract* comes abruptly to an end.

The *Social Contract* ends, but the Civil Creed that ended it leaves us with a new problem. The social contract is the only means by which political obligations can be legitimated, but its implementation turns out to be quite infeasible. Does that mean that there is no other source of personal obligation? Or can there be found in Rousseau's writings a second basis of moral obligation?

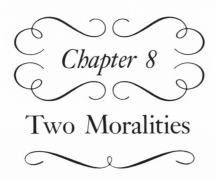

Chapter 8

Two Moralities

In the eighteenth century, as in other centuries, the vast majority of people would have equated moral obligation with religious imperatives: morality is but the will of God as revealed in the Bible or as proclaimed by the church. Because Rousseau's disdain for professional theology was so thinly disguised, it seems reasonably certain that he would not have accepted this authoritarian basis for morality. The social contract as previously interpreted provides an alternative foundation, but the contract is no longer a practical option. Because alienation of will to a government is illegitimate, morality cannot be identified with the will of the powers that be. If there is an independent basis for morality, therefore, it must be found in some theory of natural law.

Though historically there have been several varieties of natural law theory, they all have this in common: there exists a higher law that binds man's will independently of his consent.[1] It is an impersonal and an eternal law obligating all men always and everywhere. It is promulgated by reason, but 'reason' does not mean the same thing to every theorist. If Rousseau cannot be located somewhere within this broad tradition of natural law, it would seem that he is left with no basis for morality except his utopian social contract.

An extremely strong case can be made that he cannot be so located. If man is neither naturally social nor a language user, and spent unknown centuries wandering in isolation, it is hard to see the relevance of a moral law. It is hard to see how natural man, whose only language is that of grunts, groans, and gestures, can know the law or, if he knew it, how it would bear on his eremitic existence. On the other hand, and from a different point of view, it might be argued that there is a kind of moral law built into man's nature. Unlike Hobbesian man, Rousseau's natural man is neither aggressive nor acquisitive. In his original environment he lived content with himself and wished no gratuitous evil to his fellow men. In the early stages of evolution man is by nature 'moral' in that he is protected from the possibilities of those conflicts that arise only in society. He is naturally good and has no need of virtue.

There are, however, other reasons that might count as solid evidence that Rousseau rejected natural law. In his first version of the *Social Contract*, there is a chapter that contains a critique of Diderot's theory of natural law as found in an article for the *Encyclopedia*. Rousseau counterargues that neither the idea of God nor of natural law is innate, since both have to be taught to men. It may be a law of reason, but the reason sufficient to apprehend it develops only after the rise of those passions that render its dictates impotent.[2] This contention is based on Rousseau's belief that man's rational capacities develop dialectically with the passions. It is only at a very late stage that reason and language attain a perfection that in principle allows for the possibility of the independent and highly abstract pursuit of truth. But by this time, which presupposes society and all the turbulent passions it engenders, most men are, for want of the necessary discipline, practically incapable of voluntarily doing the good they might know.

It could be argued that a man who renounces natural duties must, for consistency's sake, also renounce natural moral rights, thereby reducing all human transactions to a contest of force. Rousseau concedes this but points out that in a state of nature such an individual is less at a disadvantage than if he had fulfilled the law with no guarantee that others would reciprocate. Vice generally triumphs over virtue.

Religion is hardly an adequate support for natural law, because the gods which the masses have worshipped throughout history in no way resemble that pure conception of the Godhead necessary to ground the sublime ideas of justice and goodness. But even if one admits the existence of a natural law, there is no self-evident reason why it should be obeyed. After all, the first law of nature is that of self-preservation, and this hardly motivates a man to forgo his personal interests on behalf of the counter-interests of the species.

Finally, history argues against the theory. It was only at a late date that it was introduced by philosophers, and it gained a measure of acceptance only with the spread of Christianity. For the greater part of recorded history, moral rules were peculiar to groups and applicable only among the members of the group. Behavior that was not permissible within the community was perfectly proper with respect to strangers, and, indeed, the very word *stranger* was quite often synonymous with the word *enemy*.

The above observations, if not completely decisive, provide a strong case for those who would argue either that Rousseau rejected the very idea of natural law or that he at least held the existence of a natural law to be irrelevant.[3] On the other hand, a good case can be made for the position that not only did he believe in natural law but that this belief was the core of his moral theory. Though it may be questioned whether the creed of the Savoyard vicar perfectly mirrors Rousseau's personal conviction, there is much independent evidence that he shared the vicar's beliefs on God, immortality, final judgment, and conscience.[4] As will be seen below, the paradox of Rousseau's attitude toward natural law theory is that though he strongly believes his version, he despairs of establishing it apodictically: there is always the possibility that the materialists are right.

Rousseau does not insist on the punishment of vice, but he is sure of the reward of virtue.[5] In any case, these beliefs do not make sense unless man somehow is able to know the rules of a game whose stakes are so high. Moreover, the rules in question would have to be God's rules in order to provide that objectivity of obligation which is the hallmark of any natural law theory. If the only rules that bind men are wholly of human origin, it is difficult to see either the relevance or justice of invoking God as some sort of cosmic umpire. The ultimate source of law is one with the ultimate authority of law, and if this be man, then it is a human and not a divine concern to render justice as defined by the law. Moreover, it is impossible to read *Emile* and not be convinced that in Rousseau's eyes there are objective rights and wrongs independent of society. In fact, this work can be read as a guide for a moral man forced to live in an immoral society.

The case for Rousseau's belief in natural law can be strengthened if his objections to it in the first version of the *Social Contract* can be explained. This, I believe, is possible to some degree. First of all it should be noted that Rousseau did not flatly reject the concept of natural law in general but rather those versions that demanded a sophisticated reason as a source of promulgation and, as in Diderot's case, those that implied the existence of a general society of mankind prior to established civil societies. There were many elements in Rousseau's thought that demanded that he reject the latter assumption, and, in his own eyes, he felt that he had a more satisfactory theory of natural law than that of the traditional law of right reason.

In the *First Discourse* he had rejected the rationalist version of natural law primarily on the grounds that reason is too precarious a faculty to serve as a mode of promulgation. Nature acts with far greater economy and certainty. This economy is found in the voice of conscience: "O virtue! sublime science of simple souls, are so many difficulties and preparations needed to know you? Are not your principles engraved in all hearts, and is it not enough in order to learn your laws to commune with oneself and listen to the voice of one's conscience in the silence of the passions? That is true philosophy" (*First Discourse*, p. 64). Again, in *Emile*, the vicar, discussing moral principles, says, "I do not derive these rules from the principles of the higher philosophy, I find them in the depths of my heart, traced by nature in characters which nothing can efface" (*Emile*, p. 249).

Up to Rousseau's day at least three distinct stages in the history of natural law could be identified on the basis of the way that law is promulgated. Though 'reason' is the common term that names the method of promulgation, it has distinguishable meanings. For the Roman lawyers reason was closely associated with experience. "For the medieval philosopher it was a gift of God. In both cases the evidence of reason had to be implemented, and indeed confirmed, by some other evidence—of fact or of faith. But now the evidence of reason is in itself sufficient." [6] The "now" refers to the times following Grotius. D'Entreves might have added a fourth stage, promulgation by conscience as interpreted by Rousseau. However, he reads Rousseau as completely rejecting natural law. Because he misses the cognitive dimension of the general will, he can state that where "will is made the supreme arbiter of all human value," there can be no objective justice.[7]

What complicates Rousseau's idea of conscience is that it is only one of three factors in a moral decision. Reason supplies the knowledge of the good; conscience, the love of the good; and free will, the power to effect the good. Rousseau, following Locke, rejected innate ideas but not innate feelings. Man is not born with a knowledge of good and evil, but "as soon as his reason leads him to perceive it [the good] his conscience impels him to love it; it is the feeling which is innate" (*Emile*, p. 253). It does not take a philosopher's reason to apprehend the good. "The reason which teaches a man his duties is not very complex; the reason which teaches a woman hers is even simpler" (*Emile*, p. 345). Presumably what holds true for the individual holds true for the species: at some stage of the state of nature reason has developed sufficiently to be able to distinguish good and evil.

The interrelations between reason, conscience, and free will are not very clear. But in introducing conscience Rousseau has pinpointed the limitations of any theory that would make reason a self-sufficient source of moral obligation. The demands of morality all too often conflict with the felt interests of the individual. Because man is an affective animal, he can only replace one emotion with another. Reason cannot be a sufficient source of obligation, because of each principle reason offers, it can be asked why should it be accepted. One can pile reason on reason, but an infinite regress can be checked only if a nonrational factor is introduced. Rousseau's solution has its own difficulties but it at least has the merit of adding a new dimension to the traditional theories. For a natural law to be obligatory nature must have endowed man not only with the capacity to know the law but also the affective capacity to feel obliged. This is the role of conscience. Whatever else it is, it is something in man's nature which triggers a love of the good once it is known; it is a natural feeling that certifies the validity of reason's moral pronouncements. A creature devoid of all feelings simply cannot be a moral agent.[8]

It seems appropriate to note at this point that there is an additional factor in Rousseau's approach to morality. Not only must man know the good and feel obliged, he must also be motivated to do the good. In his first version of the *Social Contract* Rousseau inextricably links two questions: Is there an objective standard of morality? And if so, why should a person be moral? As we shall see, Rousseau would deny that virtue is always its own reward—at least in this life. The knowing, the feeling, and the motivation cannot be neatly separated and compartmentalized, but, suitably combined, they activate the will so that it may seek the good.

It must be stressed that conscience is an essential element of morality only if it is a natural feeling. Rousseau realizes this, and it is for this reason that he emphatically denies that conscience is a socially induced phenomenon (*Emile*, p. 252). And this denial reinforces the argument that he believed in a natural law: nature would have acted in vain if it had equipped man with the capacity to love the good and failed to furnish an ontological ground for the good. Conscience is, as it were, a force, but it is not such a powerful force that moral behavior is assured by the predetermining power of a natural disposition. The third condition of morality is, therefore, that man has free will. Rousseau is convinced that he does, but he does not argue his case on metaphysical grounds. It is introspection that reveals a feeling of freedom too strong to be defeated by all determinist arguments to the contrary.

The three conditions of morality are thus summed up: God has "given me conscience that I may love the right, reason that I may perceive it, and freedom that I may choose it" (*Emile*, p. 257). Rousseau was aware that there were difficulties in precisely delimiting each of these elements and expressing their interrelations. To the extent that he shares the vicar's views, he saw man as a divided creature subject to drives that raised him to the sublime or reduced him to the level of sensual slavery. "No; man is not one; I will and I will not; I feel myself at once a slave and a free man; I perceive what is right, I love it, and I do what is wrong; I am active when I listen to the voice of reason; I am passive when I am carried away by my passions; and when I yield,

my worst suffering is the knowledge that I might have resisted"
(*Emile*, p. 241).

Because man is both free and driven by other passions, conscience, though ever a part of man, is not always the decisive
principle. "She [conscience] speaks to us in the language of nature
and everything leads us to forget that tongue. Conscience is
timid, she loves peace and retirement; . . . the prejudices from
which she is said to arise are her worst enemies; . . . [before
them] she is silent; . . . when she has been scorned so long, it is
as hard to recall her as it was to banish her" (*Emile*, p. 254). The
sociological factor is reintroduced. Though conscience is innate,
its efficacy can be minimized by socially induced passions and
obscured by a socially generated pseudoconscience.

But if conscience implies some sort of natural law, why, in the
unpublished version of the *Social Contract*, does Rousseau maintain that he can find no reason why a man ought to obey it in a
state of nature? The published version supplies an answer.

That which is good and conformable to order is such by the nature of
things, *independent of human conventions*. All justice comes from God, and
He alone is its source; but if we knew how to receive it from so great a
height, we should need neither government nor laws. *Undoubtedly there is
a universal justice derived from reason only*; but justice, to be admitted among
us, must be mutual. From a human standpoint, the laws of justice are
inoperative among men for lack of natural sanctions; they are but the fortune of the wicked and the misfortune of the just, when the latter observes them toward everyone, and no one observes them toward him.
Conventions and laws are necessary, therefore, to unite rights with duties, and to accomplish the purposes of justice."⁹

There is a natural law, but in order for it to be operative certain
conditions must be fulfilled; in the absence of these conditions it
is not obligatory. This idea of a conditional natural law is by itself
enough to differentiate Rousseau's version from the absolutist versions of tradition.¹⁰

A physical law is by definition self-enforcing. As related to
man it bears equally on all, so that, barring miracles, no man can
walk on water, resist the forces of gravity, and so forth. Precisely

because these limitations are universal, they cannot meaningfully be spoken of as limitations of freedom. A moral law, on the other hand, though it proscribes certain types of behavior, is not self-enforcing, since the behavior in question falls within the area of possibility, that is, the area of natural freedom.

Just as equality, universality, and impersonality are the signs of a physical law, equality, universality, and impersonality constitute the necessary conditions for the authority of a moral law. Because he had rejected all theories that implied moral inequality, Rousseau could not admit a law as legitimate if it exempted some portion of humanity, large or small. In the case of a physical law it is not necessary to distinguish the content of the law and its enforcement, since it is the de facto enforcement of the law that defines its content. The case of a moral law is quite obviously different. Built into the very notion of a moral obligation is the idea that there is no inevitable connection between content and enforcement.

Because of this split there is the ever-present threat of inequality, where some men live by the rules and others do not. Rousseau's point is that if mutuality is the essence of justice and morality, where such mutuality is not guaranteed there can be no moral obligation. An individual is morally obligated only to the extent that all other individuals are equally obligated. In a state of nature this mutuality of enforcement is assumed to be nonexistent. Because the law of self-preservation is the first law of nature, there can be no moral obligation that puts an individual at a serious disadvantage in relation to his fellows, and this is exactly the situation in which virtue finds itself in relation to vice. In short, though there is a natural law, it is not morally obligatory, because it is not enforceable in a state of nature.

This observation alone could suffice to explain Rousseau's attack on Diderot's position that in the state of nature there was not only a natural law but that it was obligatory. However, Rousseau's critique in the first version is far more detailed: it is a summary of points previously made in the *Second Discourse*. What is also at issue is the question of a general society of mankind and what that idea entails.

For Rousseau 'mankind' is a collective term that does not imply any real unity. When it is conceived to denote a moral person with a common sense of humanity and activated by a moral law, difficulties arise. Since man is not by nature social, in the early stages of the state of nature men lived as solitaries; associations were casual and temporary; since man lacked reason, there was no knowledge of the good and evil implied by natural law. What led men to unite was their common greed. "Our feeling of weakness comes less from our nature than our cupidity: our needs draw us together in proportion to the passions which divide us." [11] The very factors that cause men to unite make enemies of them. Mankind conceived as a community ordained by nature is a chimera, for the intelligence necessary to know nature's laws develops only after the passions have made compliance impossible.

The real thrust of Rousseau's argument in the first version is not to deny that there is an objective standard of justice but to question whether the state of nature embodied conditions under which there would be an interest in being just. The 'independent man' (presumably Rousseau himself) argues, "It is not a question of teaching me what justice is; it is a question of showing me what interest I have in being just." [12] Even if one were to suppose a general society in the state of nature, there would still be no compelling reason for a man to be just. But there was no such society, and whenever men did unite they became both unhappy and wicked. However, there might be some hope for man if a new form of association could be devised which reconciled justice and self-interest. This hope, of course, was the *Social Contract*.

Aside from the inherent difficulties in Diderot's position, two basic beliefs of Rousseau demanded an attack on the conception of a general society and its attendant theory of natural law. The first is psychosociological. The affective bonds which unite a society have their origin in the smallest unit, and from there expand. It is only when men find security in their own society that they can begin to look upon foreigners as humans not to be harmed. In *Emile* Rousseau criticizes Plato for downgrading the family: "Can devotion to the state exist apart from the love of those near and dear to us? Can patriotism thrive except in the soil of that miniature fatherland, the home? Is it not the good son, the good husband, the good father, who makes the good citizen?"

(*Emile*, p. 326). Before men can affectively embrace the idea of humanity they must be affectively shaped in particular societies. To argue, as did Diderot, the existence of a general society ante-dating civil society would be to reverse this order of affections. The love necessary to unite mankind in a society can only arise, if it can, from the prior love a man feels for his family and fellow citizens.

A second consideration also demanded the priority of civil society to the purported general society. The mutual respect citizens bear one another becomes concrete in actions. From these transactions are "born the rules of reasoned natural right, different from natural right properly speaking, which has its source in a feeling which though true is very vague and often stifled by self-love." [13] It is only within society that distinct ideas of justice and injustice arise. Since it is the law that shapes society, "law is anterior to justice, and not justice to the law." [14] Law, for Rousseau, is the expression of a general will, and for a general will to be heard it must be institutionalized. But how can one imagine an institution in the state of nature common to all men, spread out as they were over the face of the globe? If justice requires the strict enforcement of the law, then in the state of nature there could not have been any natural justice, because there was no institution capable of enforcing natural law throughout the world.

To summarize Rousseau's objections to Diderot: The issue is not natural law in general, but natural law as conceived by sophisticated rationalists. In the state of nature the reason sufficient to promulgate such a law is lacking. Reason develops dialectically with the passions, and these passions rule out the possibility of unorganized individuals' voluntarily obeying rules that abridge their interests. In the absence of institutions that insure equal enforcement of laws, the only obligations that bind men are prudential. Moreover, without institutions there can be no society, and thus the term 'mankind' as applied to a state of nature signifies not a general society of man, but simply the aggregate of all men. The idea of a natural law, however conceived, is irrelevant in the state of nature; if it is to acquire relevancy, certain political conditions must be met. An analysis of these conditions is found in the final version of the *Social Contract*. The law written in the heavens, then, is a necessary but not a sufficient condition of obligation; there must be in addition a reasonable assurance that it will be enforced universally, and, given the nature of things, this guarantee demands some sort of government. So insistent is Rousseau on the necessity of complete and full enforcement of the law that he denies government the right of pardon.

In an ideal state the question of a moral law becomes in a sense superfluous. Given the theory of the general will, it is difficult to imagine an assembly legislating contrary to natural law. For if natural law is directed to man's perfection and good as man, it can hardly be thought of as prescribing something all men judging with a spirit of generality would proscribe or vice versa. The general will and the process that accompanies it are a kind of collective reason and have as good a claim as any individual's reason to speak in the name of natural law when this is at issue.

But unfortunately most, if not all, states, from Rousseau's point of view, are far from ideal, and their laws for the most part bear unequally on subjects. According to his analysis in the *Social Contract*, this constitutes at least a partial reconstitution of the state of nature, and the only obligation subjects have toward rulers is prudential. Thus, from the moral point of view, subjects are technically in a state of nature vis-a-vis their rulers.

Granted that subjects are only prudentially obliged by governments, by what sort of obligations are they bound in their interpersonal relations? Due to the socializing process individuals undoubtedly feel that they are under moral obligations. But the question from a theoretical point of view is whether they really are, assuming, of course, that obligation is something more than a mere psychological phenomenon. Rousseau's answer would seem to be yes and no. Even a despotic government in its own interests enforces the law to some extent, and to this extent there is some degree of assured mutuality—bad men are punished and good men protected in their virtue. If a government for whatever reason enforces laws that an individual perceives as natural laws, then he is morally obliged by them. He is morally obliged not because of the authority of the government, which by hypothesis is illegitimate, but because of the authority of the law and also because the law is enforced. On the other hand, one can conceive of all kinds of cases where the moral way would lead to, maintain, or augment a relation of inequality. Let it be supposed that it is wrong to tell a lie, but would it be wrong for a peasant to mislead a tax collector when the tax rates are inequitable? It appears that Rousseau would allow this and much more, especially in the relations between peasants and the nobility.[15]

Once society is articulated and despotism instituted, an individual's choice for a moral life reduces to some combination of two extremes. One may withdraw as far as possible from society and, while not doing much good, at least do no evil. This is the passive morality that colors Rousseau's *Reveries*. Or one can live in the world and do as much good for others as circumstances permit. This is the life recommended in *Emile*. If the former meets the minimum demands for morality, the latter is a counsel of perfection. For Rousseau an immoral life is simply not worth living; it constitutes a kind of slavery to one's animal nature and destroys any idea of human dignity. Oddly enough, the issue of morality becomes most acute in an immoral society. The true value of man resides in his freedom. In any society much of his absolute natural freedom is circumscribed. In a despotic society he is deprived of his civil freedom. All that remains to him is the possibility of moral freedom, the voluntary submission to a self-imposed law. It is only as a moral being that a man can sustain an image of his worth and value.

But what is this self-imposed law but a variant of natural law? In the absence of rules determined by the collective decision of the people, the individual is thrown back on his own resources; he must be his own general will. The self-imposed law that gives a moral dimension to an individual is not a product of his particular will (that is, that will which looks to his advantage), but of his general will (that is, that will which never concedes him a right over others he would not willingly concede others over himself). This principle of generality and equality responds to what Rousseau means by morality. To live according to this rule is to be moral, because by so doing an individual preserves moral equality to the extent that lies within his power. Moral rules may be objective because rooted in the will of God, but the individual can be moral only insofar as he voluntarily internalizes these rules

—another instance of the relationship between objectivity and convention.[16]

The above discussion of morality under despotism can be conveniently summed up. After Emile has seen the ways of the world, the tutor explains:

> Under the name of law you have everywhere seen the rule of self-interest and human passion. *But the eternal laws of nature and order exist.* For the wise man they take the place of positive law; they are written in the depths of his heart by conscience and reason; let him obey these laws and he is free; for there is no slave but the evildoer, for he always does evil against his will. Liberty is not to be found in any form of government, she is in the heart of the free man, he bears her with him everywhere. The vile man bears his slavery in himself; the one would be a slave in Geneva the other free in Paris. [*Emile*, p. 437; italics added.]

It seems to be evident that Rousseau believed in natural law, though his version significantly differs from traditional accounts. It is also clear that ultimately he linked the fate of morality with the existence of God. In a letter to M. Paul Moulton, 14 February 1769, he firmly states that if "you reject the First Cause and have everything done through matter and motion, you take all morality from human life" (*Letters*, p. 367). Nevertheless, what is interesting to note is that most of his discussions on morality proceed independently of any knowledge of God's existence. This is true whether he is giving a purely formal analysis of moral obligation as in the *Social Contract* or a psychological analysis in terms of conscience. Conscience is an introspective fact that Rousseau interprets as an infallible guide to right and wrong. From a logical point of view, natural religion would seem to be a postulate or corollary of morality rather than vice versa. In an ideal society God would be less necessary for morality because in such a society it must be assumed that vice is always punished and virtue, if not a reward for its own sake, still does not work to the relative disadvantage of the virtuous. But as it is, this ideal is practically impossible, and virtue too often does not fare well. Under these circumstances what motive can most individuals have for being good? On Rousseau's principles the obligatory power of natural law or any law depends upon almost certain sanctions. Since this apparently is not the case in this world, it would never be the case unless there were a God who rewards or punishes after death. From this point of view religion is a practical postulate of moral experience.[17]

All of the preceding can be read in a slightly different way. *If* there is to be a moral obligation it must be defined according to the process described in the *Social Contract*. The various steps in this process "are everywhere the same, everywhere tacitly admitted and recognized" (*SC* 1. 6). This universality implies that the process and at least some of the laws that result are natural laws. However, at this stage of the argument it need not be assumed that they are natural in the traditional sense of being decreed by God. They may be viewed simply as so rooted in the nature of man that no man would as a matter of fact acknowledge a moral obligation on any other terms. This type of natural law is conditional, because there is no antecedent obligation that demands that a man enter the contract, and there is no transcendent norm that obliges him to bind himself in perpetuity. Once moral obligations are recognized as conditional obligations, the apparent paradox that some moral obligations are both conventional and natural is resolved. Though the content of the obligation is natural, its obligatory force depends upon a convention that guarantees equal enforcement. I say "some moral obligations" because every law passed in accordance with the contract morally obliges but not every law expresses a natural law. Parts of the criminal law would undoubtedly echo natural laws, but traffic regulations, though morally binding, would be wholly conventional.

Granting the content of moral obligation, it becomes fully obligatory only when it is backed by nearly infallible force. This is the principle of mutuality. From a purely rational point of view the general outlines of a naturalistic ethics are complete. They can be evaluated on their own terms without reference to a deity. But then psychological and historical considerations enter the picture. Over a period of time, is it reasonable to expect that everyone will continue to legislate in the spirit of generality and that the laws will be enforced impartially? Apparently not. Man, being what he is, is constantly tempted to seek his individual advantage to the detriment of the common good, and the fear of violating human justice is not always an adequate deterrent. To help check this tendency the Civil Creed with its promise of divine retribution becomes an integral part, even if belatedly, of the *Social Contract*. The atheist is barred from the community "not for impiety, but for unsociability, for being incapable of sincerely loving law and justice, and of sacrificing his life to his duty when necessary" (*SC* 4. 8). Religion, by itself, may not be a reliable support of equality, but without its basic tenets inequality and immorality are inevitable. In his letter to d'Alembert, Rousseau is quite explicit in stating the necessity of religion as a basis for virtue. "I do not mean by this that one can be virtuous without religion; I held this erroneous opinion for a long time, but now I am only too disabused" (*Letter to M. d'Alembert*, p. 97).

From a theoretical point of view the Civil Creed could have been dispensed with if there were an alternative way of motivating men to check their natural selfishness. Not having anticipated that nationalistic spirit of which, ironically, many have judged him the prophet, Rousseau thought there was no alternative way. But the point is that in theory the *Social Contract* can be read as a self-contained ethics without theological presuppositions and without a commitment to traditional natural law.[18] The question of religion, however, becomes vital and central in the context of moral man and immoral society. The de facto inequality that pervades contemporary states renders the *Social Contract* politically irrelevant save as a stern witness to a universal lack of legitimacy.

Under these circumstances, the purely naturalistic aspect of Rousseau's theory might advise maximization of self-interest within the limits of prudential fear. But there still remains the insistent voice of conscience, which punishes transgressions with painful remorse. For Rousseau, duty, guilt, remorse, and the like are natural, not sociopsychological, phenomena. They are as real as the pangs of hunger, but it is not empirically evident that they bear the same relation to man's well-being. Do not eat and you die. Do not listen to your conscience and soon enough its voice and remorse will be stilled. This line of thought Rousseau could not accept, but neither could he find an adequate naturalistic motive to be moral in an immoral society. In a moral society one can find happiness in the common good, and one is never disadvantaged by being virtuous. But in an immoral society there is no real common good, and vice is its own reward.

If there is no secular justification for morality and yet the desire to be moral is strong, justification must be sought elsewhere. It is here that Rousseau's leap of faith is best understood. And it is a leap of faith because, despite the natural religion expressed in the vicar's creed, Rousseau in his private letters is by no means certain that reason is capable of deciding the issue of God's existence one way or the other. In a letter to M. Jacob Vernes, 11 January 1758, he declares that he needs religion probably more than any man alive, and that his atheist friends have not succeeded in shaking his faith, though he is unable to counter their objections. But this is not decisive, for

philosophy, which has neither bottom nor shore in these matters and lacks the primary ideas and elementary principles, is nothing but a sea of uncertainty and doubt, whence the metaphysician never extricates himself. So I have abandoned reason to its fate, and consulted nature, that is to say, the internal sentiment which directs my belief independently of my reason. . . . I have no other reason for not believing them [materialist interpretations] except the fact that I do not believe. [That may be prejudice.] But what can reason do, rude though it be, against a prejudice which is more persuasive than itself? [*Letters*, p. 147]

He affirms his belief in God and the conviction that God would not be just if souls were not immortal. Even if his faith is mistaken it is salutary, because it helps him endure all the misfortunes he has experienced. In any case, "if virtue does not always make man happy, he cannot possibly be happy without it" (*Letters*, p. 148). There are other letters which express similar doubts about the efficacy of reason, but there is perhaps no more perfervid and poignant affirmation of the faith that grounds his religion than what he says in a letter to Voltaire. "All the subtleties of metaphysics will not make me doubt for a moment the immortality of the soul or a beneficent Providence. I feel it, I believe it, I want it, I hope for it, and I shall defend it to my last breath."[19]

Reason has its share in Rousseau's religious beliefs in that it provides evidence, though inconclusive, on their behalf, and also raises counterobjections to the materialist's position. But the ultimate appeal to sentiment must be interpreted as an act of faith, for what is fundamentally at issue is the justification of another sentiment, namely, conscience, and it is evident that one feeling cannot legitimate another without circularity or an infinite regress.

The fact that Rousseau's natural religion turns out to be less than natural, being ultimately based on faith, leads to an unusual dualism. The content of morality retains its natural status as revealed by a combination of reason and conscience, but its sufficient motive is to be found only in an act of faith in a God who will reward virtue. Rousseau is never in doubt about the sufficiency of nature to provide an insight into what is morally required; he knows right from wrong. The question is, "What doth it profit a man if he saves his soul and loses the world?" And the answer is that though he loses the world his faith insures him that he will be amply recompensed in heaven.

This dualism seems strange, because in the rationalist tradition the content of the law carries its own absolute imperative, and this union of content and imperative carries over into the logic of our moral discourse. Rousseau's position, however, is different. He is saying, when speaking of an ideal state in purely naturalistic terms, that *if* men would be moral, this is what they ought to do, provided the law is rigidly and equally enforced. This involves one absolute and two conditions. There is no transcendent obligation to be moral—this is a matter of convention, and this convention is binding only as long as the laws are enforced. But positing these two conditions, the content of the law insofar as it relates to morals is not really conventional at all.

Since the above conditions are not practicable, Rousseau shifts his ground without changing the content of morality. The new formulation becomes, "You are obliged by such-and-such rules if God exists, and God exists." In this syllogism the two previous conditions are removed, or, rather, they are replaced by an act of faith which in relation to reason is a kind of condition. These two positions, the naturalistic and the seminaturalistic, though formulated in different contexts, are not incompatible, because in both formulations moral rules are derived in substantially the same way, and in both formulations the full obligatory force of the law depends upon the presence of some infallible mode of enforcement.

There is, therefore, for Rousseau, a natural law that can be ascertained independently of any knowledge of God. But once again the *Second Discourse* rears its gloomy head. Why should a man be moral in a world where virtue inevitably falls prey to vice? Reason is unable to provide a definitive answer. Faith is the only court of last appeal; it alone sustains the hope that the wounds of virtue will be healed and that virtue will endure triumphantly through eternity. But what if this faith is in vain? "Justice and conscientiousness only make dupes here below. Take away eternal justice and the prolongation of my being after this life and I see in virtue nothing but a madness one gives a handsome name." [20]

Chapter 9

In Search of an Identity

Because Rousseau wrote with his thoughts pointing in so many opposite directions, it is not surprising that he is so many different and incompatible things to his countless commentators.[1] In many cases he is not the altogether-innocent victim of his confusing perspectives and powerful but deceptive rhetoric. If there is to be any hope of properly cataloguing him, it is necessary to proceed by negation and determine what he is not. To this end, one of Rousseau's basic methodological cautions must be constantly borne in mind. This may be called the fallacy of extrapolation: failing to recognize that what is appropriate to one context is inappropriate to a different context. Thus, for example, rules suitable for the management of a household economy are unsuitable for the management of general or political economy.[2] Or again, whereas a theater would prove a baneful influence in Geneva, it serves a salutary purpose in Paris.

Political, economic, and even psychological categories have little meaning apart from a given set of concrete social relations. Consider the issue whether Rousseau is a democrat or a totalitarian. In the first place the dichotomy is unfortunate, because the two are not conceptually incompatible. This becomes clear when state and government are distinguished. The state is society insofar as society is regulated by positive law. Literally speaking, 'totalitarian' refers to a state that is coextensive with society. That is, it describes a society in which every aspect of human behavior is subject to coercive law. Since this is not yet technologically feasible, it more commonly expresses an individual's judgment that the scope of the state is considerably more than it ought to be. Be that as it may, the specific content of the laws that define the scope of the state are products of government as we employ the term. Democracy, as one type of government, no longer carries its original credentials, but presumably it describes a government that is more rather than less responsive to the popular will, because it is more rather than less dependent for its existence on that will. Viewed thus, there is nothing conceptually strange about a totalitarian democracy.

In these terms, what then is Rousseau? As far as the *Social Contract* is concerned, it should be obvious that he is an advocate of democracy far beyond anything contemplated by the wildest contemporary utopian. It is true that he disparages democracy as a form of government, but government for him, be it recalled, is limited to executive and judicial functions. He is the preeminent democrat, where 'democracy' signifies the direct, legislative supremacy of all the people.

Whether he is a totalitarian in a nonpejorative sense is not clear. He specifically says that a well-governed state needs very few laws (*SC* 4. 1). But if you extend the idea of law to cover customs, tradition, and public opinion, the scope of the state is considerably enlarged. From a theoretical point of view the scope of the state cannot go beyond the area of common concerns. What this area is, is a variable depending primarily on the nature of the economy. If the social model is that of a series of privately owned and self-sufficient farms, it may be assumed that the range of law is quite small and the private realm correspondingly large. If my collectivist model is allowed, the relative proportions would be roughly reversed. But this is not really important. Totalitarianism, as we know it, is intelligible only as applied to a very complex society that is rigidly regulated by legislation that does not pertain to the whole. Given Rousseau's specialized concept of law, 'totalitarian', or for that matter 'nontotalitarian', simply makes no sense when applied to him.[3]

Because of historical shifts in meaning, liberalism, as a category, is hard to pin down. If it is interpreted in a Lockean sense as advocating a very limited state and a free (that is, legally unregulated) market economy, then Rousseau is not a liberal. His

contract can support private property but not where there is significant economic inequality or where a wage economy is conjoined with the institution of private property. If liberalism is
associated with increased governmental regulation of the economy, Rousseau is still not a liberal, for the increased complexity
of the economy that calls forth such regulation at the same time
precludes regulation by his kind of law. For Locke, liberty and
equality were for practical purposes antipodal concepts; his concept of liberty is in many respects closer to Rousseau's natural liberty than to anything else. It is the liberty one associates with
competition.

Modern liberalism, responding to its recognition that the competition is all too often unfair, locates itself closer and closer toward the equality end of the liberty-equality spectrum. This is
but a corollary of a Rousseauan awareness that liberty as natural
right is a fraud when some men by circumstances have far more
effective natural right than others. In this respect, at least, Rousseau can be called a liberal. But again, this is of doubtful help, for,
taking into account radically different socioeconomic contexts,
'liberal' can not be univocally applied both to Rousseau and our
contemporaries. How the term is to be used analogically, I will
not try to decide.

Was Rousseau a reactionary, a conservative, or a revolutionary?
Since, to repeat, none of these or like categories carry much
meaning in the abstract, it is necessary to relate them to specific
socioeconomic conditions. Unless one is to fall victim to the fallacy of extrapolation, it must be admitted that Rousseau's formal
theory of legitimacy has little political wisdom that is of direct
contemporary relevance. The *Social Contract* condemns us with a
bill of particulars that could fill volumes. But that is not very
helpful, because the principles of political right have meaning
only under the most limited circumstances, a set of circumstances
that, if they ever existed, history has long since buried. Reaction,
in the sense of reanimating dead history, is no part of Rousseau's
thought. He may have been a reactionary in his nostalgia for the
past, but he had no illusions that that past was recoverable. He
would undoubtedly have quarreled with ministers of the gospel

of progress, but he would agree with them that beyond a certain stage of development, history is a one-way street. The reactionary is a Don Quixote fruitlessly tilting with history.

I do not wish to suggest that Rousseau had an articulated philosophy of history after the fashion of, say, Marx. But he did have an attitude toward history that served to deepen his general pessimism. Let me quote George Armstrong Kelly, a scholar who has given the matter serious thought: "Rousseau hated history precisely because of its implacable momentum and unreasonable power." And again, "Rousseau saw little possibility of a 'new' history but regarded *all* history as the inevitable carrier of pernicious values."[4] This dark attitude is hardly that of a revolutionary. Reaction and revolution are equally self-defeating. The past simply cannot be recaptured, and even successful revolutions carry with them unanticipated evils that frustrate revolutionary expectations.

Think of the danger of suddenly overturning the mighty structure represented by the French monarchy! Who, once it had started, could keep such a convulsion within bounds or foresee all its effects? Even when the advantages of a new system are incontestable, what man of good sense would dare to do away with ancient customs in order to renew the State, which is what thirteen centuries have made it? Whether an existing government is what it was in the past, or whether it has insensibly changed during the course of many centuries, *it is always unwise to touch it*. If the same, it must be respected; if fallen into decay, it must be reformed by time and events, and human reason can do nothing about it.[5]

Rousseau foresaw revolution and, if you will, its moral justification, but his historical pessimism by no means welcomed it.[6]

If history were impelled solely by rhetorical forces, Rousseau might justifiably be viewed as a major influence in the progress of the French Revolution. For nothing so succinctly captures the spirit of his philosophy as the revolutionary slogan, "Liberty, Equality, Fraternity."[7] Add to this Rousseau's self-appointed prophet, Robespierre, invoking the general will, proclaiming the sovereignty of the people, and instituting a civil religion as best suited to a republic of virtue. But rhetoric too often belies reality. Given Rousseau's subtle analysis of monarchy, there was no institutional possibility of reconciling his principles with a territory the size of France. If anything, it was the more conservative elements in the early stages of the revolution who better understood their Rousseau.[8] Rousseau was far more a myth of the revolution than its architect.

The logic of Rousseau's utopian ideal demanded that he be a thoroughgoing conservative, resisting all but the most insignificant changes. Radical change can easily proceed from the relatively simple to the more complex, and complexity is a threat to the integral harmony of a community. To the extent that it articulates society, change weakens the general will, which is limited to literally common concerns. What is more, change usually arises from a part of society and differentiates that part from the whole. Differentiation of any significant kind is soon accompanied by a new corporate will that loosens social ties. A self-conscious identity is both the essence of a people and the North Star, in relation to which its common good can be fixed. Change of identity is more apt to be loss of identity. A tenacious conservation of identity, then, is a precondition of an enduring and energetic general will.

But even on a nonutopian level, Rousseau counsels a degree of conservatism that, ironically, rivals Burke's.[9] The quotation above on revolution is by no means anomalous; his recommendations for Poland and Corsica are the recognizable fruits of a mind partial to prescription. Rousseau, ever sensitive to the interconnectedness of social phenomena, despairingly regarded conscious reform as the likely agent of unanticipated and graver afflictions. His conservatism is simply a part of his pessimistic view of history; the present is bad enough, but the future will probably be worse. However, it must be cautioned that Rousseau's conservatism relates to an economy that is primarily agrarian. What his attitude toward social change would be today simply cannot or ought not to be extrapolated.

Rousseau's attack on the arts and sciences is many-sided. Here I will limit myself to two observations. Aesthetics aside, Rousseau deplored the arts because he believed that their cultivation was possible only in a luxury society, in a society where the rich few exploit the destitute many. From a great historic distance we marvel at and enjoy the glory that was Greece, while never troubling ourselves with the slave economy that made it possible. No such forgiving distance interposed to separate Rousseau's moral and aesthetic sensibilities. The works of the devil may be pretty indeed, but they are none the less the works of the devil and must, if only for that reason, be condemned. When the alternatives are beauty or justice, the moralist's choice is clear. Rousseau may well have been mistaken in judging the alternatives, but who is to fault him for ranking morality above aesthetics?

Rousseau's attitude toward reason and the sciences is quite complex. Leo Strauss in a widely read article has convincingly cleared him of simplistic charges of antiintellectualism.[10] I have nothing to add to Strauss's analysis except to emphasize Rousseau's conviction that in certain vital areas science is a most unhealthy and damaging dissolvent. When in matters of belief science is invested with sovereign authority, there is a positivistic tendency to dismiss all indemonstrable beliefs as so many pernicious myths, superstitions, and delusions. However, what are myths to a bloodless reason, may well be the salutary and vivifying truths that give identity to and particularize a people. It is not the truth of these beliefs that is important or even relevant; what is important is the communal unity they inspire. Science as individualistic, impersonal, and cosmopolitan can never provide or nourish the affective ties that are so essential for giving a unique identity to a community. Science, by depersonalizing everything it dissects, leaves man naked before a reality indifferent to his aspirations. Only commonly shared beliefs protect men against threats of meaninglessness. Science's writ runs just so far, and it must stop short of invading the innocent dogmas without which communities become disoriented and enfeebled. Symbolic beliefs are not beholden to reason; they justify themselves in the vigorous and cooperative life of a people. Rob a people of their common symbols and they become an aggregation at war with itself.

In a polemical atmosphere positions tend to polarize to a degree beyond the intentions of their proponents. What to an outsider appears at first to be overt aggression may in reality be a defensive counterattack. It seems to me that Rousseau's less-than-sanguine view of reason is more a protective posture than anything else. In the academic world reason has a tremendous advantage, because he who would question its competence must do so only in a language acceptable to reason: "What are your reasons for doubting reason's omnipotence?" If faith cannot get a fair hearing in the court of reason, then attack the court. "Philosophy . . . is nothing but a sea of uncertainty and doubt." But life is action, and commitments must be made. "I have no other reason for not believing them [materialists] except for the fact that I do not believe" (*Letters*, p. 147). Rousseau is a man of faith. But his is not a faith born of revelation or mediated by theology. It is the expression of his affective nature. In moral matters it is conscience. In suitable societies it is a patriotic love of fellow citizens. There are a thousand reasons to prefer the self. It is only affectivity that allows man to transcend the narrow confines of selfishness; it is only affectivity properly channeled that allows man to become a citizen. Reason is simply not enough. It can infallibly disclose the conditions necessary for legitimacy, but it cannot make a citizen.

Ideally, 'citizen' is the highest category; it is what a man ought to be first, last, and always. To contemporary ears this may sound like the apotheosis of the state, the subordination of a person's whole being to the political community—in a word, like totalitarianism. But Rousseau's glorification of the citizen is something quite different. In the first place, it will be recalled, the term 'citizen' applies to a man insofar as he is an active member of sovereignty. It expresses his rights and not his self-imposed duties as a subject. But more important, 'citizen' is not a political category in a restricted modern sense; it is the highest category because it pertains to the whole man. In this respect it responds to Aristotle's idea of man as a political animal, of man as fulfilling and realizing himself in the common life of a small *polis*. A man who cannot completely identify with a group is a divided man. "Ever at war with himself, hesitating between his wishes and his duties, he will be neither a man nor a citizen" (*Emile*, p. 8).

The divided man was for Rousseau a monstrosity, both the product and cause of a corrupt society. But this same divided man is in the eyes of others the very model of individualism honorifically construed. He is the individual who, solely for the sake of civil peace, submits but a fraction of his being to the state. The remainder is the measure of his independence. For him freedom has only one meaning, the absence of legal constraint. This is the gospel preached by Hobbes and Locke and later elaborated and extended by John Stuart Mill. Now every virtuous title has its antithetical wicked twin, against which it must scrupulously guard itself. Conformism is the enemy and society is its base. Whereas the individual stands against society, the conformist gladly and without question accepts all its conventions. Society is big government meddling in the economy to the despair of rugged individuals. Society is Big Brother telling me what I shall eat, what I shall wear, what I shall read, what I shall think. Society is what is not the true me, an identity that mysteriously exists in its own right and that seeks to escape the crippling shackles of conformity. Freedom is freedom for this self-subsisting ego and freedom from an alien society.

In a universe of discourse that so completely puts individualism in opposition to conformity, it is impossible not to describe the Rousseau of the *Social Contract* as a conformist. The divided man as individualist has only one will, a particular will that forever seeks self-aggrandizement. The dominant will of the citizen, formed by uniform education, is a general will whose good is the good of the community. Ideally all citizens are shaped together from the same mold; literally they are conformed. What is more, virtue, the necessary foundation of legitimacy, is nothing but the conformity of the particular will with the general will.[11] For Rousseau the more perfect the coincidence, the better. For the individualist the less the particular will is bound, the better. The respective standards of excellence are utterly and obviously contradictory. How could anybody ever have doubted that Rousseau was an extreme antiindividualistic conformist?

This conclusion is inescapable. But it is also thoroughly unenlightening, because Rousseau completely rejected the universe of discourse that gives meaning to the terms. By some ironic quirk of semantic fate, the divided man, the man at odds with social imperatives, is today called an individualist. Rousseau was on far firmer etymological grounds when he identified the healthy individual (*individuus*) with the undivided man. Because Rousseau held views that went beyond the social contract, there is room for reasonable disagreement as to what he, the whole thinker, really advocated. There was, for example, an unmistakable authoritarian dimension in his thinking. But if one narrows his attention and focuses it exclusively on the ideal, I think some criticisms and, for that matter, some praises can be laid to rest. I would argue that any commentator who consciously or unconsciously subscribes to the above universe of discourse has completely missed Rousseau's point. That universe is the one bequeathed to us by Hobbes and Locke, and in it we debate the proper proportions of law and individual freedom. But this is not the universe in which the *Social Contract* is located, and therefore it is misleading to label Rousseau as either an individualist or a conformist.

Rousseau had objected that neither Locke nor Hobbes had pressed far enough back into history in his search for natural man. Hobbes in particular had projected the aggressive acquisitiveness of his contemporaries onto natural man. Rousseau in effect accepted Hobbesean man as an accurate picture of natural man corrupted by society. Since this is the man a practical reformer must confront on a large scale, there is little pragmatic reason for him to seek absolute origins. This is Rousseau at his pessimistic worst. But he was not always consistent in his despair. There was always the theoretical level of his thought, where he could relieve his gloom with visions of what might have been. On that level it was absolutely essential to capture true natural man, if only to avoid the apparent inevitability of Hobbes's less-than-noble savage.

Despite his obvious contempt for Scholasticism there is a crucial respect in which Hobbes falls within the Aristotelean tradition. Though man is purportedly not a social animal by nature, nevertheless there is somehow a natural and socially independent development of language, reason, and emotions. And this is true also of Locke. In a word, there is a natural self that is only minimally and superficially modified by society. It is this antecedent self that gives up a measure of natural right or freedom with the hedonistic hope of avoiding the pains of anarchy and of enjoying the fruits of peaceful competition. There may be other ways of expressing this process, but the essential point is that for both Hobbes and Locke there is a significant core of individuality that exists independently of society. It is only on some such assump-

tion that the individualist-conformist and individual-society an-
titheses carry any credence whatever. Only if individuals exist in
their own right does it make sense to distinguish those who accept
and those who resist social imperatives.

This of course is not a single, pure position. Thinkers can differ
in any number of ways about the relative influence of society on
character formation. But there is an upper limit, and it is this
limit that Rousseau seized: there is no aspect of individuality that
is not socially conditioned. Man minus society is the mindless
hominid of the *Second Discourse*. Every accretion beyond this animal minimum is due to society, and the proliferation of human
varieties strictly correlates with a like proliferation of different societies. It is meaningless to oppose the individual and society, because the individual is precisely what society has made him. He
has his whole being only in and through society. There are few
words with as tyrannous a hold over our thought as *society*. We pit
the individual against society much as one team is pitted against
another: the sacred individual *vs.* unholy society; autonomy *vs.*
conformity—a doubleheader.

Up to a point this makes some sense when society is all of a
piece. In such a case all nonrebels literally conform, that is, they
are formed from the same identical mold. It may seem facetious
to add that they are nonconformists with respect to some alien
society. But in a less extreme way this is the existential situation
of individuals in a modern, complex, pluralistically fragmented
society. No one person can recapitulate internally such a society,
because there is no one, homogeneous, consistent society to mirror. An individual's revolt against society is most usually a revolt
against some part or aspect of his society, and it is only sus-
tainable, with rare exceptions, by identification with, that is,
conformity to, some other part or aspect of society. Vis-a-vis a
participating individual, a counterculture is no less a social reality
than the established culture. The individualist, the rebel, the conformist are all equally social products.

Emile is an individualist of sorts. His education enables him to
stand above the conventions of society and to judge them rather
than be shaped by them. Nevertheless, his individualism is no
less a product of society, albeit a most peculiar and unlikely so-

ciety, namely, his tutor. Emile is as close to being an undivided man as is possible in the real world. But this is second best, because the real world is the world of corrupt societies. The key to his undividedness lies in the fact that his tutor, as Emile's society, speaks with only one, consistent voice. All competing influences are carefully screened out.

To many readers this sounds more like indoctrination than education. So it may be. But let us not deceive ourselves that indoctrination is no part of a free society. It is there, though it is not always recognized as such and hence the delusion of individuality. This delusion arises because there are so many party lines, so many alternative institutions, so many associations, so much variety that when combined in different ways, often haphazardly and by chance, a corresponding proliferation of types is produced. We sometimes brag of our pluralistic society, but this may well be an unconscious acceptance of an unalterable historical situation not of anyone's conscious choice, design, or even desire.

If man is willy-nilly thoroughly a social creation, it is impossible to interpose a no man's land between him and society. The question for Rousseau was not conformity but conformity to what. The sooner we realize that our society is not a seamless, homogeneous whole but rather a patchwork of diverse, competing, incompatible, sometimes noncommunicating elements, the sooner we will realize that we are all conformists to some social pattern or other. Rousseau above all his contemporaries saw this, and that is why it was a matter of indifference whether he attacked society in general or the vices of individuals; it was the same battle. He was never so naive as to conceive of society as a mysterious thing apart from individuals. Like the general will, it was the dialectical product of men interacting among themselves and with their institutions.

Hobbesean man was not all men but man as corrupted by a particular type of society. Could a new, better man be socialized? The social contract supplies part of the answer, for it indirectly establishes the conditions that must prevail in an ideal society. It must be a small society, where all the citizens collectively shape their own destiny. It must be a society that has a general will, that is, a common will, a will shared by all. It can have a general will only if there is no specialized division of labor or incompatible associations competing for a citizen's loyalty. In a word, there must be a perfect correspondence between individual and society. But this can only occur if all citizens are conformed from the same mold. Under such circumstances an individual is at one with himself, because he is at one with his society as a whole. There is no division between man and the citizen; the citizen is the total man. This is roughly how Rousseau would reconcile individuality and conformity: the undivided man, the true individual, is he who conforms in exactly the same way as do all his fellows. The problem of legitimacy thus cannot be separated from the problem of society, because only the undivided man *can* share in sovereignty.

If one must append a tag to what Rousseau the theorist was advocating, I suppose 'communal direct democracy' is less distorting than any other. The sovereignty of the people means nothing if it does not mean democracy. Rousseau the theorist, if not the man, is unquestionably a democrat in the more radical sense of that word. And that's the rub. Today one seldom reads about representative democracy because a direct democracy on a large scale is unthinkable, and so we take for granted that there can be no democracy without representation. Representation, however, violates the contract because will cannot be represented. The ideal, no matter how impractical, is a direct democracy.

Even this is not enough to specify what sort of democrat Rousseau was. All citizens must not only vote on every issue, they must vote their general and not their particular will. Moreover, this will can only be expressed by law in the very strict sense of the term. Now these requirements can only be met if there is an objective common good to will. These conditions mark off a special type of association, a community.

Community is an especially rubbery concept, stretching all the way from voluntary conformity in all aspects of life through successively looser versions until a point is reached where community passes over to a mere organized aggregation of nonintercommunicating bodies. The same parallel holds with respect to the subjective side of community, namely, individuality. At one end is the individual whose whole being is identified with the community; at the other end is the individual whose whole being is imprisoned in his own ego. It is well to remember that Rousseau's idea of political freedom is not that it is a value that relates to the individual qua individual; it is a value that accrues to the individual through the mediation of the community. Or to put it another way, a man is free in obeying the community only if there is a basic identification of his will with the communal will.

Can Rousseau be said to have solved the problem of legitimacy? Perhaps on some highly abstract plane, but otherwise no. In chapter 4 I argued that something of a general will must be a part of the social contract because without it a general will could never be generated by the other terms of the contract. What this means in effect is that the contract does not create a people. On the contrary, without an already existing people the contract is meaningless. Though Rousseau seems to say otherwise (*SC* 1. 5), his lengthy treatment of the legislator and a people fit for legislation is strong proof that he realized that the contract presupposed a people. The total implausibility of conjoining the legislator and a malleable people is proof enough that Rousseau failed to solve his problem. As he himself said, "the effect would have to become the cause; . . . and men, before laws existed, would have to be as the laws themselves should make them" (*SC* 2. 7). But if the legislator is no solution, his role symbolizes the very heart of the problem: unless the individual and society are perfectly integrated, legitimacy is impossible.[12]

In discussing the role of the legislator Rousseau makes an interesting statement: the legislator must be capable of changing human nature. Given his description of natural man in the *Second Discourse*, one wonders what aspect of this minimal nature is to be changed. As far as I can see, there is only one thing that needs changing, and that is man's self-referential will, his particular will. The objects of this will may be socially determined, but the will itself is intractably natural. Even if there were an initial solution to the problem it would not long endure, because as much as we act to suppress nature, sooner or later it will reassert itself. The *Second Discourse* may well be Rousseau's most powerful and comprehensive indictment of a corrupt society, but it also foredoomed any lasting solution to the problem of legitimacy. More accurately, it foredoomed a solution in *Rousseau's* eyes, because it is really quite easy to reject his account of human nature.[13]

Though Rousseau failed to find a realistic solution to the problem of legitimacy as propounded, his very failure reintroduced into political theory a dimension that had been largely ignored since Aristotle. Like Montesquieu, he realized the futility of analyzing governments apart from social facts. Going beyond Montesquieu and Aristotle, he made legitimacy a function of society as a whole. Legitimacy is no longer an isolated relation, holding or not holding between government and citizens; it is a relationship between the individual and society as a whole. This cannot be found in either Hobbes or Locke. If the government keeps the peace or protects private property, it is legitimate and that's about all there is to it. With Rousseau it is otherwise. If society is illegitimate then the government is illegitimate. It is true that Rousseau attributes more initial causative responsibility to the government than may be the case. But however culpability is apportioned, society as a whole is man's natural habitat. No matter who deformed society, society is none the less deformed. Even if there were no theoretical and practical obstacles to an ideal legitimatization of the state, there is no longer a way of legitimating the state without a parallel process of legitimating society.

It is, I take it, obvious that the conditions Rousseau laid down for legitimacy are in a formal sense irrelevant to modern nation-states. But that does not mean that the social contract lacks all value as a regulative ideal. I would suggest, however, that it would be a mistake to think of it as a scale ranking governments higher as they become progressively more democratic. Political rhetoric pays homage to the sovereignty of the people, but on Rousseau's terms there is no people; there is instead a vast, complicated web of associations, each with its own general will. Literal common goods are minimal and hardly visible beneath a flood of private interests. Under such conditions the people ought not be sovereign, because sovereignty is legitimate only when there is a corresponding general will. Even were it technologically possible to establish a direct legislative democracy, this would not be justified by the social contract, for what will does an individual have for the most part but his particular will shaped by his own special social location?

Our democratic theory is in large measure based on Benthamite principles: the primary aim of government is to establish the greatest good for the greatest number. But this good by the nature of the case is a mere summation of individual wills; it is not and it cannot be an expression of the general will. I have described Rousseau as a democrat, but I must emphasize that the democracy I had in mind was his own unique brand and not Benthamite democracy.[14] My own opinion is that, given the modern alternatives, Rousseau would have judged our government to be very bad but at the same time the least bad. But this I think can never be proved, because he had no idea of modern governments.

The social contract may not *directly* help us to judge existing governments, but if we look to the ideal man, the citizen, who is a presupposition of the contract, the situation is different. The citizen ideally is the undivided individual whose communal identity enables him to transcend the narrow limits of his ego. This unity is achieved by a dialectical process: the community creates the individual, and the individual creates the community. The problem of legitimacy thus is not just a problem of formal political organization; on a more substantive level it is a problem of the types of personality that various societies produce. On this level an acquisitive society that is formally free might be less legitimate than an authoritarian religious community.

If the social contract is to function as a regulative idea, it must be reexpressed as a philosophy of community, for only communities give birth to undivided citizens. I have not thought it part of my task to reconstruct a theory of community from the scattered observations of Rousseau. It is easy enough to catalogue the obstacles to community, and I would agree that "Rousseau is the first great thinker to focus his thoughts on the condition of man as it has been shaped by the uncontrolled conflict of private economic interests."[15] He was a caustic, bitter critic of the havoc wrought by the embryonic capitalism of his day, but it is an unwarranted extrapolation to conclude that he was a socialist in a contemporary sense. He was against the personal constraints that capitalism generated; it is yet to be seen whether any form of socialism in a modern economy can dispense with them. What form a new philosophy of community will assume I do not know. But the chances are it will owe much to Rousseau. It is not an accident that cries for community control and participatory democracy invoke Rousseau's name.

The irony is that, though Rousseau offers us a communal ideal, he himself despaired of attaining it. The *Second Discourse* leaves us with a picture of man as inherently selfish. Fortunately its arguments are not compelling. Rousseau had criticized Hobbes and other contract theorists for not having ventured far enough back into prehistory in their search for human nature. Modern historians and anthropologists might equally charge Rousseau with having vaulted over long stretches of known history that were relevant to his problem. Rousseau in his quasi-historical moments viewed that problem as one of communalizing naturally egocentric men. Had he been less agile his pessimism might have been softened. The selfish men of his experience were not continuous with original man; they were late emergents from long periods of time when the community was the natural expression of individuality. Rousseau's pessimism need not be ours, but his insight that community is fundamentally a politicomoral concept warrants the attention of an age that is plagued by "collectivization, functionalization, commercialization, disruption of all human and organic coherence."[16]

Notes

Introduction

1. Representatives of the various positions noted in the Introduction will be identified in the body of the text, where they are considered in more detail.

2. In a letter to Father Dom Deschamps, 12 September 1761, Rousseau locates the roots of this ambiguity. "You are very good to chastise me on the score of inexactnesses in reasoning. Is it the first time you noticed that I see certain objects very well but that I do not know in the least how to compare them, that I am fertile enough in conceiving propositions without ever being able to see their logical consequences, that order and method which are your Gods are my furies, that nothing ever presents itself to me save as an isolated thought, and instead of relating my ideas in my writings I employ juggler's tricks of passing from one thing to another so that I make an impression on you other great philosophers? *Citizen of Geneva: Selections from the Letters of Jean-Jacques Rousseau*, ed. Charles W. Hendel (New York: Oxford University Press, 1937), p. 198. Hereinafter abbreviated *Letters*.

3. The distinction between good and legitimate will be pursued in chapter 3. It will be seen there that the full import of Rousseau's attack on monarchy depends upon premises that are elaborated outside of the *Social Contract*.

4. *Men and Citizens: A Study of Rousseau's Social Theory* (New York: Cambridge University Press, 1969).

1 · The Unique Basis of Political Obligation

1. *Social Contract*, book 1, chapter 1, in *Rousseau: Political Writings*, trans. Frederick Watkins (New York: Nelson, 1953). All subsequent cita-

tions from the *Social Contract* are from this translation, hereinafter abbreviated *SC*.

2. *SC* 1. 8. I see nothing to distinguish Rousseau's idea of natural liberty from Hobbes's conception of natural right. Both are coterminous with a man's ability to effect his desires, and neither, at least in a state of nature, has any moral significance. However, Rousseau in the *Second Discourse* employs 'natural right' (*droit naturel*) in a sense that suggests moral overtones. *The First and Second Discourses*, ed. Roger D. Masters, trans. Roger D. Masters and Judith Masters (New York: St. Martin's Press, 1964), pp. 95–96. Subsequent citations from the *Discourses* are from this edition.

Rousseau at one point even rejects his own frequent use of the phrase 'natural liberty' on the grounds that when doing what one wants hurts another, it should not be dignified by the term 'liberty'. *Lettres de la Montagne*, in *The Political Writings of Jean Jacques Rousseau*, 2 vols., ed. Charles E. Vaughan (1915; reprint ed., Oxford: Blackwell, 1962), 2:234. However, I see no reason not to treat 'natural freedom', 'natural liberty', and 'natural right' as interchangeable phrases when the context clearly reveals that what is in question is man's physical endowments.

3. This position is forcibly argued by Peter T. Manicas [*The Death of the State* (New York: Putnam's, 1974)] and by Robert Paul Wolff [*In Defense of Anarchism* (New York: Harper and Row, 1970)]. Both assume a transcendent morality, and it is in relation to this conception that the idea of authority is rejected. It is interesting to note that for both the meaning of legitimacy is much the same as for Rousseau.

4. *SC* 1. 6. Rousseau goes on to add that the terms of this contract are everywhere at least tacitly admitted and recognized. As a reading of history this is a truly mystifying pronouncement, all the more so in view of the fact that he had just finished examining countertheories. Could it be that he considered all rival theories as so many rationalizations of narrow-minded interests? In any case, his belief that the contract is universally recognized comports with his assumption that the meaning of legitimacy is uniquely determined in some Platonic heaven.

5. In rejecting Grotius's claim that a people can alienate their collective freedom to a ruler, Rousseau argues that such a grant, lacking any quid pro quo, is irrational. This implies that a rational motive is a necessary condition for true consent (*SC* 1. 4).

6. *SC* 1. 6. 'Property' does not seem to be the correct translation of *biens*, at least in this context.

7. *SC* 4. 2. On at least two important occasions Rousseau employs the term 'law' (*loi*) in a manner inconsistent with his more technical usage.

Because law is what the sovereign creates, it cannot itself create the sovereign. Moreover, laws may be changed; the terms of the contract cannot.

8. Considering the times and Rousseau's negative attitude toward female capacities, it may be that by 'the people' he means adult males. Women and children would presumably be represented by fathers, brothers, husbands, and uncles.

9. *SC* 2. 5. If the sovereign were to decide on a total and direct democracy, the membership of the sovereign and the membership of the government would exactly coincide. Nevertheless, the two bodies would be distinguishable by their functions. As will be seen in chapter 2, the sovereign speaks one language and the government another.

10. I know of no commentator who shares this position. Most inferentially reject it by their silence. Some reject it explicitly. See, for example, Alfred Cobban, *Rousseau and the Modern State*, 2d ed. (Hamden, Conn.: Shoestring Press, Archon Books, 1964), p. 73, and Rousseau, *Rousseau: Political Writings*, trans. Watkins, pp. xx–xxi.

11. The Civil Creed, which I take to be an afterthought, tends to undermine this continuing option.

12. Cf. H. L. A. Hart, *The Concept of Law* (London: Oxford, 1961), pp. 85–88. My disjunction between a person's psychologically consenting to the contract or remaining in a state of nature bears some similarity to Hart's contrast between internal and external points of view toward a legal system.

13. This idea of a unique convention bears some similarity to a language system. Any language is conventional in the sense that it is not given in the genes (or, *pace* Noam Chomsky, at least not its vocabulary), for there are hundreds of different languages that can express the same meanings. But each language is obligatory in the sense that if one is to be a member of a language community, he must subscribe to the rules of that language. To the extent that he fails to internalize the rules, he misunderstands and is misunderstood. Rousseau's point is that *if* you wish to speak the language of legitimacy, the contract provides the only acceptable grammar. Anything less or other than these imperatives only approximates in various degrees the sounds of legitimacy.

2 · *Freedom, Law, and the Citizen*

1. *SC* 1. 6. It should be remembered that there is a third scenario recounting man's transition to civil society. In Rousseau's description of a people fit for legislation there is no indication of a war between rich and poor, or of obstacles that needed to be overcome.

2. Rousseau explicitly notes that the contract increased man's effective freedom (*SC* 2. 4).

3. *Emile*, trans. Barbara Foxley (New York: Dutton, 1966), p. 49. Subsequent citations of *Emile* are from this edition.

4. Leo Strauss, *Natural Right and History* (Chicago: University of Chicago Press, 1953), pp. 281–82.

5. *SC* 1. 7. This conjunction cannot be dismissed as a careless piece of rhetoric because it recurs in *Emile* (p. 290). I think, however, that there is a theoretical lapse here. Noncompliance is a particular fact, and, as the contract demands, the force that ought to be exerted ought to be exerted by the government and not by 'the whole body', that is, the sovereign. Roger Masters in treating this conjunction fails to distinguish between a reluctance to do one's duty (for example, to pay taxes) and an actual commission of a crime (for example, a fatal assault). A citizen can be forced to pay his taxes; he cannot be forced to undo the effects of his assault. Though I believe that Rousseau can theoretically extend his formula to crimes already committed, the two cases are different. Masters also fails to distinguish between a citizen who breaks the law but still wills the contract and "a rebel and a traitor to his country" (*SC* 2. 5) who is executed as an enemy of the state. A dead man is hardly politically free. Roger D. Masters, *The Political Philosophy of Rousseau* (Princeton, N.J.: Princeton University Press, 1963), p. 331.

6. For example, John H. Hallowel concludes that this conjunction is "a conception entirely congenial to tyranny." *Main Currents in Modern Political Thought* (New York: Henry Holt, 1957), p. 179.

7. I think that John Plamenatz (*Man and Society*) is mistaken on this point. Though I have no quarrel with his analysis of the relation between freedom and discipline, it seems obvious to me that, in any given instance, when obedience to a law is other-imposed, it is not self-imposed. This is not to deny that forced discipline may over a period of time result in self-discipline. Jean Jacques Rousseau, "*Ce qui ne signifie autre chose sinon qu'on le forcera d'être libre*" in *Hobbes and Rousseau*, ed. Maurice Cranston and Richard S. Peters (New York: Doubleday, 1972), pp. 324ff.

8. *SC* 2. 6; italics added. The same point in almost identical words is made in *Emile* (pp. 225–26).

9. *SC* 1. 6. Rousseau is not always consistent in distinguishing the citizen as sovereign from a subject as bound by the sovereign. For example, he says that "*subject* and *sovereign* are identical correlates whose meaning is conjoined in the single word *citizen*" (*SC* 3. 13).

10. Lester G. Crocker believes, on the contrary, that Rousseau's theory of law can give rise to a prejudicial distribution of social burdens and

benefits. His main textual support is the *Social Contract* (*SC* 2. 6), where Rousseau says that law can assign privileges and establish several classes of citizens. This need not be interpreted as an invitation to inequality. *Rousseau's Social Contract* (Cleveland, Ohio: The Press of Case Western Reserve University, 1968), p. 82.

11. *SC* 3. 16. There is no international law when 'law' is used in a strict sense. Given a looser interpretation of 'law', Rousseau was quite concerned with international law. Cf. *L'état de guerre*, *La paix perpetuelle*, and *Jugement sur la paix perpetuelle*, in *Political Writings*, ed. Vaughan, 1: 293–307, 364–87, 388–96.

12. *SC* 2. 2. In the light of contemporary experience, one may wonder why Rousseau would invest the government with such an awesome power. It must be remembered, however, that Rousseau had a precedent. Locke in theory assigned foreign relations, including the power of war, to the federative branch of government. But for practical purposes this power was under the control of the executive branch. John Locke, *Two Treatises of Government*, ed. Peter Laslett (New York: New American Library, 1965), pp. 411–12 (*Second Treatise*, sections 146–48). It seems to me that Rousseau's position is more a theoretical nicety than anything else. The type of society the contract was designed to organize would be too poor to wage aggressive war. Its abiding problem would be to forestall the aggressions of its neighbors.

13. This is not quite accurate, because the mere form of law does not necessarily guarantee equitable treatment for all. Consider an example: "All citizens must wear similar uniforms." If similarity is further specified to include the same size, the law must inevitably work a hardship on some, be they the fat or the thin, the short or the tall. In such cases equity must determine the proper formulation.

14. Though the context is different, Rousseau comments on the impersonality of lotteries: "For then, since the conditions are equal for all, and the choice depends on no human will, there is no specific application to impair the universality of the law" (*SC* 4. 13).

15. Rousseau was only too aware of the unjust tax structure of his day; the power to tax was the power to oppress. Sovereignty could not possibly be a viable idea unless this power resided ultimately with the people. It is this necessity that both justifies and explains what otherwise must seem to be a convoluted effort to express tax policy in the form of criminal law.

16. *Political Economy*, in *Rousseau: Political Writings*, ed. Vaughan, 1:273.

17. *Considerations on the Government of Poland* in *Rousseau: Political Writ-*

ings, trans. Watkins, pp. 176–77; italics added. Subsequent citations are from this edition.

18. The nature of sovereignty and law rigidly circumscribe the authority of government. The only language the sovereign is authorized to speak is the language of law. Because sovereignty is inalienable, this means that no one else, and in particular no government, may legislate. Since the legitimate scope of sovereignty is formally defined by the logical structures of the language it may speak, it follows that, from a syntactical point of view, government and the sovereign can never speak the same language. The former may never speak the language of law and the latter may speak nothing else. The inalienability of sovereignty signifies nothing unless it means that what the sovereign can do, no one else may do. Every governmental 'sentence' is a specification of some general principle that can be expressed in a form of law. If a government specifies a law that lacks the sovereign's approval, it has exceeded its authority. It cannot, for example, imprison jaywalkers if the sovereign has not proscribed jaywalking. There may, however, be cases where the government commands without a formally approved law to justify the command. If the sovereign is free to oppose and does not, the command may be accepted as an expression of the general will. But the implicit law that justifies the command is not the government's law (*SC* 2. 1).

19. What follows must seem, as it does to me, highly artificial, but I have been unable to think of an alternative. Unless the sovereign's right to regulate noncitizens is established, the social contract is seriously deficient.

20. The dependent status of the child is not in question (cf. *SC* 1. 2). The problem is whether the law can stand as a legitimate surrogate of the father.

21. The implication that women never fully emerge from a state of nature will hardly endear Rousseau to the hearts of feminists. John Plamenatz denies that Rousseau's conception of law can meaningfully require that it apply to all citizens. He cites Rousseau's approval of privilege and notes that laws rewarding veterans and nursing mothers would not pertain to all citizens. See Plamenatz's *Man and Society*, 2 vols. (New York: McGraw-Hill, 1963), 1:404–5. In my view the law need not affect all citizens actually, only potentially. This addition takes care of privilege legislation. I also argue that law satisfies the principle of universality if it affects all citizens either actually or potentially *at one time or another*—as in the case of a draft law that produces veterans. It is true that when a draft law is passed there would undoubtedly be citizens who would never be eligible because of old age, for example. But if you look at the law as

it affects future generations, universality will be secured. Exemptions based on physical disabilities could be explained on a similar, though not identical, basis. Since women apparently are not citizens, a law concerning mothers would either have to bear on citizen-fathers or be a law whose ultimate reference is an 'object'. I am sure that Plamenatz is right in arguing that there would be cases where not all citizens could seriously view themselves as potential subjects of law. Practical considerations invariably escape even the best-formulated regulative ideas. I apologize for my casuistical interpretation of law, but I take very seriously Rousseau's repeated emphasis on universality. What my interpretation cannot accommodate I leave to the spirit of what Rousseau means by law, and I assume this includes fairness.

22. The fact, if it is a fact, that the original contractors' citizenship rights are inviolable cannot be due to law, because any law is subject to change by the sovereign. It would have to be a curious part of the original contract—curious because with the death of the last original citizen, it would cease to be referential.

23. *SC* 3. 2. This scenario is certainly not intended to suggest that this contraction is substantively legitimate: the general will, in the concrete sense of an objective common good, would undoubtedly rule that out. But the point is that there is nothing in the formal character of law that prevents this extreme contraction.

24. Rousseau, *Political Writings*, ed. Vaughan, 2 : 377.

25. But even in the case of Poland the ideal is still a universal franchise. Some classes cannot be enfranchised at this time, "but the law of nature . . . does not permit legislative authority to be thus restricted, nor does it allow laws to be binding on anyone who has not voted for them" (*Poland*, p. 185). Eventually, when education has "freed their souls," even serfs should be given the vote (ibid., p. 187).

26. *Constitutional Project for Corsica*, in *Rousseau: Political Writings*, trans. Watkins, pp. 301–4. Subsequent citations are from this edition.

27. The qualification 'resident' as distinguished from 'foreigners' is used because residency is prima-facie evidence of consent. Nonconsenters may be considered foreigners (*SC* 4. 2).

28. The sovereign's right, if he has it, to disenfranchise becomes the odd right to release a moral agent against his will from moral obligations.

29. *SC* 2. 5. Cf. 1. 4, where this right of war is denied: wars can only occur between states.

30. Since the prosecution of a crime is a particular act, and the determination of continuing consent is a matter of fact, they are not matters of sovereign concern (*SC* 2. 4).

31. Like his use of the term 'law', Rousseau's use of the terms 'citizen' and 'consent' does not always respond to common usage.

32. So strict is Rousseau's construction of the social contract that I cannot see how a convicted citizen, even if jailed, can be denied participation in the assembly. The right to vote is "a right of which the citizens can *in no circumstances* be deprived" (*SC* 4. 1; italics added).

33. My argument is that this clause is demanded by the logic of the *Social Contract*. I do not claim that Rousseau in practice identified the people with all the male adults of a territory. On the contrary, I agree with Alfred Cobban that he did not. See Cobban, *Rousseau and the Modern State*, pp. 44–45.

John Plamenatz holds that no adult may be excluded from the assembly, because participation is a moral, not a legal, right. I, too, argue that it is not a legal right, and with certain theoretical reservations would agree that it is a moral right, but one that must be explicitly written into the contract because of Rousseau's fear of reserved rights. Plamenatz qualifies this moral right by saying that it can be forfeited by breaking the law and that it remains suspended for the terms of the punishment (*Man and Society*, 1:395–96). However, he later speaks of exclusion as a breach of contract (ibid., p. 434).

3 · Government

1. Rousseau does recognize that hereditary aristocracy in the strict sense is incompatible with sovereignty. The sovereign, should it designate an aristocratic class, puts itself under no obligations. "The form it gives to the administration is provisional, and continues until the people is pleased to ordain otherwise" (*SC* 3. 18). But then this is a form of elective aristocracy and not, strictly speaking, a hereditary aristocracy.

2. If mixed forms of governments are disregarded, elective aristocracy turns out to be one of only two possible forms of magistracy. Monarchy and democracy, it will be seen, are not governments, that is, magistracies. Hereditary aristocracy is the second possible form, and it is the worse because there is a greater probability of finding meritorious talent among the citizenry as a whole than in some predefined part of the whole. Moreover, the corporate will of a hereditary aristocracy would be far more concentrated than that of an elective aristocracy and thus pose a greater threat to the general will.

3. *SC* 2. 6, note 1. 'Republic' is Rousseau's general designation for a legitimate government.

4. Sheldon S. Wolin, *Politics as Vision* (Boston: Little, Brown and Co., 1960), p. 70.

5. *SC* 3. 9. Note that this criterion is an independent variable and can be applied without regard to standards of legitimacy. Moreover, it turns out to be less than infallible: China is an admitted exception (*Emile*, p. 342). Montesquieu had noted before Rousseau a correlation between population and governmental character. *The Spirit of the Laws*, trans. Thomas Nugent (New York: Haffnar, 1966); cf. book 23, chapters 19, 24, 28. In the *Second Discourse* (pp. 196–203) Rousseau presents several causes of depopulation, all of which he took to be operative in the France of his day. Ominously he concludes, "Thus the State, enriching itself on the one hand, weakens and depopulates itself on the other, and thus the most powerful *monarchies*, after much labor to become opulent and *deserted*, end by becoming the prey of poor nations" (p. 200 note i; italics added).

6. *Corsica*, p. 282. I am sure the reader will be interested to learn that the healthy, virtuous rustic is more prolific than his debauched counterpart in the city (ibid.). That is why the city does not do its fair share in maintaining population levels.

7. *Emile*, p. 433. If there is a constant theme that runs through Rousseau's several works, it is his emphasis on the radical, thoroughgoing differences that separate city and countryside. The city is the symbol of just about all evils. Here my concern is with the adverse economic effects of urban concentrations, but it might be noted in passing that the differences that split city and provinces are so many and so fundamental that there can be no single, general will uniting them. This is why one would not find cities in a legitimate state.

8. Ibid. Beyond this assumption Rousseau was definitely not a physiocrat. He had little competence as an economist. He never, for example, entertained an idea of economic development and progress, believing on the contrary that one man's gain was necessarily another's misfortune (Lucio Colletti, *From Rousseau to Lenin* [New York: Monthly Review Press, 1972], pp. 157–62).

9. An aristocracy and an inefficient bureaucracy are integral parts of Rousseau's conception of monarchy (*SC* 3. 6). 'Luxury' is a moral category (evil) by reason of its economic entailments.

10. *SC* 3. 9. The criteria of suitability that Rousseau offers for monarchy really only mark off the realm of the possible and not that of the necessary, because theoretically an area that might support a monarchy might also support two republics. The assumption underlying his transition from possibility to necessity seems to be a Hobbesian principle that nations, like individuals, never voluntarily limit the exercise of their

power. Thus there is a 'natural' tendency for power to seek its limit in such a way that what is not impossible is in effect necessary. If this is true, Rousseau's faith in confederations becomes problematical. On the expansion tendencies of societies, cf. *Second Discourse*, pp. 160–61.

11. *SC* 3. 9. All further references to the conditions favorable to monarchy may be found here.

12. Cf. *Second Discourse*, pp. 212–13 note j, where Rousseau proposes that anthropological expeditions be sent to those parts of the world about which Europe knows virtually nothing. His list of such places pretty much covers what reasonably might be taken to constitute the south. So much for the empirical basis of his argument that the south is suitable for monarchies!

4 · The General Will

1. This, if I understand it correctly, is the view of Lester G. Crocker (*Rousseau's Social Contract*, p. 83). It is also the view of Allan Bloom, who equates the general will with a pure will devoid of content—whatever that means. See his article "Jean-Jacques Rousseau" in *History of Political Philosophy*, ed. Leo Strauss and Joseph Cropsey (Chicago: Rand McNally and Co., 1963), p. 524.

2. I have not included in this book a detailed discussion of the legislator because the chapters in the *Social Contract* on the legislator and a people fit for legislation, if taken seriously, doom the social contract as historically irrelevant. If only the most primitive people are fit for legislation, one can understand the necessity of a legislator, though not where he is to be found. Then Rousseau confronts us with an insoluble dilemma. The social contract is a very sophisticated instrument and is intelligible only on a high level of reason. But a people capable of this measure of reason are no longer a people fit for legislation. Thus, if a people can understand the contract they cannot embody it, and if they cannot understand it, what efficacy can it have? Rousseau was not unaware of this dilemma (*SC* 2. 7).

3. In *Poland* (pp. 163–66) Rousseau analyzes the distinctive contributions of Moses, Lycurgus, and Numa. Each, faced with a mere aggregation of individuals, scarcely held together and existing to no purpose, transformed their material into tightly knit and cohesive societies. What they did was to create distinctive peoples, peoples with unique identities. Cosmopolitan philosophers notwithstanding, exclusivity was for Rousseau a principle of political necessity.

4. *Second Discourse*, p. 163. Rousseau further argues that it would be unreasonable for people to accept masters without prior agreements as to the conditions of submission.

5. John C. Hall, *Rousseau: An Introduction to His Political Philosophy* (Cambridge, Mass.: Schenkman Publishing Co., 1973). Though on different grounds, Hall also argues that the general will must have some publicly acceptable content before the contract can become effective (pp. 112–15). There are also some obvious differences between us.

6. Cf. Rousseau's *Letter to M. d'Alembert on the Theater* in Allan Bloom, trans., *Politics and the Arts* (Illinois: Free Press, 1960). All further references to the *Letter to M. d'Alembert* are to this edition.

7. *SC* 4. 2. Crocker (*Rousseau's Social Contract*, p. 84) criticizes Rousseau for assuming that some will is always or axiomatically right. But the extent to which Rousseau does make this assumption is limited to a very special type of society. He by no means assumed that the wills of existing governments were infallible.

8. Wolff, *In Defense of Anarchism*, pp. 56–57.

9. *SC* 4. 1. It is not always possible to identify unambiguously the general will. Suppose some citizen suggests to the assembly that it might be a good idea to establish a public theater. Three positions can be conceived: (*a*) Tom believes that a theater is in the public interest and should be supported by a public tax; (*b*) Dick believes it would be detrimental to the common good; (*c*) Harry believes that it is a matter of public indifference and therefore beyond the competence of the sovereign. Tom and Dick agree that the issue is one of common concern, though they differ as to the effect of a theater. Harry disagrees with both, but he implicitly agrees with Dick that a theater ought not to be publicly financed. One can imagine a sequence of three questions that our three-man assembly must answer. (*a*) "Is the issue one of common concern?" (Recall that one of the clauses of the contract limits sovereignty to matters of common concern and that it is the sovereign that makes this determination.) If the answer is yes, then it must next be asked, (*b*) "Is a theater in the public interest?" If the answer is once more yes, a third question is demanded, (*c*) "How ought it to be financed?"

The first vote would result in an affirmative: Harry's no would be overridden by two yeses. But how is the second question to be resolved? The yes and no of Tom and Dick cancel each other, leaving Harry with the deciding vote. His first vote shows that he has no positive general will on the subject at hand. Yet that vote proved he was mistaken. He might argue that since he is against a public tax he ought to vote no at this stage rather than chance a vote on a third question. On the other hand, he might argue that since he sees no positive evil in a theater and might personally like to attend a play now and then, he ought to vote yes. Suppose he votes in the affirmative. Can this be unambiguously said to be the declaration of a general will? I think not, but what else can he do but express his particular will? The third question is at this stage not simply one of finances; it is a question of how to support what has been declared a public good. Tom, of course, voted for a public tax in good and consistent conscience. Dick's position is less clear. Having voted no to question *b*, it hardly seems consistent that he would now vote to support what he judged evil. On the other hand, he might argue that the vote proved him wrong and that as a general principle what is in the public interest ought to be supported publicly. Or again, he might argue with lawyerlike precision that question *c* is implicitly a reopening of question *b* and that since any law is subject to repeal or modification, he could honorably vote against public support. Harry's vote is similarly plagued. Since the final vote and the one before could have legitimately gone either way, the common good at issue is less a cognitive question and more a procedural decision.

5 · *Property and the Division of Labor*

1. Charles E. Vaughan (Rousseau, *Political Writings*, ed. Vaughan, pp. 64–65) sees the limitations that the formal conditions of law put on sovereignty but thinks that these limitations automatically increase the power of individuals and groups. If that were permissible, it is hard to see how the personal dependencies Rousseau condemned could be avoided. A sovereign that cannot regulate the economy is not much of a sovereign.

2. Rousseau on the surface seems to picture the arts and sciences as unmoved movers creating corruption and vice ex nihilo. Similarly, in his *Letter to M. d'Alembert* it would seem that the theater would by itself cause wide and radical changes in Geneva. But this appearance does not do justice to his basically dialectical view of social causation. Thus, in a letter to Voltaire, 10 September 1755, he notes the relation that holds between corruption and the arts. "The love of letters and arts arises in a people from an internal weakness which it only augments." Moreover, corruption thus augmented by the arts can reach a point where "the evil is so great that the very causes which give rise to it are needful to prevent it from becoming worse" (*Letters*, p. 135). Note also that Rousseau had

explicitly traced the origins of certain arts and sciences to various vices (*First Discourse*, p. 48).

3. It might be speculated that Rousseau's strongly negative attitude toward money derives in part from his reading of Locke, where the introduction of money is the ultimate cause for the transformation of his state of nature from a condition of equality to one of continuing and progressive inequality. John Locke, *Two Treatises*, pp. 210–13 (*Second Treatise*, sections 48–50).

4. *SC* 3. 15; italics added. Recall that 'republic' is the term Rousseau reserves for legitimate states and that the luxury that characterizes monarchies is derived from monied economies.

5. *Emile*, p. 148; italics added. Note the dialectical relation between economic exigencies and society.

6. Rousseau and Marx differ in their terminology. 'Impersonal dependence' as used by Rousseau is a good phrase. For Marx it describes the depersonalization that results when a wage earner is reduced to the status of a commodity, a mere thing. 'Impersonal dependence' in Rousseau's sense is associated with the warm interpersonal relations that characterize small communities. My colleague Peter Manicas brought these different usages to my attention.

7. Rousseau calls hunters, savages, and herdsmen, barbarians in his *On the Origin of Language*, trans. John H. Moran and Alexander Gode (New York: Frederick Ungar, 1966), p. 38. In *SC* 3. 8, he maintains that savages and barbarians inhabit lands such that "no form of polity would be possible there."

8. This is yet another example of Rousseau's inability satisfactorily to combine principles of right with his several versions of history.

9. *SC* 1. 9. This quote by itself suffices to prove that Rousseau would never endorse a nineteenth-century laissez-faire society. A sovereign that does not control the economy is a sovereign in name only.

10. In his *De l'économie politique* Rousseau seems to be operating under the assumption that property is a sacred right antedating civil society and that the end of government is its protection (*Political Writings*, ed. Vaughan, 1:238). However, it turns out that property as an inviolable right does not reach beyond what subsistence requires. Everything beyond that is justifiably subject to taxation (ibid., p. 267). Supposedly this is self-taxation based on consent, but this consent is automatically given by the mere possession of a superfluity (ibid., p. 273). A right that must be waived on demand is really no right at all. In the last analysis the sacred right on which civil society rests is the prior right of self-preserva-

tion and the means thereto. And this right does not necessarily imply private property in a capitalist sense.

11. Pëtr Kropotkin, *Mutual Aid* (Boston: Extending Horizons Books, 1955), pp. 223–61 (chapter 7).

12. Ibid., p. 232.

6 · *The Search for Human Nature*

1. Descartes's cosmogony begins with a few assumptions. "These few assumptions are, I think, enough to supply causes from which all effects observed in our universe would arise *by the laws of nature previously stated*" (René Descartes, *Principles of Philosophy*, trans. Elizabeth Anscombe and Peter T. Geach, in *Descartes' Philosophical Writings* [Indianapolis: Library of Liberal Arts, 1971], p. 225 [part 3, section 46]; italics added).

2. *Emile*, pp. 234, 234 note 1, 235, 236. I have included the quotation from the note because it is Rousseau's comment, and it seconds the vicar's position. Cf. Descartes: "For in my opinion nothing without which a thing can still exist is comprised in its essence" (*Reply to Objections IV*, in *Philosophical Works of Descartes*, trans. E. S. Haldane and G.R.J. Ross, 2 vols. [New York: Dover, 1955], 2:97).

3. The similarity of these criteria to those Descartes employed to determine the nature of a piece of wax cannot be accidental.

4. If rest is matter's natural state, initial motion can only be explained by recourse to a nonmaterial cause. Rousseau is at least consistent on this point: the ultimate explanation of motion "is a will which sets the universe in motion and gives life to nature" (*Emile*, p. 236). This is essentially a Cartesian explanation of the origin of motion. Though Descartes was the first to explicitly formulate the principle of inertia, his purely geometrical conception of matter demanded that he deny that inertia was an active force of resistance intrinsic to body, the *vis insita* of Newton. Rest and motion, accordingly, are states of bodies, the determination of which depends upon an extrinsic 'force', namely, motion, that is imparted by God. Though Descartes does not characterize either rest or motion as the natural state of body, were he to find the question of which state is the natural state intelligible, he would probably choose rest. In any case, Cartesian physics explains why Rousseau can distinguish between the nature of a thing and its state, natural or otherwise. See S. V. Keeling, *Descartes* (London: Oxford University Press, 1968), pp. 149–50, 282, 306.

5. *Second Discourse*, pp. 140–41; italics added. Was Rousseau merely echoing Descartes's methodology? Descartes, too, admits that God could

have effected cosmic evolution in several ways. "Therefore, we are free to make any assumptions we like about them, so long as all the consequences agree with experience" (*Principles*, p. 225 [Part 3, section 46]). And again: "In any case, it matters very little what suppositions we make; for change must subsequently take place according to the laws of nature; and it is hardly possible to make a supposition that does not allow of our inferring the same effects (perhaps with more labour) according to the same laws of nature. For according to these, matter must successively assume all the forms of which it admits; and if we consider these forms in order, we can at last come to that which is found in this universe. So no error is to be apprehended from a false supposition at this point" (ibid., p. 226 [section 47]).

6. This would have to be qualified, I suppose, in the case of some domestic animals.

7. Not being a zoologist, I ought not to be so dogmatic. But even if some animals are subject to induced needs, these needs would be insignificant in comparison to their natural needs.

8. In many life situations a concern for the common good is irrelevant. But when the common good is in question Rousseau believed that for the most part particular and general interests are mutually exclusive. *Geneva Manuscript* in *Political Writings*, ed. Vaughan, 1 : 450.

9. Plamenatz (*Man and Society*, 1 : 376–77) also argues the impossibility of viewing self-love and vanity as two different species. For a less pessimistic account of *amour de soi*, see Ronald Grimsley, *The Philosophy of Rousseau* (London: Oxford University Press, 1973), pp. 67–69. I find it difficult to agree that "Rousseau's philosophy is essentially optimistic" (ibid., p. 163).

10. The primacy of self-love can be seen in the following: "The origin of our passions, the root and spring of all the rest, the only one which is born with man, which never leaves him as long as he lives, is self-love; this passion is primitive, instinctive, it precedes all the rest, which are in a sense only modifications of it. In this sense, if you like, they are all natural" (*Emile*, p. 173).

11. Though I have closely equated Hobbes and Rousseau with respect to social psychology, three important qualifications must be given. Rousseau took great pains to refute Hobbes's version of the state of nature and thus of man's original nature, while not wholly disputing his version of contemporary civilized man.

Hobbes grounds his theory of absolute sovereignty on his account of human nature: if man is naturally an evil beast, then only despotism backed by force can keep peace in the jungle; it is the least of all evils. For

Rousseau this is a reversal of cause and effect: despotism is not justified by human nature; on the contrary, despotism is a cause of the perversions of human nature. People are only what governments make them (introduction to *L'état de guerre*, in *Political Writings*, ed. Vaughan, 1 : 286–87). Second, though a man's character is shaped by social structures, it does not follow that all institutional patterns are equally corruptive. Cupidity is one of the cardinal sins, and it is awakened by superfluities; the more one has the more one desires. Savages brought to Europe find no pleasures in what delights society, for they are closer to nature and as yet unspoiled (ibid., 1 : 306–7). On the same principle, peasants living off the land are less vicious than the urbanely civilized. Whenever I equate Rousseau's version of man's second nature with Hobbes's account of man's original nature, I have in mind the civilized man that is the object of Rousseau's wrath in so many of his works.

Third, there is at least a hope that the more blatant expressions of self-interest may be rechanneled into more useful courses. A good part of man's selfishness is his desire for esteem; it is not so much wealth in itself that a man seeks as it is a desire to be esteemed as rich. If only the criteria for distinction could be changed along more publicly fruitful lines, a man in indulging his love of esteem would be serving the public good (*Fragment*, in *Political Writings*, ed. Vaughan, 1 : 333–34). Rousseau attempted to institutionalize this insight in his proposals for Corsica. Here he distinguishes self-referring vanity, the *amour-propre* of the *Second Discourse*, from a pride justified by the intrinsic value of the objects it seeks (*Corsica*, pp. 325–26).

12. For example, *Second Discourse*, pp. 192–94 note i.

13. But it ought to be recalled that the loyal Spartan lived off the labor of enslaved helots, in relation to whom he had ample opportunity to indulge his personal pride. Economic competition, it appears, is a serious threat to liberty. If a people can transcend this competition by assigning all economic functions to slaves, they may perhaps enjoy liberty. "What is this? Can liberty be maintained only on the basis of slavery? Perhaps" (*SC* 3. 15).

14. John W. Chapman, *Rousseau, Totalitarian or Liberal?* (New York: Columbia University Press, 1956), p. 75.

15. Rousseau was not unaware of his problem: how to relate an all-pervasive self-love and virtue. "The love of oneself is the most powerful, and in my opinion, the sole motive that makes human beings act. But how virtue, taken absolutely and as a metaphysical thing, is founded on that love of self, that passes my comprehension" (*Letters*, p. 273). If virtue is, as Rousseau holds, some kind of countervailing force, I do not under-

stand what it means to consider it absolutely and as a metaphysical thing.

16. In *SC* 2. 10, Rousseau claims that Corsica is the only country in Europe that is still capable of legislation. Because the Corsicans were far more advanced than his description of a people fit for legislation, it must have been their brave, patriotic resistance to the common enemies that engaged Rousseau's attention.

17. I am tempted, but only in a footnote, to ask, "Could Rousseau have written the *Second Discourse* if he had understood the principle of inertia?"

18. Vaughan (Rousseau, *Political Writings*, ed. Vaughan, 1 : 5) sees Rousseau as moving from individualism to the supremacy of the community.

7 · *The Civil Creed*

1. Crocker, *Rousseau's Social Contract*, pp. 98–99.

2. Cobban, *Rousseau and the Modern State*, p. 56.

3. Rousseau, *Political Writings*, ed. Vaughan, 1 : 90–92.

4. Green, *Rousseau: A Critical Study*, p. 304.

5. Rousseau, *Political Writings*, ed. Vaughan, 1 : 87.

6. *SC* 4. 8.

7. Rousseau repeats this position: "It seemed to me to rest with the Sovereign alone in each country to settle the form of worship and the unintelligible dogma as well" (*The Confessions of Jean-Jacques Rousseau*, trans. J. M. Cohen [London: Penguin Books, 1955], p. 365; all further references to the *Confessions* are to this edition). This is far less liberal than the Civil Creed, which, aside from a few basic dogmas, leaves each man free to believe and worship as he pleases.

8. This is from the first version of the creed (*Political Writings*, ed. Vaughan, 1 : 499).

9. For example, see his letter to Madame de Crequi, 5 February 1761 (*Letters*, p. 181).

10. Today the political fanatic replaces the religious fanatic of old. His "truth" justifies bombings, disruptions of lectures, hijackings, and bank robberies.

11. Willmoore Kendall notes that in *The Government of Poland* Rousseau pays scant attention to the role of the church, though he well knew that it was a pivotal institution. Seeking to lessen the church's importance as an alternative locus of loyalty, Rousseau proposed "a comprehensive system of state controlled education" (*The Government of Poland*, trans. Willmoore Kendall, [Indianapolis: Bobbs-Merrill, 1972], p. xxxiii). It

might be added that the Communists faced with the same problem chose a similar solution.

12. That this is consciously a civil and not a religious creed becomes apparent when it is contrasted with what seem to be Rousseau's personal convictions. These did not include any strong belief in the eternal punishment of the wicked. And the creed makes no mention of a love of humanity; it is not the business of the state to inculcate a love for foreigners who may someday be enemies.

13. John Locke, *A Letter concerning Toleration*, 2d ed. (New York: Liberal Arts Press, 1955), p. 27. All further quotations of Locke are from this edition.

14. Crocker, *Rousseau's Social Contract*, p. 99.

15. *Political Writings*, ed. Vaughan, 2:163.

16. Ibid., 2:164.

17. Bishop Warburton, Rousseau notes, was wrong. Religion and politics do not have a common purpose, for "in the creation of nations, the one [religion] serves as the instrument of the other [state]" (*SC* 2. 7).

18. The case of sovereignty is a different matter. Though sovereignty cannot retroactively sanctify the social contract, there is a conditional and metaphorical sense in which the contract can be said to sanctify sovereignty. Granting the contract, sovereign law at any given time is so absolutely obligatory that it may be described as 'sacred'. And even before the creed is introduced Rousseau so describes sovereign power (*SC* 2. 4). But he also makes explicit that this sacredness is derivative. "But the social order is a sacred right. . . . And yet this right does not come from nature; thus it is founded on conventions" (*SC* 1. 1). The conventions that create this 'sacred right' are the terms of the contract. But without appeal to a higher principle the contract itself cannot be sacred, because what a mortal god has joined a mortal god may put asunder. The civil creed makes just such an appeal and in so doing transforms the secular version of the contract.

19. *Political Writings*, ed. Vaughan, 2:297; italics added. Vaughan also notes the incompatibility between the irrevocability expressed here and the explicit right to withdraw consent found in the *Social Contract*.

8 · *Two Moralities*

1. There are those who hold that nature certifies rights rather than duties. Leo Strauss, for example, has argued that the fundamental difference between modern and classical political philosophy consists in this:

modern political philosophy substitutes right for law, that is, duty, as its starting point. Starting with a right of nature, and without recourse to divine or natural law, Hobbes establishes a sovereign whose will is law (*The Political Philosophy of Hobbes* [Chicago: University of Chicago Press, 1961], pp. 156–60). I think this is quite misleading. Natural right for Hobbes is not a justified claim; it is a fact, namely, the actual power one man has relative to another. It has no moral significance because it does not entail a corresponding duty. To the extent that Hobbes might be interpreted as having generated moral obligations, the basis of morality is not a natural right but the duty to keep promises. In any case, Rousseau's moral theory has nothing to do with natural rights as thus conceived. His overriding moral principle is a principle of equality, and equality is attainable only if natural 'right' is severely limited by duties. Moreover, Rousseau was quite explicit in rejecting natural rights; see, for example, *SC* 1. 6.

2. *Political Writings*, ed. Vaughan, 1:449.

3. Vaughan (Rousseau, *Political Writings*, ed. Vaughan, 1:16) claims that Rousseau swept away the theory of natural law "root and branch." Masters (*The Political Philosophy of Rousseau*, p. 270) qualifies this, holding that "Rousseau rejects the 'root' of the traditional natural law, but not the 'branch.'"

4. The first three beliefs are reaffirmed in the Civil Creed of the *Social Contract*. In the third promenade of his *Reveries*, he states that the vicar's creed is essentially his, though he admits that there are objections he cannot answer. But these objections are "nothing but quibbles and metaphysical subtleties, which are of no weight after the fundamental principles adopted by my reason, confirmed by my heart, and which carry the seal of interior assent in the silence of my passions" (*The Reveries of a Solitary*, trans. John G. Fletcher [New York, 1927], pp. 68–69. Charles Hendel has pointed out the circumstances that led Rousseau to include the vicar's creed in *Emile*, a creed which is a clear disavowal both of formal Christianity and of the materialist position of many *philosophes*. Hendel notes that from a dramatic point of view the length of the creed is far more than the unity of *Emile* demands, and can be explained only as a general profession of Rousseau's personal creed (Charles W. Hendel, *Jean-Jacques Rousseau: Moralist* [New York: The Library of Liberal Arts, 1962], 2:124). Finally, there is the clear testimony of the *Moral Letters*, addressed to Mme. d'Houdetot, which contain a reasoned defense of a belief in God, immortality, and the supremacy of conscience. Because of Rousseau's skepticism toward all empiricist or rationalist metaphysics, his own position is offered with even less certitude than the relatively

cautious presentation of the vicar (ibid., 1:298–316). But the issue at hand is not what Rousseau felt he could satisfactorily prove but what he personally believed.

5. Man's weakness and God's justice rule out the possibility of eternal damnation (letter to M. Jacob Vernes, 18 February 1758 [*Letters*, p. 148]).

6. A. P. d'Entreves, *Natural Law* (London: Hutchinson University Library, 1961), p. 49.

7. Ibid., p. 75.

8. It is interesting to note that something of Rousseau's analysis of conscience is incorporated in contemporary evolutionary theory. Konrad Lorenz, for example, says that "in reality, even the fullest rational insight into the consequences of an action . . . would not result in an imperative or in a prohibition, were it not for some emotional, in other words, instinctive, source of energy supplying motivation. . . . Man, as a purely rational being, divested of his animal heritage of instincts, would certainly not be an angel!—quite the opposite" (*On Aggression* [New York: Bantam, 1966], p. 239).

9. *SC* 2. 6; italics added. Note that Rousseau does not see any incompatibility between a natural law "derived from reason only" and a conventional basis for justice.

10. There is a striking structural similarity between Rousseau's conception of law as conditional and Hobbes's distinction between the obligatory character of natural law *in foro interno* and *in foro externo* (*Leviathan*, ch. 15). Assured enforcement of the law is a necessary condition for transforming a conditional into a categorical imperative. Covenants without the sword are purely verbal (ibid., ch. 17).

11. Rousseau, *Political Writings*, ed. Vaughan, 1:447–52.

12. Ibid., 1:452.

13. Ibid., 1:494.

14. Ibid.

15. Recall the incident from the *Confessions* where Rousseau approved the precautions a peasant took to hide taxable goods (*Confessions*, pp. 159–60).

16. Recall that this idea of freedom as obedience to a self-imposed law has nothing in common with those subjectivist versions which see each individual as a law unto himself. As already noted, there is no question of moral obligation where the 'law' an individual imposes upon himself is purely self-referential. The formal characteristics of the law in question have been previously analyzed. The law may be self-imposed, but it is not self-authorized: "that which any man . . . ordains on his own authority is not a law at all" (*SC* 2. 6).

17. Rousseau's religious views do not seem to harmonize with the *Second Discourse*. If God is a providential God, why is the emergence of man as a moral agent due to accidents that might not have occurred? How do heaven and hell relate to eons of hominids who knew nothing of virtue? Man's highest freedom is moral freedom, but to make religion a necessary condition of morality is to conflate the important distinction between a moral and a prudential obligation. A man who obeys the law out of fear of divine retribution or in hopes of an eternal reward is not obeying the law for its own sake. But this is a problem that has perennially engaged Christian theologians and is not peculiar to Rousseau.

18. I mean by traditional natural law in this context the medieval conception, where natural law, being a part of the eternal law of God, presupposes God. On the other hand, there is a sense in which at least some of the laws that proceed from the social contract may be described as natural. Rousseau's formal requirements for law very closely anticipate Kant's principles for determining duty, and it can be and has been maintained that Kant's ethics fall within the scope of natural law. See d'Entrèves, *Natural Law*, p. 115.

19. Quoted in Peter Gay, *The Party of Humanity: Essays in the French Enlightenment* (New York: Alfred A. Knopf, 1964), p. 125.

20. Letter to M. L'Abbé de Carondelet, 4 March 1764 (*Letters*, p. 273). This belief by itself explains why Rousseau would bar atheists from his ideal society.

9 · In Search of an Identity

1. William T. Bluhm argues that Rousseau's conception of the political order is totalitarian (*Theories of the Political System* [Englewood Cliffs, N.J.: Prentice-Hall, 1965], p. 373). Karl Popper refers to Rousseau as a collectivist (*The Open Society and its Enemies*, 2 vols. [New York: Harper and Row, 1963], 2:91). Charles E. Vaughan agrees that Rousseau is a collectivist but not, strictly speaking, a socialist, and definitely not, in his mature thought, an individualist (Rousseau, *Political Writings*, ed. Vaughan, 1:111). J. L. Talmon argues that Rousseau's principles give rise to totalitarian democracy (*The Origins of Totalitarian Democracy* [New York: Praeger, 1960], p. 43). Lester Crocker perceives Rousseau as a nondemocratic totalitarian (*Rousseau's Social Contract*, pp. 163–86). Zevedei Barbu reads Rousseau as a democrat (*Democracy and Dictatorship* [New York: Grove Press, 1956], p. 56). John W. Chapman views Rousseau as attempting to achieve liberal goals by totalitarian means (*Rousseau, Totalitarian or Liberal*,

p. 139). For Alfred Cobban, Rousseau is an advocate of one meaning of individualism, a conservative, and a champion of community (*Rousseau and the Modern State*, pp. 162–70). If political tags are necessary, my view of Rousseau comes closer to Cobban's than to any of the others listed above.

2. *De l'économie politique*, in *Political Writings*, ed. Vaughan, 1:237–38.

3. There are, of course, other, nonetymological ways of characterizing totalitarianism. Carl J. Friedrich's and Zbigniew K. Brzenzinski's list of six characteristics common to all totalitarian dictatorships includes, either singly or in combination, just about all the reasons that are used to condemn Rousseau as a totalitarian (*Totalitarian Dictatorship and Autocracy* [New York: Praeger, 1961], pp. 9–10). But of these six characteristics only one, namely, an official ideology, might possibly be credited to him. Even if one views social ends and ideals as an ideology, it is hardly likely that Rousseau would recommend a chiliastic dimension, and it is even less likely that he would approve an ideal of world conquest. It is difficult to provide a blanket defense for Rousseau against the charge that he is a totalitarian, because that term means different things to different critics. Supposedly illiberal doctrines such as 'forced to be free' and the Civil Creed are sometimes taken as sufficient justifications of the charge. Frederick Watkins apparently equates totalitarianism with the assimilation of the individual by the collectivity (Rousseau, *Rousseau: Political Writings*, trans. Watkins, p. xxx). On the other hand he notes the liberal side of Rousseau (ibid., pp. xxiii–xxvi).

4. "Rousseau, Kant, and History," *Journal of the History of Ideas* 29, no. 3 (July–September 1968): 351; his italics.

5. Rousseau is quoted in Gaetano Salvemini, *The French Revolution: 1788–1792*, trans. I. M. Rawson (New York: W. W. Norton and Co., 1962), p. 77; italics added. The French text can be found in Rousseau, *Rousseau: Political Writings*, ed. Vaughan, 1:416.

6. It should be carefully noted that *if* Rousseau would have judged a revolution to be morally justified, that justification could not be entirely linked with his principles of legitimacy. A morally justified insurrection is a function of two quite independent variables: the present regime must be illegitimate and the revolution must have prospects of reconstructing society in conformance with the exigencies of legitimacy. The first condition is all too easily satisfied; the second condition is, this side of Armageddon, a historical condition contrary to prospective fact. If there is a justification for revolution in Rousseau's thinking, it has to be tied to less stringent conditions, for example, criteria of economic justice.

7. Plamenatz, *Man and Society*, 1:428–29.

8. Cf. Joan McDonald, *Rousseau and the French Revolution*, (London: Athlone Press, 1965).

9. Burke's most telling arguments against a fictional Rousseau were essentially Rousseauan. See A. M. Osborn, *Rousseau and Burke: A Study of the Idea of Liberty in Eighteenth-Century Political Thought* (London: Oxford University Press, 1940). There are really two sides to Rousseau's pessimism. One side made him extremely cautious with respect to deliberate radical social change. This is the side Burke failed to see. The other side grows out of his wide-ranging and radical criticism of just about every aspect of existing society. Rousseau may have despaired of righting injustices, but few could equal his eloquent and impassioned denunciations of them. The revolutionary potential of this side of his pessimism was not overlooked by subsequent radicals such as Robespierre. In sum, Rousseau was a radical with regard to social analysis but a conservative in his prescriptions.

10. Leo Strauss, "On the Intention of Rousseau," *Social Research* 14 (1947): 455–87.

11. Rousseau, *De l'économie politique*, in *Political Writings*, ed. Vaughan, 1:248.

12. Rousseau is quite insistent that the legislator must not resort to force. It is thus sadly ironic that it has been totalitarian movements that have consciously sought to integrate subjects and states to the fullest.

13. Aside from the fact that the parallel roles played by the legislator and Emile's tutor are quite implausible, it may be argued that through them Rousseau is merely expressing his penchant for authoritarianism. It is true that both may be described as manipulators, but it must be borne in mind that it is one thing to manipulate a child and something quite different to manipulate an adult. If a child is not manipulated, indoctrinated, forced, or whatever, he will never develop a stable personality that ought not to be manipulated. If he is not consistently and comprehensively shaped by an external force, he will soon enough become one more proof of the alleged wretchedness and perversity of mankind (*Emile*, pp. 15–16). Rousseau's point is that no man is what he is independently of socializing forces. But usually these forces are haphazard and unrecognized. If manipulation (socialization) there must be, why not manipulate in a rational and moral fashion?

If it is proper to speak of Rousseau as authoritarian in this context, the question of motive still remains. To locate the motive in his personality is to do less than justice to his intellectual life. The truly sad significance of the legislator and the tutor is that, given Rousseau's principles, they are apparently the only conceivable solutions to the problem of legitimacy on the one hand or to the problem of creating the autonomous man on the other. Though Rousseau passionately believed in free will, this belief does not sit comfortably with his theory of human nature. There is a tension between this belief and what seems to be the inner logic of all societies.

In the *Second Discourse* man is endowed by nature with free will, but it is difficult to distinguish this faculty from man's perfectibility, a principle that is not self-actuating. In the early stages of the state of nature there is no need to postulate free will: biological promptings alone suffice to explain man's limited behavior patterns. At some later date man exists in society, and this same society has already corrupted him. Perhaps there was a point when man could have chosen a different path, but that is now a moot subject because beyond some point of social evolution, a point that has been reached and passed, there is no turning back. More and more, society enslaves man by inflaming his desires. Man is ruled by the opinion of others; he is inextricably caught up in a competition for that which society esteems; to be successful he must shun virtue and embrace vice. History is irreversible, and it promises only further evils. Man's destination is not of his choosing.

Probably no man before Rousseau had a deeper understanding of society's all-pervasive grip on the individual. But that is precisely the problem. Society for the most part cannot reform or redirect itself, because it lacks the will. Like the slave it soon comes to love its chains. Nor can corrupt societies be reformed from without.

These beliefs of Rousseau strictly limit the conditions under which legitimacy can be instituted. The case of Emile is instructive. He is given into the hands of the tutor before his normal environment has a chance to misshape him. He is carefully guarded against alien influences; he is, if you will, manipulated. The details of his education are not important here. The point is that he supposedly reaches a stage of independence. That is, there will always be a psychic distance between him and whatever society he visits, as if he were a stranger to the world. He is his own man because no real society has had a chance to claim him as its own. But such is the intensity of Rousseau's pessimism that even Emile is eventually crushed by society and rendered miserable.

Now one can rob a cradle and sequester the baby, but where is one to find an infant society not yet developed beyond the point of inevitable corruption? Even if there were such a people, whence springs the legislator and what motivates him? How has he managed to escape the corrupting influence of society? Who was his tutor? Where does he get the ideological blueprint from which this nascent people's general will is to be shaped? Contemplate these and like questions, and see just how impossible it is to solve the problem of legitimacy with premises borrowed from the *Second Discourse!* The practical absurdity of the legislator and the tutor is but the measure of Rousseau's despair. Without tutors and legislators the world cannot avoid the evils that Rousseau catalogues in his several writings.

14. Rousseau explicitly denies that the general will is the greatest good of each part (*De l'économie politique*, in *Political Writings*, ed. Vaughan, 1:418).

15. Mario Einaudi, *The Early Rousseau* (Ithaca, N.Y.: Cornell University Press, 1968), p. 143. Natural freedom, the absence of legal restraint, would be an effective freedom if indeed man could pursue his destiny independently of society as a whole. But where society is divided into rich and poor, powerful and weak, the less the legal scope of the state, the more the poor and powerless are subject to the personal restraints of the rich and powerful. Because Rousseau rejected the myth of the self-sufficient individual in modern society and realized that the great majority are constrained one way or another, he could never view the absence of legal coercion as a guarantee of freedom. On the contrary, what absence of legal constraint in fact produces is a situation where the powerful few legitimately exploit the many. Though Rousseau was not a professional economist, he emphatically rejected the ideas of Mandeville and others that the public welfare was served, even if unintentionally, by the free and unhampered play of individual acquisitiveness (*Second Discourse*, pp. 194–95 note i). If the natural freedom of the few is the personal slavery of the many, then if there must be restraints, let them be the impersonal restraints of legal control.

This maximization of restraint, even if it is impersonal, seems excessively constrictive, but only because it is so difficult to break out of Locke's universe of discourse. If the natural freedom of the great majority of men is limited in any case, why is it not better to be impersonally constrained in such a way that one is free of the arbitrary control of others? At least one has a voice in determining the nature of the restraints. "The more you are subject to law, the freer you are" and "one must be forced to be free" are paradoxes, nay, absurdities, in a Lockean universe of discourse. They are but truisms in Rousseau's universe of discourse, where the main threat to freedom is a biased legal system that allows the powerful to exploit the weak.

16. Erich Kahler, *The Tower and the Abyss* (New York: Viking Press, 1967), p. 243.

Selected Bibliography

Rousseau's Writings

Citizen of Geneva: Selections from the Letters of Jean-Jacques Rousseau. Edited by Charles W. Hendel. New York: Oxford University Press, 1937.

The Confessions of Jean-Jacques Rousseau. Translated and with an introduction by J. M. Cohen. Harmondsworth, England: Penguin Books, 1953.

Emile. Translated by Barbara Foxley. London: Dent, 1911.

Essay on the Origin of Languages. In *On the Origin of Language*. Translated by John H. Moran and Alexander Gode. New York: Frederick Ungar, 1966.

The First and Second Discourses. Edited with an introduction and notes by Roger D. Masters and translated by Roger D. and Judith R. Masters. New York: St. Martin's Press, 1964.

The Government of Poland. Translated with an introduction and notes by Willmoore Kendall. Indianapolis: Bobbs-Merrill, 1972.

Political Writings. Translated and edited by Frederick Watkins. Edinburgh: Nelson, 1953.

The Political Writings of Jean Jacques Rousseau. Edited by Charles E. Vaughan. 2 Vols. 1915. Reprint. Oxford: Blackwell, 1962.

Politics and the Arts: Rousseau's Letter to d'Alembert. Translated and edited by Allan Bloom. Glencoe, Ill.: The Free Press, 1960.

The Reveries of a Solitary. Translated with an introduction by John Gould Fletcher. New York: Burt Franklin, 1971.

The Social Contract. An eighteenth-century translation completely revised, edited, with an introduction by Charles Frankel. New York: Hafner, 1947.

Of the Social Contract. Translated by Richard W. Crosby. Brunswick, Ohio: King's Court Communications, 1978.

On the Social Contract with Geneva Manuscript and Political Economy. Edited by Roger D. Masters and translated by Judith R. Masters. New York: St. Martin's Press, 1978.

Commentaries on Rousseau's Writings

Cassirer, Ernst. *The Question of Jean-Jacques Rousseau*. Translated and edited with an introduction and additional notes by Peter Gay. Bloomington: Indiana University Press, 1963.

Chapman, John W. *Rousseau, Totalitarian or Liberal?* New York: Columbia University Press, 1956.

Cobban, Alfred. *Rousseau and the Modern State*. London: George Allen and Unwin, 1934.

Cohler, Anne M. *Rousseau and Nationalism*. New York: Basic Books, 1970.

Colletti, Lucio. *From Rousseau to Lenin*. Translated by John Merrington and Judith White. New York: Monthly Review Press, 1972.

Cranston, Maurice, and Peters, Richard S., eds. *Hobbes and Rousseau: A Collection of Critical Essays*. New York: Doubleday, 1972.

Durkheim, Emile. *Montesquieu and Rousseau: Forerunners of Sociology*. Translated by Ralph Manheim. Ann Arbor: University of Michigan Press, 1965.

Einaudi, Mario. *The Early Rousseau*. Ithaca, N.Y.: Cornell University Press, 1967.

Green, F. C. *Jean-Jacques Rousseau: A Critical Study of His Life and Writings*. Cambridge: University Press, 1955.

Grimsley, Ronald. *Rousseau and the Religious Quest*. Oxford: Clarendon Press, 1968.

Hall, John C. *Rousseau: An Introduction to his Political Philosophy*. Cambridge, Mass.: Schankman Publishing Co., 1973.

Hendel, Charles W. *Jean-Jacques Rousseau: Moralist*. 2 vols. London: Oxford University Press, 1934.

Lemos, Ramon M. *Rousseau's Political Philosophy: An Exposition and Interpretation*. Athens: University of Georgia Press, 1977.

McDonald, Joan. *Rousseau and the French Revolution 1762–1791*. London: Athlone Press, 1965.

Masters, Roger D. *The Political Philosophy of Rousseau*. Princeton: Princeton University Press, 1968.

Plamenatz, John. *Man and Society*. Vol. 1. New York: McGraw-Hill, 1963.

Roche, Kennedy F. *Rousseau: Stoic and Romantic*. London: Methuen, 1974.

Shklar, Judith N. *Men and Citizens: A Study of Rousseau's Social Theory*. Cambridge: University Press, 1969.

Spurlin, Paul M. *Rousseau in America 1760–1809*. University: University of Alabama Press, 1969.

Strauss, Leo. *Natural Right and History*. Chicago: University of Chicago Press, 1953.

Talman, J. F. *The Origins of Totalitarian Democracy*. London: Secker and Warburg, 1952.

Wright, Ernest H. *The Meaning of Rousseau*. London: Oxford University Press, 1929.

Index